Teaching 3–8
3rd Edition

Also available from Continuum

Teaching 3–8

3rd Edition

Mark O'Hara

Reaching the Standard Series

continuum

Continuum International Publishing Group

The Tower Building   80 Maiden Lane, Suite 704
11 York Road   New York, NY 10038
London
SE1 7NX

www.continuumbooks.com

First published 2000, second edition published 2004
Reprinted 2003, 2006

British Library Cataloguing-in-Publication Data
A catalogue record for this book is available from the British Library.

ISBN: 9780826483447 (paperback)

Library of Congress Cataloging-in-Publication Data
O'Hara, Mark.
  Teaching 3-8 / Mark O'Hara. — 3rd ed.
      p. cm. — (Reaching the standard series)
  Includes bibliographical references and index.
  ISBN-13: 978-0-8264-8344-7 (pbk.)
  ISBN-10: 0-8264-8344-5 (pbk.)
  1. Preschool teaching. 2. Elementary school teaching. 3. Preschool teachers—Training of. 4. Elementary school teachers—Training of. I. Title. II. Title: Teaching three-eight. III. Series.
  LB1140.3.O36 2008
  372.1102—22

                                                            2007036522

Typeset by Ben Cracknell Studios | www.benstudios.co.uk

Printed and bound in Great Britain by Cromwell Press, Wiltshire, UK

Contents

Acknowledgements

I would like to thank colleagues at Sheffield Hallam University for their advice and suggestions in compiling this book. I would also like to thank friends, former colleagues and Debbie Curtis, for providing samples of work, documentation and planning sheets, some of which illustrate the text. I am particularly grateful to Frances Hunt for her insight and commentary on the ever changing policy environment.

Preface

This book is aimed at teacher-training students on 3–8 courses, and newly qualified teachers working with the same age range. This age range is a crucial time in children's development, and effective teaching in Foundation Stage and lower primary education will help to lay the foundations for their future success both as learners and as citizens.

Good teaching is a complex, highly skilled activity, and one of the devices by which initial teacher training (ITT) students are required to develop a positive and proactive approach to their own professional development is to demonstrate achievement against the competences set out in the Standards for the Award of Qualified Teacher Status, and to use this process to compile a Career Entry and Development Profile (CEDP). Once in post, newly qualified teachers (NQTs) are also required to address a further set of competences in order to complete their induction year successfully. This book uses the Standards for the Award of Qualified Teacher Status and the subsequent Induction Standards as the basis for discussing key aspects of 3–8 teaching and for directing trainee and newly qualified teachers towards further reading and sources of information.

The Standards for the Award of Qualified Teacher Status comprise a set of statements outlining the required knowledge, understanding and skills necessary for the award. Student teachers wishing to look at the detail of the latest Standards can find them on the Training and Development Agency for Schools' website: http://www.tda.gov.uk/teachers/

The Standards are grouped under three headings: **Professional attributes**, **Professional knowledge and understanding** and **Professional skills**. The statements and competences described under these three headings can help student teachers and NQTs to establish exactly what areas should be covered and to set clear goals and targets to aim for. They also help trainees and recently qualified practitioners to gain greater confidence about the skills and knowledge that they have already acquired. Competence models may even give teacher trainers and future employers some assurance about what a student or an NQT can do.

However, competence approaches to teaching and teacher training are not without their shortcomings. It is possible for some competence statements to mean different things to different readers. In addition competence statements tend to emphasize outcomes – they are statements about what teachers must achieve. On their own the statements do not always provide any insights into the process or processes by which these achievements are to be attained, nor can they necessarily guarantee that a competence, once demonstrated, will be demonstrated again at other times and in other contexts.

Teaching is not just about the unthinking mastery of a set of competences and the acquisition of teaching skills and curriculum knowledge; it is also about the values and attitudes that impact upon a teacher's decision-making processes, values which are not always fully identified in a competence approach to training. Teachers need to have lively intellects and should be able to exercise understanding and judgement. They have to be adept at problem solving and communication, and be able to make links and connections between theory and practice. Good teachers are thoughtful, creative, self-critical and believe that all children can make progress. They need to be reflective in their practice and engage in self-appraisal, reading and research, rather than simply ticking off a list of competences.

One of the difficulties facing a writer of an introductory text on 3–8 teaching is the temptation to try to cover every aspect in depth. This is clearly impossible in the space available. Consequently this book offers an introduction to some of the issues and ideas relating to both the Standards for the Award of Qualified Teacher Status and the Induction Standards and then directs the reader to further sources of information (TDA, 2007a, 2007b). It aims to provide a platform from which trainees and NQTs can launch themselves into the further research and investigation that will be necessary if they are either to achieve qualified teacher status (QTS), or to complete successfully their induction period in nurseries and schools.

How to Use the Book

This book addresses policy and practice across two different age phases with different, albeit related, curricula. In the interests of inclusivity both the terms *nursery* and *school* are frequently used together. The introduction of the Foundation Stage has resulted in some changes in terminology relating to year groups, with some practitioners beginning to talk about FS1 instead of *nursery* and FS2 instead of *reception*. The book makes use of both when talking about children in the 3–5 age range.

The book follows the broad structure of the Standards documentation and each of the competences raised in the Standards is addressed in the book (TDA, 2007a). However, the sequence may be slightly different in the book. Where particular aspects of practice and the role of the teacher appear in more than one location within the Training and Development Agency documentation, some of the commentary on individual Standards in the book has been combined in some chapters to avoid duplication. In other instances, where it seems more appropriate, the reader is directed to related sections elsewhere within the text. For example:

- Standard Q5 requires teachers to understand the contribution that colleagues, parents and carers can make to the development and well-being of children and young people and to raising their levels of attainment. Standard Q33, however, requires teachers to ensure that colleagues are appropriately involved in supporting learning and understand the roles they are expected to fill (TDA, 2007a). In this case the reader will find that commentary relating to learning support staff and other professionals is largely combined and located within Chapter 1.
- Standard Q1 meanwhile states that teachers should have *high expectations* of pupils; they should respect different social, cultural, linguistic, religious and ethnic backgrounds; and they should be committed to raising the educational achievement of all the children. Standard Q19 requires teachers to know *how to make effective personalized provision* for those who have special educational needs or disabilities, and Standard Q25a concerns the need for teachers to *use a range of teaching strategies and resources* to promote *equality and inclusion* (TDA, 2007a). In this instance the reader will find commentary on teacher expectations and inclusion in more than one chapter and is therefore directed to the relevant sections in other parts of the text.

Each of the chapters begins with a brief introduction outlining those aspects of the Professional Standards for the Award of Qualified Teacher Status that are discussed.

Within each chapter the major sections also begin with their own brief audit statement to narrow down the connection to the Standards.

At various points throughout the text, grey shaded boxes indicate the use of exemplar material linked to the topic under discussion. All the identities of pupils, teachers, nurseries and schools have been altered or deleted to ensure anonymity.

At other points – in the boxes with black outline – there are questions, further exemplar materials and suggestions on how trainee and newly qualified teachers can begin to address the competences set out in the Professional Standards for the Award of Qualified Teacher Status and Induction Standards.

Each chapter also contains suggestions on further reading and other sources of information that trainee and newly qualified teachers can use to enhance and extend their knowledge and understanding of the different topics covered.

Chapter 1 deals with the professional expectations and requirements to which all teachers, including 3–8 teachers, are subject. Teachers have to conduct themselves within an environment governed by extensive regulation, laws and systems. Trainee and newly qualified members of the profession need to:

- have high expectations of all their pupils, irrespective of their social, cultural, ethnic backgrounds or their abilities;
- be effective at establishing partnerships with parents;
- engage in whole-school and team approaches to delivering the whole curriculum;
- have an understanding of how schools and nurseries are managed;
- be aware of the inspection framework for nurseries and schools;
- have a working knowledge of the legislation relating to equality of opportunity, health and safety, and children's welfare;
- know about a range of special educational needs that may be encountered in 3–8 settings and be familiar with the SEN Code of Practice;
- fulfil their responsibility to maintain good order in the classroom, without which there can be no successful teaching.

Chapter 2 deals with knowledge and understanding of children as learners and the 3–8 curricula. The chapter uses the broad areas of learning from the Early Years Foundation Stage as a framework for the discussion. Student teachers and NQTs need to:

- be familiar with ways in which children's development can affect teaching and learning in 3–8 settings;
- know about the importance of first-hand experience, play, talk and good quality adult intervention in learning and teaching;
- be familiar with the principles and structure of the Early Years Foundation Stage;
- be familiar with the principles and structure of the National Curriculum for primary pupils;
- know about the structure and delivery of literacy and numeracy in primary settings;
- know about the other areas of learning in the Foundation Stage and the range of National Curriculum subjects to be taught.

Chapter 3 deals with learning, teaching and assessment in the classroom. Knowing *how* to teach something effectively to young children is every bit as important as knowing *what* to teach. Teachers of 3–8 pupils need to:

- know how to create the right conditions for learning in the nursery/classroom;
- be able to plan lessons and sequences of lessons that contain appropriate yet challenging learning objectives;
- be able to make accurate assessments of children's learning and to record the results;
- be able to give constructive feedback to pupils and to make accurate reports to parents;
- be able to differentiate during teaching, taking into account the needs and abilities of pupils, including pupils with special educational needs (SEN);
- be efficient organizers and managers of the learning environment;
- have a good grasp of the different aspects of their role during teaching and learning.

Chapter 4 deals with the early stages of a teacher's career. Trainee teachers need to:

- know where to look and how to apply for their first post;
- be familiar with the arrangements for the induction year including the creation of a Career Entry and Development Profile (CEDP);
- be aware of their responsibility for their own continuing professional development.

1 Professional Attributes

Introduction

Teaching is about much more than a set of competences, such as the mechanics of planning a lesson or organizing a display board. Teaching is a profession, not just a job, and as such its members are subject to certain professional standards, expectations and codes of conduct as outlined in the Standards for the Award of Qualified Teacher Status (TDA, 2007a).

✔ **Audit**

By the end of this chapter you should:

- know why having high expectations of all your children matters;
- know about communicating and working with parents and other adults;
- know about playing a full part in the corporate life of the nursery/school; and
- know about legislation, policies and practices affecting the work of 3–8 teachers.

Having high expectations of all children

All children have a right to expect that their teachers will provide them with every opportunity to achieve their full potential irrespective of their gender, race, ability or social class. Education may be one of the best routes out of poverty and social exclusion but the very social, economic and health problems that we want children to leave behind frequently create barriers to learning hence the need for a *joined-up*, more unified approach to the removal of these barriers.

✔ **Audit**

By the end of this section you should:

- understand the impact that teacher attitudes can have on pupil attainment;
- understand the importance of motivation in children's learning;
- be familiar with the concept of personalized learning.

Every Child Matters

Children are entitled to an education that will enable them to participate fully in society; an education that prepares them for the opportunities, responsibilities, choices and experiences of adult life (QCA, 1999). The ethos in nursery and primary settings is informed by legislation and national strategies, including a series of Education Acts and the Every Child Matters agenda (DfES, 2004c). Current policy is an attempt to create an integrated system involving health, social care and education services to ensure that every child is given the best possible start in life irrespective of any inequalities in terms of background or circumstance. Underlying this attempt is the belief that academic attainment and well-being are interrelated. Schools have a duty therefore to do everything possible to support and contribute to children's rights to:

- **be healthy** (physically, mentally, emotionally, sexually);
- **stay safe** (from neglect, ill treatment, violence, exploitation, injury, death, bullying, discrimination, crime and anti-social behaviour);
- **enjoy and achieve** (by being ready, willing and able to participate in schooling, achieving national standards and reaching personal and social goals);
- **make a positive contribution** (by developing autonomy, decision-making skills, self-confidence, positive relationships and by displaying law abiding and enterprising behaviour);
- **achieve economic well-being** (by being ready and able to progress to further education, training or employment; living in decent homes and sustainable communities, with access to transport and goods) (DfES, 2004c).

Teachers may make a somewhat indirect contribution to the longer-term economic well-being of young children but they have a major part to play in children's health and safety in the setting and their abilities to enjoy and achieve as well as making a positive contribution. Adult conduct is central to the task of establishing an enabling learning environment characterized by positive relationships in which children are valued as individuals (DfES, 2007d). Trainee and newly qualified teachers need only to think back to their own school days to appreciate the important role that teacher expectations played in their achievements, motivation and self-esteem.

Having high expectations of general behaviour

Teachers expect children to:

- walk, not run, around the classroom;
- seek permission before leaving the room or area;
- listen to others;
- converse in normal voices without shouting;
- take care when handling tools and materials;
- show care and consideration for their peers irrespective of race, gender, ability or class;
- show care for the learning environment.

Communicating your high expectations to the children and others

- Make it clear that you expect all children to try their hardest, take pride in their work, concentrate, listen and participate.
- Ensure that the principle of equality of opportunity and high standards for all permeates planning and teaching and that the curriculum is enriched and enhanced by positive reference to diversity.
- Include learning support staff (e.g. learning mentors, TAs and lunchtime supervisors) in discussions about Every Child Matters, the Early Years Foundation Stage (EYFS), the nursery/school equal opportunities policy and help to develop appropriate strategies to translate the principles into practice.
- Work to develop a shared understanding of the nursery/school policy and practices among parents, governors and other staff.
- Make concerts and assemblies inclusive of all groups in the nursery/class, including good work assemblies.

Motivating children to succeed: Excellence and Enjoyment

Children who are stimulated, interested, excited and keen are likely to learn better than those who are not (DfES, 2004a). Although motivation may be a difficult concept to define and measure it lies at the heart of learning and can be both intrinsic and extrinsic in nature. Extrinsic motivation may be related to completion, achievement or rewards, while intrinsic motivation entails a child having an inner desire to participate in a task regardless of any end product or outcome and becoming fully immersed in that task, often losing track of time in the process (Passey *et al.*, 2004). Intrinsic motivation may be longer lived and almost certainly involves aspects of pleasure or enjoyment. Teachers can have a big impact on children's motivation to learn:

- by planning interesting learning experiences using their knowledge of the children;
- by providing plenty of opportunities to talk about their learning;
- by offering good quality and timely feedback.

It has been suggested that one way of gauging learning is to look at the level of motivation and involvement a child demonstrates in a task. Involvement means intense mental activity and concentration, during which time children are strongly motivated and are engaged in deep-level learning. Laevers has suggested a scale consisting of five levels ranging from *activity that lacks energy*, which is simple, repetitive and passive, to *total involvement*, where children are concentrating, creative, energetic and determined. In this model the level of involvement is assessed by looking at key signals such as concentration, creativity, expression, posture, persistence, precision, language, energy, reaction time and satisfaction. Although based on individual teachers' judgements regarding *levelness*, the involvement scale below can provide a fascinating insight into the children in your class, the learning and teaching approaches they respond well to, and the curriculum areas that interest and motivate them the most (Laevers, 1994 in Bertram and Pascal, 2002).

Involvement levels and signals

Levels of involvement	The child involvement signals
Level 1. Low activity Simple, stereotypical, repetitive and passive. Child is 'absent'; displays no energy. An absence of cognitive demand.	**Concentration**: child's attention is directed towards the activity. Nothing can distract the child from his/her deep concentration.
Level 2. Frequently interrupted activity Child is engaged in activity but half of the observed period includes moments of non-activity (e.g. not concentrating/ staring into space).	**Energy**: child displays effort and is eager and stimulated (e.g. loud talking or pressing down hard on the paper). Mental energy can be deduced from facial expressions which reveal 'hard' thinking. **Facial expression and posture**: distinguished between 'dreamy empty' eyes and 'intense' eyes. Posture revealing high concentration or boredom.

Level 3. Mainly continuous activity
Child is busy at an activity but at a routine level and the real signals for involvement are missing (e.g. some progress but energy is lacking and concentration is at a routine level). Child can be easily distracted.

Complexity and creativity: child freely mobilizes his/her cognitive skills and other capabilities in more than routine behaviour. Child involved cannot show more competence – he/she is at his/her very 'best'. Child exhibits an individual touch and what she/he does furthers his/her creative development. Child is at the very edge of his/her capabilities.

Level 4. Continuous activity with intense moments
Child's activity has intense moments and this level of activity is resumed after any interruptions. Stimuli from the surrounding environment, however attractive, cannot seduce child away from the activity.

Persistence: the duration of the concentration at the activity (e.g. he/she will not let go of the activity easily and wants to continue with the satisfaction/ intensity it gives him/her). Prepared to put in effort to prolong it. Not easily distracted. Duration/persistence can be dependent on age/development of the child.

Level 5. Sustained intense activity
Child shows continuous and intense activity. Not all signals for involvement need be there but the essential ones must be present: concentration, creativity, energy and persistence. This intensity must be present for almost all the observation period.

Satisfaction: child displays sense of pride/achievement.

Precision: child shows special care for his/her work and is attentive to detail.

Reaction time: child is alert, reacts quickly to any stimuli introduced (e.g. child 'flies' to activity and shows prolonged motivation and keenness).

Language: child shows activity has been important by his/her comments (e.g. asks for activity to be repeated/states that he/she enjoyed it.

(Bertram and Pascal, 2002)

Personalized learning

A key concept emerging from policy developments such as Every Child Matters, Excellence and Enjoyment and the Early Years Foundation Stage is the notion of personalized learning or the unique child (DfES; 2007c). The terms are intended to describe the act of supporting and challenging every pupil to achieve in education and to gain the skills, knowledge and attitudes essential for their future success and happiness as adults. The paradox at the heart of having high expectations of all children is that this apparent equity may only be possible if one treats them differently on occasion. In their desire not to be unfair to children, some teachers adopt the position of trying to *treat everyone the same*. Unfortunately, treating all children in the same way may not be respectful of the children's varied backgrounds and capabilities nor does it ensure equality of opportunity, but could have quite the reverse effect (Miller *et al.*, 2002). Such a policy ignores and fails to tackle the individual needs and differences of children. It is also a mistake to think that children themselves are ignorant of the differences between them; they can be very conscious of them and may have their attention drawn to these differences outside school and nursery.

However, personalized learning does not mean that teachers only plan and teach one-to-one, individual lessons and programmes of work. In part this is because the resources do not exist to make this a feasible proposition, but just as importantly it is because children benefit from the social dimension to learning. In some ways the idea of personalized learning is really a restating of traditional good practice; the best teachers have always sought to tailor the curriculum and their teaching to the needs of individual children in the class. The purpose in making the term explicit in recent curriculum documentation therefore is to support efforts to make such practice increasingly common across all settings.

Educators of young children have to consider the ways in which learning takes place and is experienced by children as well as the content of the curriculum. How children are encouraged to learn is every bit as important as what they learn. Teachers' expectations ought to be based on a professional appraisal of the needs and capabilities of individuals and not on stereotypical assumptions about the children's intellectual, emotional, social and physical attributes. Engaging in conversation with children, listening to them, as well as monitoring and observing their work, will assist you in seeking out materials and experiences likely to be both challenging and exciting for pupils from a wide range of backgrounds.

Which children:

- are highly inquisitive and curious?
- are self-confident, adventurous, and enjoy decision-making?
- are in need of more support and encouragement to take risks and respond positively to new things and experiences?
- thrive on practical problems?
- prefer intellectual problems?
- are quiet, steady, composed?
- are gregarious?
- enjoy the written word?
- prefer the spoken word?
- find visual information most instructive?

If personalized learning can be made to work widely across education it could play a valuable part in motivating children to learn. However, other factors could conspire to impede this process. In infant schools, for example, teachers are still working with classes of 25–30 children, trying to cover a predetermined diet of curriculum content at set points during the week and within a limited period of time, for example during literacy and numeracy sessions. Equally children are still tested and schools are still judged and compared in league tables. The pressure of accountability may make some practitioners reluctant to encourage the level of pupil autonomy implied by truly personalized learning for fear of being seen as lacking academic rigour and failing children, their families and society as a whole. Many of these issues are beyond the ability of individual settings and teachers to resolve as they require action on a national scale. However, there is much that teachers can do in their own classrooms to work towards a more personalized educational experience for children.

Personalizing learning in the classroom

Learning and teaching approaches:

- help children to learn about learning itself;
- make effective use of learning support staff and mentors in the classroom;
- plan interesting, stimulating and interactive lessons and experiences for children using a wide variety of techniques, approaches and resources (including ICT).

Assessment:

- provide useful and timely feedback to children on their work and their attitudes;
- use classroom assessments to inform future planning;
- set learning targets with the children.

Partnerships:

- involve parents in children's learning.

Working with parents and other adults

Children's Workforce Reform and the drive to create more coherent multi-agency and multi-disciplinary services for children and their families, brought about as a result of Every Child Matters and the Children Act, are creating new working environments for teachers. These policies and practices may develop and evolve in unexpected ways in future years as a result of a range of professional, historical, structural and political factors, yet what seems certain is that teachers will increasingly be faced with the need to rethink their inter-professional working arrangements, their role as part of multi-disciplinary teams, and partnership arrangements with parents and carers (DfES, 2004c). The Early Years Foundation Stage makes clear the importance of partnership with parents of 0–5 year olds in its initial principles and the arguments in favour of partnership are no less meaningful for children between 5 and 8 years of age, where successful partnership with parents is also cited as a vital component in education (DfES, 2007d).

✔ Audit

By the end of this section you should know about:

- parental roles in children's learning;
- effective ways of liaising and communicating with parents;
- some of the other professionals involved in the care and education of young children and the contribution that learning support staff can make to children's education;
- working as part of a team and managing the work of other adults in the nursery/classroom.

Partnership with parents

Home and nursery/school are the two most important contexts for learning in a young child's life. Families contain relationships that are not replicated anywhere else, while nurseries and schools offer children an introduction to group life where they can acquire new skills and knowledge. Although the roles of teachers and parents are different, their aspirations for the children are similar. Educators of young children are building on a learning process that has been begun by parents; consequently parents should be valued as potential partners in the continuation of that process. Effective partnership between parents and teachers can help parents to exert a positive influence on their child's progress through their attitudes towards education and the support they give. The potential gains for children and their teachers include greater motivation, better behaviour and positive relations. These outcomes may help to avoid conflict between the home and the nursery/school and minimize confusion for the children that can result from differing expectations and norms. Good liaison can also help to keep parents informed about children's learning and the part that they can play in supporting it (Fitzgerald, 2004). For example, parents can be introduced to the value of play as a vehicle for learning, or can undertake activities with their children that will help to prepare them for entry into education.

> ### Ways in which parents can help to support their children's education
>
> - Spending time with and showing an interest in the child
> - Listening to the child
> - Talking with and asking questions of the child
> - Exploring feelings and ideas with the child
> - Reading to and with the child
> - Encouraging the child to try new things and solve simple problems
> - Playing with the child
> - Creating time and space for the completion of simple homework tasks.

A key concern for parents will be that their child will be safe and secure while in nursery/school. There is an apparent tension here between a school's desire to be open and welcoming to parents, while at the same time ensuring a secure environment for the children using in some cases security fences, CCTV systems and combination locks. Parents may wish to know about:

- the timing of the school day, equipment and clothing expectations, and arrangements for the collection/non-collection of children;
- the physical arrangements to prevent intruders and escape attempts;
- the supervision arrangements while in the nursery/classroom;
- the supervision arrangements out of the classroom (e.g. during outdoor play, local walks, trips and visits);
- school policies including the behaviour policies and codes of conduct for staff, parents and children;
- teaching and learning methods: 'Why are they playing?'; 'Why aren't they all sitting at desks?'; 'Why aren't they all silent?';
- curriculum and assessment arrangements: 'Why teach a broad and balanced curriculum, shouldn't you be concentrating on English and maths?';
- partnership arrangements: 'How can I get in touch with my child's teacher and when?'; 'What can I do to help my child learn?'; 'Is there a way in which I could help the nursery/school?'

(Roffey and O'Reirdan, 2001)

Enquiries about teaching methods and the curriculum in particular may constitute a potential source of tension between nursery/school and home if parents anticipate particular educational practices based on their own (possibly secondary) schooling. Should they then perceive a mismatch between their ideas on education and existing practice in their child's class they may well raise this with the class teacher. Teachers may have to become advocates for developmentally appropriate teaching and learning on occasions and challenge preconceived ideas about educational practice. Similarly some parents may feel they have little to offer their children in terms of support as a result of their own experiences of schooling, or worries about recent curriculum developments. Communicating the purpose of different activities, explaining the teaching and learning process and offering advice on how they can help their child may help to assuage some of these concerns.

Although effective partnerships with parents has much to recommend it, it is by no means unproblematic either to initiate or to maintain these relationships. It is important for 3–8 teachers to keep clearly in mind the powerful arguments in favour of effective home/school links given some of the impediments to cooperation. In some cases the challenges to partnership may originate in schools. There may be a lack of will on the part of some teachers who feel threatened at having their work exposed to public scrutiny, while others may regard partnerships as a relatively unimportant and even peripheral feature of their role. Lack of training for teachers in working and liaising with parents could be a contributory factor to attitudes such as these. Alternatively, schools may be willing to develop partnerships but find themselves struggling to find the necessary resources and strategies.

Real partnership requires real dialogue

Ben, a newly qualified teacher (NQT), keen to encourage parents into the classroom, invited a parent to visit the class. When the parent arrived Ben asked her to supervise a group of six reception/FS2 children doing a baking activity in an adjacent utility room. The activity was intended to give the children experience of exploring and handling equipment and materials, and talking about how materials change when mixed and/or heated, but this was not communicated to the parent. When Ben went into the utility room a little later to check on how the activity was proceeding he found that the children had had almost no hands-on experience with the tools and materials and all the discussion was purely procedural in nature. It became clear to Ben that the parent was primarily concerned with the end product and that he would have to make a point in future of explaining and communicating the purposes of tasks properly instead of using parents as little more than a spare pair of hands.

In other situations the challenges to partnership originate elsewhere. Parents are no more homogeneous than the diverse society from which they and their children's teachers come: what works well in one place, for one set of parents, may not be so effective in a different context. There may be a lack of will on the part of some parents to be involved in partnership with the nursery/school. Some parents may have had negative experiences in relation to their own schooling or may be anxious about their own skills and knowledge, for example a parent whose first language is not English or who feels his/her own knowledge and skills in particular curriculum areas are weak. In other cases parents might welcome the opportunity for greater involvement but find themselves unable to, due to other commitments or problems, for example those in full-time employment; those caring for younger siblings or elderly relatives; those wishing to re-enter education themselves now that their children have started nursery/school; or those who are experiencing personal traumas of one kind or another such as marital breakdown, ill health or bereavement.

A further set of challenges to partnership can arise from differing priorities, expectations and clashes of culture between schools and parents. While there is certainly much common ground between teachers and parents, there may also be some key differences: the parents' starting point is their own child but the teachers have to consider the happiness and success of all the children. There can also be differences in terms of beliefs, with some activities valued by teachers but not valued or appreciated by some parents, for example promoting anti-racist policies in an area characterized by endemic racism, or defending parity of esteem for the wider curriculum in the face of preoccupations with SATs scores for English and mathematics.

> ## Understanding between teacher and parent?
>
> Philip's father accompanied him to school on the day that he started in Year 2. He explained to Philip's teacher that Philip had not always been well behaved in his Year 1 class and that he wanted the school to know that he was in complete support of their efforts to get Philip to improve his behaviour. He told Philip's teacher that she had his permission to give Philip a 'good hiding' if he misbehaved. Philip's teacher explained that such an act would be illegal and would run counter to the school's policy of promoting responsibility and self-discipline among the children. 'I see,' replied Philip's father. 'Well, in that case, if he messes you about, tell me and I'll give him a good hiding.'

Communication and sharing information are vital in promoting positive parental involvement and this can take place in writing or during events, some formal, others informal, at which both parents and staff are present.

Communication with parents

- **Regular parent–teacher contact**

Everyday interactions between parents and practitioners can produce considerable insight into home circumstances, needs and problems as well as children's achievements and interests beyond the classroom. Parents can give teachers useful information when they arrive at the start or end of the day on topics ranging from local problems to children's learning. Parents who are knowledgeable and have a positive attitude towards education can also be highly effective in promoting the nursery/school in the rest of the community. It is important to deal promptly and effectively with everyday queries on such things as pupil progress, transition to new classes and teachers, seating arrangements, or lunchtime problems. Parents need to be made to feel welcome when they come into the school/classroom; well-signposted, attractive and friendly looking environs can help.

- **Joint teaching/work in the classroom**

Inviting parents into nursery/school to work with the children offers opportunities for shared classroom experiences. Teachers need to be professional and to adopt a partnership approach which includes explaining to, taking advice from, and working cooperatively with parents. They should be prepared to discuss current educational ideas and practices with parents; things may well have changed dramatically since the parents' own school days. Remember that you might feel you are approachable, but others may not share that view. Be open with parents, show them that you can be discreet and will refrain from gossiping. Parents need to be sure that they can talk to you in confidence. Show parents that you listen to their comments and take their concerns seriously by taking action where necessary. Offer parents opportunities to contribute to children's learning in a range of ways including working with groups, listening to readers or talking to larger groups and classes about their experiences or interests. Although this is a time-consuming approach, it is more likely to make parents feel valued than an approach where they are in the classroom but are engaged only superficially on the margins of teaching and learning.

- **Home visits**

These can be an effective, albeit resource intensive, approach to sharing information and establishing close links between parents and practitioners. Such visits can help to ensure that parents, carers and children are properly inducted into the life of the nursery/school, for example in terms of understanding the ethos and approach to good behaviour and discipline. They also help teachers to acquire an understanding of the children's linguistic or cultural background. Home visits may provide a less threatening forum in which early years teachers can discuss ways of preparing children for entry into the Foundation Stage and ways of supporting their continued progress once they have made the transition.

- **Nursery/school events**

Less formal opportunities for parental involvement include fund-raising events such as jumble sales, sports days, summer fairs, and invitations to assemblies and concerts. Formal events such as parents' evenings, open evenings, talks and curriculum events are also useful venues at which parents and staff can share information and concerns. Such evenings can give teachers a greater insight into children's attainment, interests and actions outside the classroom. These events can also enhance parents' perceptions of how and what their children learn in nursery/school. Remember that parents have many commitments and be sensitive to the dangers of overloading them with unreasonable demands on their time or resources. The timing of events needs to take account of the constraints many parents find themselves under, such as going out to work and caring for other children. Furthermore, during parents' evenings the numbers invited ought not to preclude meaningful dialogue with staff; many schools run parents' evenings over two or three evenings to ensure that there is sufficient time for parents and teachers to talk meaningfully about children's progress. The atmosphere should also be conducive to positive and productive communication; providing refreshments and things to look at or do while they are waiting helps to make parents feel less awkward.

- **School handbooks/prospectuses**

Handbooks can provide valuable information for parents on the curriculum their children will experience, supervision arrangements in and out of the classroom and school policies and codes of conduct (e.g. dealing with incidents of bullying). Documentation should be attractive to encourage parents to look at it and including illustrations of children's work is one way of doing this. At the same time, the content should be clear, brief, easy to find, and the booklet should not be overly large as this can be off-putting, as indeed can inappropriate text that is too dense or badly spaced. Where parents' first language is not English, text in alternative languages should also be used.

- **Letters, notices and circulars**

Much of the communication from nurseries/schools to parents is in written form including letters, notices and reports. Children should be encouraged to remember to give letters and notices to their parents. Putting names on documents helps, so too does following up and checking that delivery has actually taken place. This can be particularly important with the youngest children, who may have more important things on their minds. It is a good idea to include return slips at the bottom of letters where answers are needed, and to keep copies for future reference. As with school handbooks, text in alternative languages should be available where needed.

How would you respond to these concerns?

- 'I'm not happy about Chris reading the books that you're sending home. They're too easy for him.'
- 'I want you to give me some homework for Irfaan [aged 6] so that I can do lessons with him at home.'
- 'That Wendy from Mrs Smith's class has been threatening our Claire and taking her sandwiches at dinner time.'
- 'We're worried about Daniel. He's spending all his time in the structured play area wearing dresses, high heeled shoes and carrying a handbag. His dad's really upset. Can't you stop him and get him to do normal things?'

Managing other adults in the nursery/classroom: working as part of a team

Having other adults in the classroom is nothing new for 3–8 teachers. In some instances, the additional adult support available to 3–8 teachers is on a voluntary basis, for example parents. At other times, the support is professional in nature and may involve a wide variety of staff, both internal and external. Education and training for Teaching Assistants (TAs), Higher Level Teaching Assistants (HLTAs) and Early Years Professional Status (EYPs) all raise questions about the nature of the teacher's role in the classroom. National efforts to integrate health, social care and education services also mean a raft of new practices and procedures for teachers to digest and possibly new skills and knowledge to be learned (TDA, 2007c).

While the eventual outcomes of workforce reform remain to be seen, some principles of good practice should remain constant. To begin with, trainees and NQTs need to recognize that having other adults in the nursery/classroom can significantly enhance children's learning. Teachers should value such support and treat those involved with respect. To be able to make the most of this expertise you will need to become effective both as leaders of and as members of a team. In nurseries especially, the teamwork required is particularly noticeable, including both the core nursery team (e.g. nursery teachers, nursery nurses and TAs) and the wider team (e.g. language support staff, special needs staff and parents). While not necessarily trained as teachers themselves, other adults can bring new and useful skills and experiences to the learning environment. In the case of planning, for example, a team approach enables staff to:

- produce a more comprehensive set of learning opportunities;
- improve their individual capabilities by learning from one another;
- utilize particular strengths;
- promote continuity and progression;
- ensure a unified and coherent philosophy and ethos.

It is the teacher's job to take responsibility for managing this valuable human resource. At one level this involves decisions about which activities and pupils learning support staff should be responsible for, and discussing the purposes and processes of lessons or activities with team members. However, teachers also need to think about the wider curriculum, which includes the ethos and philosophy of the setting. Learning support staff and other adults can be very effective in helping teachers to inculcate certain values and attitudes in young children such as positive relationships, fairness, respect and honesty (DfES, 2007d).

The job of managing, leading and taking responsibility for a team, some of whose members might be only occasional visitors, is a demanding task. It is a real test of teachers' interpersonal and communication skills as well as their professional expertise to do this successfully, and is particularly challenging for trainees and newly qualified teachers.

Leadership and team working skills and qualities

- Assertiveness
- Determination
- Consideration towards the feelings of others
- Energy
- Creativity
- Flexibility
- Ability to focus clearly on a task
- Good organizational skills
- Excellent communication skills
- Ability to delegate
- Knowledgeable about young children and the curriculum
- Good negotiating skills
- Being thoughtful and reflective
- Good problem-solving abilities
- Ability to motivate and support others.

Improving your expertise in working with other adults

- Think ahead: planning and preparation enhance your chances of success.
- Participation: the whole team should be involved (in appropriate ways) in planning, organizing and managing the learning environment.
- Communication: if you fail to discuss your intentions and ideas with learning support colleagues or fail to listen to their ideas and observations, there is a danger of inconsistency in approach and outcomes.
- Lead by example: this is something that you are already experienced in through your interactions with children. If you wish to foster a positive, supportive and calm manner in other adults it helps to exhibit those qualities and characteristics yourself.
- Review: being a reflective practitioner and reviewing the outcomes of directing the work of learning support staff are essential if your skills and capabilities in this area are to improve.

Very often, schools must share learning support staff between classes, although this may become less common as the numbers of non-teaching practitioners seems set to rise (DfES, 2003a). The following sections provide additional information on some of the other adults who may also be involved in 3–8 settings.

Core team members

Nursery nurses are trained in child development and healthcare, including early language development, numeracy, and personal and social development. They are also knowledgeable about the organization and management of early learning environments, as well as being very well trained in a range of observation techniques useful in the monitoring and assessment of children's needs and attainment. They are an important part of the teaching team in a Foundation Stage setting. In terms of their interactions with the children, the responsibilities are very similar to those of teachers, i.e. preparing materials, setting out equipment and facilitating children's learning. It can sometimes be difficult at first glance in many nurseries to distinguish between the teachers and the nursery nurses. The teacher, however, is ultimately responsible for planning and organizing both the curriculum and the day-to-day running of the nursery/classroom, albeit in consultation and collaboration with the nursery nurse(s).

Learning mentors work closely with individual children and small groups to support their learning and to help motivate and encourage children who are at risk of underachievement. They have a particular brief to help children to try to overcome any barriers to learning that are caused as a result of emotional, social and behavioural problems.

Teaching Assistants (TAs) and **Higher Level Teaching Assistants (HLTAs)** can take on some of the daily classroom tasks and routines to free more teacher time for planning and teaching. Equally important, however, is their ability to work alongside the teacher. In so doing they can extend and enhance the quality of educational provision for children by targeting groups and individual pupils who need extra support, providing them with access to valuable one-to-one attention, and encouraging children to talk, discuss and extend their speaking and listening skills (e.g. when reading stories and listening to readers). HLTAs may also be involved in the assessment and recording of pupil progress and may take on responsibilities for managing some of the work of other learning support staff in the classroom. In some settings HLTAs may supervise whole classes.

Wider/occasional team members

Liaison needs to take place between teaching staff and support staff not directly involved in classroom activities, such as **school secretaries**, **administrators**, **lunchtime supervisors** and **caretakers**. Both groups may need to talk about problems that particular children have and to discuss what might constitute appropriate action in particular circumstances. For example, new children can be supported in adapting to a new school/nursery environment by special and friendly attention during lunchtimes. Other pupils may have medical conditions such as allergies which the teacher knows about and which also need to be communicated to other responsible adults in the wider team.

At various times nurseries and schools will also be visited by a wide variety of adults from outside nursery/school in both professional and voluntary capacities, all of whom may need to be included in a team approach, albeit on a temporary basis. These visitors include:

- Nurses
- Speech therapists
- Health visitors
- Educational Welfare Officers (EWOs)
- Educational psychologists
- Special needs staff
- Language support staff
- Librarians and technicians
- Students
- Occasional visitors (e.g. community police officers, local theatre groups)

Health visitors and **nurses** conduct medical examinations of children when they start nursery/school and oversee immunization programmes. They also carry out screening for possible problems such as hearing loss or visual impairment at regular intervals and may work closely with practitioners to support children with specific health issues. Although many children with health difficulties are identified prior to starting school, others are not, and teachers have an important part to play in helping health professionals to identify and assist pupils with difficulties.

Educational psychologists work directly with children and their families and indirectly with teachers and other practitioners to tackle problems that children encounter in education as a result of learning difficulties or emotional and social problems. Their work may involve their testing and assessing children's needs and abilities, supporting teaching staff in understanding and responding to these needs, and writing reports to help determine the allocation of special needs resources to particular children within Children and Young People's Services (CYPS). Local CYPS also provide access to other peripatetic special needs staff for nurseries and schools to help them respond effectively where children need some additional specialist teaching or support. **Specialist support teachers** provide a range of expertise and can visit schools to assist in assessments of need, drawing up Individual Education Plans (IEPs), working with individuals or small groups and offering advice and guidance to practitioners. **Special Needs Teaching Assistants** meanwhile can work alongside class teachers and other practitioners during particular sessions in the week; they are often focused on helping specific individuals with complex needs or difficulties to access the curriculum during learning and teaching.

Educational Welfare Officers (EWOs) are mainly concerned with the enforcement of compulsory school attendance. However, they can also be involved in wider aspects of child welfare such as neglect or illegal employment. In addition, EWOs may be involved in supplying adequate clothing, meals and transport for pupils from disadvantaged homes. EWOs are a useful link between teachers and the local social services.

Visitors (individuals from outside the world of education) can help schools and nurseries to make the curriculum more relevant and exciting; some of these experts may be parents or relatives. A good visitor can do much to motivate and enthuse children but teachers must bear in mind that while a visitor may have considerable expertise in his/her particular field, it is the teacher who is the child specialist. There is an onus upon the teacher to liaise with outside experts beforehand to ensure that the content will be appropriate for the children and that it will be presented in a suitable manner.

Poor liaison, poor teaching

An education officer from one of the public utilities was asked to come and talk to a class of Y1/2s about his industry as part of a project that the children had been doing. When the education officer arrived he set up his slide projector and overhead projector. He then delivered the same 45-minute talk that he used with secondary school leavers to a class of stunned infants and their equally stunned teacher. Thereafter, this particular NQT made a point of liaising properly, and in advance, with such visitors.

Strategies for making the best use of learning and other adult support in the classroom

- Gather information on the roles of learning support staff and their expectations of you. Promote a teamworking approach by utilizing the particular skills, talents and expertise of these colleagues.
- Find out the procedures for briefing learning support colleagues.
- Explain what children should be learning and not just what they should be doing.
- Ensure that children understand the adult's role and behave properly when they are with them.
- Prepare lessons which include plans for the work of other adults and review these in lesson evaluations.
- Remember that communication is vital and involves listening as well as talking. You need to value the different perspectives that other adults bring.
- Develop shared policies on discipline, organization and assessment.
- Avoid stereotypical or negative assumptions about non-teaching colleagues.

The corporate life of the nursery/school

This section is primarily concerned with the development of whole-school documentation, the role of the governing body and Ofsted inspections. Many 3–8 settings also make use of time outside the normal school day to offer additional activities for the children and the wider community such as after-school clubs or residential visits. The reader can find further commentary on out-of-school activities in Chapter 3.

✔ **Audit**

By the end of this section you should:

- know about the structure and function of governing bodies, including their role before, during and after inspections by the Office for Standards in Education, Children's Services and Skills (Ofsted);
- know about your professional responsibilities in relation to school policies and practices, including those concerned with pastoral and personal safety matters such as bullying.

Governing bodies

The governing body has responsibility for the overall management and conduct of a setting. The governors are not concerned directly with the day-to-day running of the nursery/school as this is the responsibility of the headteacher; they deal with more strategic issues related to monitoring and evaluation of a school's performance. The exact nature of the governors' responsibilities will vary depending upon whether the nursery or school has **county**, **special** or **voluntary aided** status, and the details of the governing body's duties and powers will be set out in the nursery/school Articles of Government. Some of the areas in which governing bodies have a role to play include:

- Standards of attainment (including comparisons against national averages)
- Health and safety
- Racial equality and inclusion
- Parents
- Links with the community
- The curriculum
- Resourcing, finance and budgets
- Staffing
- Development planning
- Premises
- Child welfare and discipline
- Admissions
- Extra-curricular activities.

The exact size of the governing body will be determined by the size of the nursery or school and those elected and appointed to be governors will represent a range of interests. Trainee and newly qualified teachers can obtain up-to-date information on the constitution of governing bodies by accessing the Department for Children, Schools and Families sponsored website (www.governornet.co.uk).

Categories of governor

- **Parent governors** are elected by a vote of all parents with a child at the nursery/school, and they too must have a child in the school/nursery to be eligible to stand for election.
- **Teacher governors** are elected by the staff in the school and report back to their colleagues on the discussions and actions of the governing body. Schools and nurseries are required to ensure that non-teaching staff are also represented.
- **Appointed governors** are chosen by the Local Authority (LA), and any other bodies with authority to appoint, such as the church in the case of voluntary aided schools.
- **Community, partnership and sponsor governors** are co-opted by other governors from a wide variety of backgrounds, the aim being to broaden and strengthen the expertise of the governing body. At least one member of the governing body should be a member of the local business community.
- **Foundation governors** represent the views of churches or trusts in, for example, voluntary aided schools.
- **Headteachers** can opt to be a governor or not as they see fit. Whatever decision they make, they are entitled to attend all governors' meetings.

Each year the governing body of the school or nursery must elect a Chair and Vice-Chair (neither an employee) to lead meetings and oversee the business of the governing body, and employ a clerk. The clerk's tasks include arranging meetings, circulating agendas and papers, and taking minutes. Normally papers will be circulated to members of the governing body prior to meetings to enable the discussion to be chaired more efficiently. Due to the extensive nature of the governors' responsibilities, most nurseries and schools set up a number of sub-committees, for example finance, premises, recruitment and staffing, and curriculum sub-committees, in order to delegate some of the decision-making and preparatory work.

Once a term, the headteacher must make a report to the governing body. This report is a way of keeping governors up to date with events in the nursery/school, and places issues before the governors for advice or decisions. Curriculum coordinators may be asked to report back to governors on developments in their area of responsibility, particularly when the coordinator is involved in meeting targets set out in a development plan or identified as needing attention by an inspection team from the Office for Standards in Education, Children's Services and Skills (Ofsted). The governors themselves have a duty to keep all parents informed about their actions and the work of the nursery/school. This is done formally through an annual report supported by an annual parents' meeting at which parents can discuss the report and any matters arising from it with members of the governing body. Parent governors and the headteacher are also likely to be approached on a more informal basis whenever an issue of concern to parents arises.

Being inspected

It is a governing body's responsibility to ensure that nurseries and schools are prepared to be inspected by teams from Ofsted and that they respond to the findings of these teams. Not only do inspection teams make judgements about existing standards but they also comment on the extent to which a nursery/school has improved since its last inspection and on its capacity to improve still further in the future. The inspection teams, led by a Lead Inspector, visit nurseries and schools usually for one or two days depending on the size of the school, approximately every three years to inspect standards. The size of inspections teams can vary from one to five inspectors and will be determined by the size of the school. Not surprisingly, schools and nurseries have no right to choose their own inspection team, although they can request the CVs of team members. Governing bodies can draw the inspectors' attention to particular aspects of the school/nursery which they would like the inspectors to comment on, and can even ask Ofsted to conduct an inspection, although there is no guarantee that it will do so. Schools deemed to be in special measures as a result of an earlier inspection, for example, may seek to bring forward the next inspection if they believe the outcome will raise them out of special measures.

Normally schools/nurseries receive between two and five days' notification of a forthcoming inspection. In part this is to prevent schools becoming distracted by an inspection for weeks or months before it happens; in part it means inspection teams are more likely to see schools as they really are. Having been notified, the school must provide the Lead Inspector with a copy of its self-evaluation form (SEF). Schools therefore need to update their SEFs annually. This document combined with the school's previous inspection report and any performance and assessment data through Raise on-line provide a basis for initial discussions with school managers and governors and help the Lead Inspector to plan and direct the inspection. The focus for the inspection should be shared with the school prior to the start. Schools are reminded that the SEF must be more than descriptive; the best SEF documents are reflective and analytical about a school's view of its own strengths and areas for development. Nurseries and schools are encouraged not to produce additional documentation specifically for an inspection but depending on its focus the team could require copies of any existing documentation pertaining to the running of the nursery/school which could include:

- school/nursery development plans;
- schemes of work;
- policies and guidelines;
- pupils' records;
- details of in-service training for staff during the previous three years;
- the school prospectus;
- the programme of staff meetings;
- financial details;
- monitoring and evaluation outcomes.

Prior to an inspection a questionnaire is sent to all parents by the governors to elicit comments and responses concerning their children's education. The responses are returned to the Lead Inspector, who will incorporate the feedback into her/his deliberations concerning the focus for the inspection. Parents may also request meetings with inspectors during the inspection period, although given the short timescale of the inspection, inspectors may not be able to accommodate every such request.

The inspection itself will focus upon:

- the overall effectiveness of the school and its ability to meet the Every Child Matters agenda;
- how well learners achieve;
- the effectiveness of teaching and learning;
- how well the curriculum meets the needs and interests of pupils;
- the quality of guidance and support for learners;
- the efficiency and effectiveness of school leadership and management.

Class teachers are not the only staff to be inspected; the headteacher, deputy headteacher, members of the governing body, the nursery team leader and curriculum coordinators may all be interviewed about their roles. Inspectors will also make comments on the class teachers' ability to effectively deploy learning support staff within the classrooms. Furthermore, inspectors may also make use of pupil interviews. While in school/nursery, inspectors will observe teaching, talk to children and make comments on an observation schedule. Given the focus on standards, inspection teams will be particularly interested in prior attainment and the progress made by children. Consequently Foundation Stage settings will be looked at carefully for data on prior attainment and Year 2 and Year 6 classes will also be closely examined as a means of gauging pupil progress and achievement.

Inspectors would normally be expected to spend a minimum of 30 minutes observing any lesson and to be present at the start of the session. Teachers need to have their plans and records available and inspectors are instructed to share the purpose of their observations. Teaching may be judged **outstanding**, **good**, **satisfactory** or **inadequate** and inspectors are expected to give teachers clear and constructive feedback face to face. It is worth noting that in the context of an inspection the term *satisfactory* indicates competence; it should not be imbued with any of the everyday connotations sometimes associated with the term. This said, inspection teams will be looking for learning and teaching that is *good* or better, rather than satisfactory.

In addition to classroom observations the inspection team will look at Standard Assessment Tasks (SATs) results in primary settings and examine teacher assessments and samples of work that reflect the ability range in classes. The inspection team may also wish to examine the Individual Education Plans (IEPs) and Statements for children with special educational needs and may even track case studies of individual children. This work is undertaken in order to enable the team to make judgements concerning continuity, progression, coverage of the Foundation Stage early learning goals and educational programmes and/or National Curriculum and the extent to which pupil achievement is in line with national expectations. As the inspection team begins to arrive at its findings the Lead Inspector has to discuss these with the headteacher and/or governors, who then have the opportunity to provide additional information if they wish to do so. Once the inspection team has reached its final conclusions these are outlined verbally to the school's management.

During the post-inspection period the nursery/school receives a full written report and must prepare its response to the team's findings. Final reports are expected to be completed within three weeks of the inspection's conclusion. A final draft is sent to the school before publication and schools have one day in which to respond. This is a final opportunity to correct any factual inaccuracies but not to challenge or query any of the inspectors' judgements. At this point the report becomes a public document and appears on the Ofsted website (www.ofsted.gov.uk/reports). Copies are also sent out to the school, CYPS or other appropriate authorities. While most schools will be judged satisfactory, good or outstanding a few are judged to be failing to meet the needs of learners. In these cases inspection teams have two options. Where they feel the management in a school lacks the capacity to make the necessary changes they can place a school in **special measures**. Where the team believe the school's management can make the changes needed the school can be issued with a **notice to improve**. Both categories result in subsequent intervention and follow-up visits to check on progress.

Once the inspection report has been received, there is a statutory requirement upon the governors to send copies out to all parents and to draw up an action plan to address those areas identified by the inspection team as requiring change. Newly qualified teachers with curriculum coordination responsibilities may find themselves leading aspects of this action planning. Even if the governors disagree with an inspection finding they must still institute action to bring about the change required in the final report.

Action plans identify:

- clear targets and criteria for success;
- the action to be taken to meet the targets including personnel involved in monitoring, evaluating and controlling the process;
- an indication of the timescales involved;
- possible funding or resources needed.

Coping with an inspection

- Make sure the learning environment is attractive and stimulating for the children.
- Make sure your planning is available for an inspector to look at. Session planners should show clear and appropriate learning objectives.
- The quality of your teaching and the children's learning will be of prime concern to an inspector during an observation. Make sure you consider the different needs and abilities in your class. How are you going to differentiate for them?
- Your questioning and exposition skills are important elements in ensuring that learning takes place. Have you thought through your questions, explanations and vocabulary?
- The structure and organization of the lesson/session needs to be well thought out. Is there a clear beginning, middle and end? How are transition times going to be managed? Are your instructions clear? Is your timing and pacing suitable for the age and abilities of the children? Have you made effective use of any adult support in the nursery/classroom?
- You need to maintain the children's interest and enthusiasm and keep them on task. This might be more difficult if you play it safe and plan a staid, completely risk-free lesson. How can you make your lesson motivating, interesting and exciting without losing control of events?

Ofsted inspection comments and related action plan

Remarks on teaching and learning in history:

107 Attainment in history in both Key Stage 1 and 2 is in line with national expectations. In Key Stage 1 pupils are developing a sense of chronology. They can also give some valid reasons for people's actions and past events. By the end of Key Stage 2 most pupils are able to combine information from a variety of sources and make inferences and deductions. They have a sound general knowledge of the Tudors, Vikings and Ancient Egypt. Progress in both Key Stages is good.

108 Pupils' attitudes to learning history are good. They are interested in the topics and study units, answer questions with enthusiasm and concentrate well.

109 In the small number of lessons observed, the quality of teaching was sound. Teachers' subject knowledge is secure. Individual lessons are well planned with clear learning objectives. More precise references to the Programmes of Study would aid both progression and assessment of pupils' attainment and progress.

110 The new coordinator has not yet had time to make a significant impact, nor has she had the opportunity to benefit from in-service training. The policy and guidelines for the subject need updating to bring them into line with the rest of the school's documentation. The role of the coordinator in monitoring curriculum development and the quality of teaching is not yet in place. The subject is adequately resourced and pupils' work is displayed well. The history curriculum is significantly enriched by school visits.

Action Plan

Targets	Criteria for success	Action
To improve documentation for history in the school	• Produce policy and guidelines for history • Produce scheme of work for history	• Draft action plan to be reviewed/adapted/approved by staff • Draft documentation to be produced by coordinator • Draft documentation to be reviewed/adapted/approved by staff
To enhance subject expertise of History Coordinator	• Attend LA training courses for history	• Agree funding for staff training with governors • Obtain copy of LA Inset provision and apply
To institute monitoring of the history curriculum	• Planning for history is reviewed • History teaching is observed in classrooms • History resources are recorded	• Arrange staff meeting to discuss and agree systems for coordinator to review history planning • Draw up timetable for classroom observations • Conduct audit of history resources across the school
To make increased use of National Curriculum documentation in planning for history	• Long-term plans clearly state relevant PoS • Medium-and short-term planning is based on whole-school plans	• Use new policy and guidelines and map out history coverage across the year groups • Check that reference to relevant PoS appears in planning • Check that lesson objectives are informed by the National Curriculum during peer observation
To improve assessment and recording of pupil attainment in history	• Class records to include history • Agreement among staff about levels at Key Stages 1 and 2 • Informative reporting to parents	• Create resource of benchmarked history work • Organize moderation meetings • Develop exemplar material to support report writing

Member(s) of staff	By when	Completed on
History Coordinator All staff	End of autumn term	
Headteacher History Coordinator All staff	By end of academic year	
HT/coordinator in consultation with staff Coordinator	By end of academic year	
Coordinator All staff Coordinator Coordinator	By end of spring term	
Coordinator All staff	By end of summer term	

(O'Hara and O'Hara, 2001)

Whole-school policies and practices

Teachers of 3–8 pupils are required to play their part in drawing up, and adhering to, whole-school documentation on a range of matters such as Foundation Stage early learning goals, core and foundation subjects in the National Curriculum, and generic issues that cut across subjects and areas of learning such as bullying, special educational needs, health and safety, behaviour, and transition to, within and between schools. Such documentation will be composed of policy statements and guidelines, and in the case of National Curriculum subjects and areas of learning in the Foundation Stage it will also include schemes of work/educational programmes.

Policies and guidelines

A policy is a succinct description, outlining the overall rationale for teaching a subject or tackling an educational issue. It should be to the point and written in plain English. A policy consists of broad principles which underpin the way in which a subject or issue is approached in a nursery/school. In effect it answers the questions 'What is it?' and 'Why do we do/teach it?' Guidelines set out how staff are expected to approach a subject, an area of learning or generic issue with their pupils and they are usually attached to the policy statements. Guidelines address the question 'How do we do it?' by providing a general framework to deal with a range of issues including organization, cross-curricular links and assessment. Possible headings for guidelines will vary depending on whether the guidelines in question relate to a National Curriculum subject (e.g. mathematics), an area of learning (e.g. Creative Development) or a generic issue (e.g. bullying).

Possible guideline headings

- Links to the early learning goals or National Curriculum Programmes of Study and Attainment Targets. Links with other subjects.
- How the subject or issue is planned for in the nursery/school.
- Classroom organization, management and teaching methods.
- Marking, monitoring, assessment and recording.
- Continuity and progression across the nursery/school.
- Equal opportunities and multicultural/anti-racist strategies.
- Provision for special educational needs (SEN).
- Provision for children in the Foundation Stage.
- Use and provision of ICT and other resources.
- Health and safety.
- Links with the cross-curricular elements.
- Links with the wider community.
- The role of the headteacher.
- The role of the subject coordinator.
- The role of parents and other adults.

Policy and guidelines on generic issue: Bullying

Policy statement

. . . . School believes that it is against the interests of all children, the bullied and the bullies, to allow bullying to take place unchallenged. No child can learn properly and achieve their full potential when they feel threatened and vulnerable. We regard bullying as particularly serious and the school will always take firm action against it. In addition, our school believes that we do a long-term disservice to a pupil if we allow them to continue to bully others and avoid facing up to the consequences of their actions.

Guidelines

1 Identifying incidents of bullying

Staff need to be aware that there can be a fine line between bullying and boisterous or bossy behaviour. A child being bossy will try to dominate whoever is around at the time and will often grow out of this behaviour as they mature and develop wider social skills. A bully will target younger or weaker children and will display a conscious desire to hurt or frighten these children. A boisterous pupil displays a high spirited, uncontrolled and not unfriendly presence in the classroom. A bully will deliberately engage in a concerted campaign to spoil other children's activities, displaying hostile, rough, intimidating and targeted behaviour.

Bullying can take many forms. It can be physical, emotional or verbal in nature and can involve a single bully or a group of pupils. Possible examples of bullying include:

- name calling, malicious gossip and taunting;
- stealing or damaging other children's property and work;
- coercion, threats, extortion and intimidation;
- punching, kicking and other violent behaviour;
- ostracizing children.

Signs of distress that might indicate that bullying is taking place include:

- pupils acting in a withdrawn manner and appearing isolated;
- deterioration in standards of work;
- fake illnesses and a deterioration in attendance and punctuality;
- a desire to remain close to adults;
- apparent unhappiness, anxiety and fear.

2 Reasons for bullying

Bullying can occur in children of all ages and there are a variety of reasons why some pupils become victims of bullying and some pupils become bullies. In some cases the bullies themselves are the victims of bullying. The children targeted are often (although not always) timid, anxious or less assertive, in other words those children deemed unlikely to fight back or resist the bullying, the children who are younger or smaller than the bully, or the children who are loners and not part of a particular group.

The reasons why children are targeted include:

- differences in race, sex, or social class;
- other differences, including physical disability, general appearance or being new to the school;

- differences in ability, including academic, physical and creative;
- vulnerability, perhaps as a result of suffering other problems.

Children may become bullies because:

- they are themselves victims of bullying or violence;
- they obtain a sense of power and control through the act of bullying;
- they are copying the behaviour of others (either in school, at home or on television and in films and videos);
- they are jealous; or
- they are insecure and have low self-esteem.

3 Strategies for eliminating bullying in the classroom

- Use lots of praise and recognition to reward cooperative, non-aggressive behaviour.
- Encourage the caring side of pupils' development.
- Discuss and promote friendships and cooperation.
- Maintain proper supervision both in the classroom and outside.
- Make children aware that standing by while bullying takes place is to support the bullying.
- Give support to the victim and help them to regain and develop their self-esteem and confidence.
- Try to find out why the bully is bullying. Do not bully the bully. Help the child to see another's point of view: 'How would you feel if . . .?'
- Give support to the bully by encouraging and supporting them to work positively with other children, for example giving responsibility for looking after someone or something.
- Work to involve parents. Explain why certain actions have been taken and discuss with parents what they can do to reinforce and support the efforts of the nursery/school to resolve the problem successfully. If necessary, help parents to understand the distinction between bossy or boisterous behaviour and bullying. However, make sure that parents know that you take their concerns seriously, are aware of the situation and will take steps to stop their child being made to feel unhappy.
- Serious or persistent incidents should be monitored, recorded and reported to the headteacher or the responsible member of staff.
- In very serious cases bullying needs to be reported to the governing body and if necessary will involve an official complaints procedure.

Policy and guidelines on a National Curriculum subject: English

Subject: English

Date of publication:

1 The aims of English teaching

English is the basic language of communication in this country and throughout much of the world. The mastery of this subject is a prerequisite for educational progress in all other curriculum areas and is vital for pupils' future adult lives as citizens, producers and consumers in society. Through the teaching of English at . . . . School pupils will build on the language opportunities provided in the home and will develop into more proficient and discriminating readers, writers, speakers and listeners.

Pupils will:

- be introduced to a wide range of text, materials and information technology resources to enrich and challenge their learning;
- be given opportunities to develop their competence in standard written English;
- be made aware of the differences between spoken and written forms of language.

2 Interpretation of the statutory orders

The National Curriculum provides the basic framework for our programme of teaching and assessment in English for both key stages.

> In studying English pupils develop skills in speaking, listening, reading and writing. It enables them to express themselves creatively and imaginatively and to communicate with others effectively. (QCA, 1999, p. 43)

In addition the school follows the National Literacy Strategy to underpin wider teaching and learning in English. All pupils from Year 1 to Year 6 will experience shared reading and writing tasks, word/sentence level work, individual pupil tasks, and guided writing tasks as part of the school's daily literacy sessions. Guided reading sessions are also incorporated into the school's English provision on a daily basis.

In English pupils will be taught:

- how language works so that they can understand how people write and speak;
- to use formal and impersonal forms of language;
- to adapt writing and speech to a range of different audiences;
- to use conventional letter formation, spelling and grammar;
- to use punctuation;
- comprehension and composition;
- the meaning of individual words, groups of words, sentences, groups of sentences and whole texts.

3 Planning for English

We have a mixed approach to our planning and teaching of English. In delivering the National Literacy Strategy teachers are required to adhere to the national documentation to support their planning. In addition staff will plan for wider English teaching and learning in their remaining medium-term and lesson plans.

4 Classroom organization and management

The English curriculum is organized into:

- learning of reading, writing, speaking and listening in literacy lessons;
- additional and wider learning which goes on throughout the school day and throughout all curriculum areas.

Equal importance is given to both these aspects of the English curriculum in terms of organization and management.

5 Teaching methods

The school uses a range of teaching methods in English based on fitness for purpose. These methods include whole-class, group and individual teaching. English can be a collaborative subject and pupils will be taught the skills required to work both as individuals and as members of a team.

6 Differentiation

At .... School we aim to provide for the needs of individual children and the following strategies are used as appropriate:

- children with difficulties in English receive extra support in the classroom from a specialist teacher and/or external agencies;
- children are supported within their class by their own class teacher and differentiated work is given as appropriate;
- extra help is provided in the classroom by learning support staff and parent volunteers;
- able children are encouraged to develop their full potential by being provided with challenging work appropriate to their needs.

7 Assessment, recording and reporting

a Assessment *for* learning

Formative assessment is mostly carried out by teachers in the course of their teaching through:

- hearing children read;
- small-group and class discussions;
- short tests;
- specific assignments;
- individual discussions with the teacher in which children are encouraged to appraise their own work and progress.

b Assessment *of* learning

Formal summative assessment is carried out at the end of each National Curriculum Key Stage through the use of SATs and/or teacher assessments. The school also makes use of commercially produced testing systems to measure pupil progress and performance midway through each school year.

c Marking

Feedback to pupils about their own progress in English is achieved through discussion and through marking of work, sometimes done while a task is being carried out. Marking should:

- be constructive, continual and consistent;

- be done sensitively and with discretion so that a child can assimilate a limited number of corrections at one time. This will vary according to age and ability.

d Recording and reporting

The records of progress in English kept for each child include:

- home/school diaries annotated by the child or parents as appropriate to age and ability;
- a record of books read which takes the form of a reading diary and is maintained by each child;
- a portfolio of written work, dated and annotated with teacher comments and containing one item for each term which shows achievement and progress;
- reading progression records.

8 Use of ICT in English

This is in line with the school's ICT policy. In addition to the use of class based computer resources, the school's ICT suite is used to support teaching and learning in English. Pupils will use ICT in English to:

- handle information;
- communicate information.

9 Meeting the needs of pupils in the Foundation Stage

Language development for the under-fives and early years children receives a very high priority at . . . . School. Teaching and learning in the school's nursery and reception settings follows the Early Years Foundation Stage (EYFS). Teaching encourages the children to extend their vocabulary, speak clearly and confidently and listen carefully. The children are provided with numerous play-based opportunities to improve their skills in this area through discussions and conversations, structured role-play activities, listening to stories and poems, singing songs, handling and looking at books and writing. The children are helped to recognize letters and write simple words including their own name.

10 Resources for English

Classroom resources for English include:

- a class reading library containing fiction, non-fiction and poetry;
- dictionaries;
- textbooks and workbooks to support comprehension activities;
- a selection of paper and guidelines for writing activities;
- the class computer;
- speaking books and tape recorders are also used in the early years settings.

Central resources for English are the responsibility of the English Coordinator in consultation with staff and the headteacher. The school expects these resources to be kept in good condition and to be replaced when worn. Staff are responsible for returning resources to central areas when they have finished using them.

11 Links with the cross-curricular elements

Links will be made with appropriate cross-curricular elements, particularly personal, social and health education (PSHE) and citizenship. These links will be identified on the school's schemes of work.

12 Equal opportunities, multicultural education and English as an additional language
Where children speak English as a second language the teaching will be adapted and differentiated to meet their needs and ensure that they achieve their full potential. In addition the school provides a range of literature including stories and tales from different cultures and geographical and historical periods.

13 Continuity and progression in English
At . . . . School continuity and progression are ensured by using the revised literary framework in planning for English. In addition, staff use after-school meetings and in-service training days when appropriate to discuss the English curriculum and ensure consistency in approach and standards.

14 Time allocation for English
The formal time allocated each week is 7 hours in Key Stage 2 and 7 hours in Key Stage 1. In addition pupils will be given opportunities to apply their learning about reading, writing, phonics, speaking and listening during linked (integrated thematic) work.

15 Links with the wider community
Opportunities are provided for the children to enhance their learning in English through links with local businesses and organizations, through visits and by inviting parents and other adults into school.

16 The role of the English Coordinator
The coordinator, working alongside the headteacher, has the responsibility for ensuring quality in the teaching and learning of English in the school. He/She will take the lead role in the production of whole-school documentation and in addition will support colleagues in the production of short-term planning. He/She has responsibility for the maintenance of resources and equipment, and for the purchase of new equipment and materials. He/She will attend courses, be a resource of subject knowledge and provide in-service training for his/her colleagues. He/she will be familiar with standards of achievement in speaking and listening and reading and writing in each year group. He/she will monitor pupils' achievement against age related expectations and National Curriculum levels.

17 The role of the headteacher
The headteacher will support the English Coordinator in encouraging colleagues to teach English effectively. He/She will be responsible, through the English Coordinator, for ensuring that the policy and guidelines are used and for bringing the policy and guidelines to staff for periodic updating. This policy will be reviewed every two years. The next review will begin in . . . . and the revised policy will be in place by . . . . The headteacher will ensure that the school's policy is in line with national policy and that of the LA.

Schemes of work

A scheme of work constitutes long-term planning (see Chapter 3) and gives details about what is taught, where and when across the school or nursery. It provides for the sequence of teaching in order to ensure progression and continuity while avoiding repetition. Schemes are based on relevant national documentation such as the EYFS early learning goals, National Curriculum Programmes of Study or Revised Literacy and Numeracy Strategies. More specific, medium-term planning for individual classes or year groups is based upon this framework. It is worth noting that with the increasing emphasis on English and mathematics, including the introduction of literacy and numeracy strategies, many primary schools are using commercially produced schemes such as those published by the Qualifications and Curriculum Authority (QCA) to help them deliver the non-core foundation subjects which make up much of the wider curriculum.

Section from scheme of work for Key Stage 1 geography

Programme of Study (PoS) requirements	Year 1 Local area study	Year 1 On the farm	Year 1 Improving the school grounds	Year 1/2 Barnaby Bear	Year 2 Bangladesh
1a. Ask geographical questions	•	•	•	•	•
1b. Observe and record	•	•	•		•
1c. Express own views	•	•	•	•	•
1d. Communicate in different ways	•	•	•	•	•
2a. Use geographical vocabulary	•	•	•	•	•
2b. Fieldwork skills	•	•	•		

(Owen and Ryan, 2001)

The responsibilities and legal liabilities of the 3–8 teacher

This section will introduce the reader to some of the legislation, systems, legal liabilities and responsibilities governing teachers' actions, including the maintenance of good order in the classroom.

✔ Audit

By the end of this section you should have a working knowledge and understanding of:

- teachers' professional duties as set out in the current School Teachers' Pay and Conditions document, issued under the School Teachers' Pay and Conditions Act 1991;
- teachers' responsibilities and legal liabilities relating to the Race Relations Act 1976, the Race Relations (Amendment) Act 2000, the Sex Discrimination Act 1975 and the Disability Discrimination Act 1995;
- the potential range of needs that are included under the heading of SEN and the operation of the Code of Practice;
- the Health and Safety at Work Act 1974 and teachers' common law duty to ensure that pupils are healthy and safe;
- teachers' responsibilities and legal liabilities relating to the promotion of children's welfare as set out in the Children Act 1989, the role of the education service in protecting children from abuse and appropriate physical contact with pupils (DfEE, 1995);
- teachers' responsibilities relating to discipline and control, including appropriate physical restraint of pupils (DfEE, 1998);
- how to establish a presence in the classroom and how to promote positive values, attitudes and behaviour.

The School Teachers' Pay and Conditions Act (1991)

The School Teachers' Pay and Conditions Act (1991) sets out the pay and conditions of teachers in England and Wales. The Act provides for the constitution of a Review Body and defines the powers and responsibilities of the Secretary of State for Children, Schools and Families to make Statutory Orders on teachers' pay and conditions. The function of the Review Body is to consider matters relating to pay and conditions and to report its findings and recommendations to the Secretary of State. This is intended as a way of trying to ensure a rational basis for policy-making based on balanced consideration of the evidence. Although the Secretary of State has the power to override and ignore the Review Body, to do so completely could prove politically embarrassing.

Not only may the Review Body consider issues for itself, but also the Secretary of State may ask it to examine a particular matter and report back within a given time period. In such cases those affected – teachers, their unions, school governors and

Local Authorities – have to be given the opportunity to submit evidence to the Review Body. Once the Secretary of State has received the report and advice from the Review Body there is a legal requirement to publish the report and subsequently seek to make a Statutory Order based on that report. In so doing, the Secretary of State has the power to modify or change the recommendations. In addition to seeking recommendations from the Review Body, the Secretary of State also has the power to make Statutory Orders in his/her own right. Whenever a Statutory Order is made, teachers must be paid according to the pay scales laid down in it, and any conditions set out in the Statutory Order become part of teachers' contracts.

Pay

Teachers' salaries are determined by the number of points a member of staff has reached on the pay scale. These points will be assessed and awarded by a local authority if a teacher is employed centrally or if the school or nursery at which he/she is employed does not have a delegated budget. Where a school has a delegated budget, or in the case of grant-maintained schools, it is the governing body's responsibility to make the points assessment. In parts of the country where schools and Local Authorities are experiencing difficulties with teacher recruitment and retention the basic salary package may be augmented by the offer of additional monies to tempt applicants into the area. If trainee or newly qualified teachers are uncertain as to their points entitlement, their teaching unions will be able to offer advice.

Pay

- Since the introduction of the revised 6-point pay scale, newly qualified teachers start at point 1.
- Governing bodies can award extra points where recruitment and retention is difficult (in certain parts of the country and in certain subject areas) and in cases of excellence.
- An additional point is added for every year's satisfactory performance until the teacher reaches point 6 on the scale. Scale point 6 is the maximum point a teacher can reach by virtue of experience and qualifications alone. This yearly increment is not automatic and can be withheld by the governing body if they feel that a teacher's performance is not satisfactory.
- Once teachers reach point 6 on the scale they can apply for their performance to be assessed in order pass the **threshold**. If successful they move to point 1 on the upper pay scale. Progress in pay rates after this point is performance related and not automatic, with a minimum period between incremental increases of two years. To progress through the upper pay scale teachers have to demonstrate that they have sustained or enhanced their substantial contribution to the working of the nursery/school.

- Many teachers are expected to take on posts of responsibility during their teaching careers and some of these posts can also carry additional points, for example English Coordinator, Nursery Team Leader, Key Stage 1 Coordinator.
- Teachers who wish to advance their career without moving into school management are also able to apply for advanced skills teacher (AST) posts, which have their own pay scale.
- Teachers who are primarily engaged in teaching children with special educational needs are entitled to an extra point on the pay scale and could receive two such points should the governors so decide.

(NUT, 2002)

Conditions of service

Under the terms of the 1991 Act all teachers must carry out their professional duties as well as any particular duties that can be *reasonably* assigned to them by the headteacher. The term reasonable will appear repeatedly in the remainder of this chapter in relation to teachers' duties and responsibilities and as you will see, it is invariably open to interpretation. Teachers employed on a full-time basis are expected to work for 195 days (a total of 1,265 hours) during the school year (NUT, 1998). Five of these days are allocated for staff and curriculum development. In addition to the 1,265 figure, teachers are required to work any additional hours needed to enable them to discharge their professional duties effectively. These additional hours would normally be taken up by tasks such as report writing, attending staff meetings and, of course, planning, preparation and marking.

In 2005 changes to teachers' contracts as part of ongoing workforce reform meant that they were also now entitled to time during the week for planning, preparation and assessment (PPA). Early years and primary practitioners had long pointed out that unlike secondary schools, in nursery and primary settings all such activity had previously to be conducted outside of the school day and outside of term time. The introduction of PPA time will not remove such out-of-hours work but it should ease the pressure on 3–8 teachers and is also intended to provide opportunities during the working day to liaise with colleagues, direct the work of learning support staff and to plan new and improved ways in which to raise standards of pupil attainment.

Teachers' professional and particular duties

- Teachers are expected to promote the well-being and educational achievement of individual children, irrespective of ethnicity, gender or social class, and to maintain good order and discipline in the classroom.
- They must safeguard the health and safety of the children in their care, both in school and on outside visits.
- Teachers are expected to take part in activities such as registration, playground supervision and attending assemblies.
- During teaching, staff must ensure that lessons are properly planned. They must also be prepared to take part in medium-term planning and preparation, and whole-school approaches to the curriculum. This planning and teaching must take individual needs and abilities into account.
- Staff must engage in assessing and reporting on children's progress and attainment, for example recording and reporting on the personal and social needs of children, liaising with parents and working with outside agencies and individuals such as special needs colleagues. For teachers of Y2 pupils, this will include participating in arrangements for Standard Assessment Tasks (SATs), while in reception it will mean completion of the Foundation Stage Profile.
- Beyond the classroom, teachers of young children are required to take part in appraisal activities aimed at improving their own professional competence and, as part of this, to review from time to time their current practice and their training and development needs.
- Participation at staff meetings and in-service training days is mandatory for teachers.
- Teachers can also be asked to take part in the selection and recruitment of new staff, mentoring newly qualified colleagues and taking responsibilities across the school for coordinating a curriculum area, which would involve ordering resources, developing documentation and supporting the staff development of colleagues.

Professional body membership

All teachers wishing to work in the maintained sector and special needs education must now by law be registered with the General Teaching Council (GTC), which involves the payment of a small annual fee. The stated aims of the GTC are to raise both standards of teaching and the status of teachers. The GTC is an independent professional body with duties to maintain a register of recognized teachers with Qualified Teacher Status (QTS), to rule on certain discipline or competence cases and to advise the government on educational policy associated with professional practice, teacher supply, retention and career progression. The GTC also regulates on standards of professional competence and conduct. In a case of professional misconduct, for example, the GTC could decide to remove a teacher from the Register thus effectively blocking him/her from future employment in the maintained sector. Students on teacher training courses are offered the chance to be automatically registered with the GTC once they have been awarded

QTS. It is possible to opt out of this process but if you do you will have to register at a later date if you intend to teach in the maintained sector.

Promoting equality of opportunity and inclusion

Discriminatory behaviour must be opposed by teachers as it creates barriers and obstacles that disadvantage and exclude children. Legislation in recent decades has given increasing prominence to the issue of special educational needs (SEN) and how best to respond to such needs to enable all children to realize their full potential. In addition, both the Race Relations (Amendment) Act 2000 and the Sex Discrimination Act 1975 make discrimination on the grounds of race or sex illegal. Although the various Acts relating to equality of opportunity are under review at the time of writing and may well be superseded by a new Single Equality Act which will unify and simplify the existing legislation, any changes that take place will not alter the fundamental fact that discrimination can be either direct or indirect in nature and that both are prohibited.

✔ Audit

By the end of this section you should:

- know about the implications of the Race Relations (Amendment) Act 2000 and the Sex Discrimination Act for your practice as a teacher;
- know about the need to remove barriers to achievement in the classroom for children with special educational needs (SEN);
- know about the Code of Practice for children with SEN;
- know about some of the ways in which you can promote equality of opportunity and inclusion in your practice.

Ethnicity

The Race Relations Act 1976 makes illegal any direct or indirect discrimination on the grounds of race, colour, ethnic or national origins. Direct discrimination is considered to have occurred in any instance where an individual is overtly treated unfavourably, such as racial abuse or bullying in the playground. Indirect discrimination relates to those instances where individuals are ostensibly being treated equally, but where the outcome is actually discriminatory in nature. Indirect discrimination, through admissions policies, for example, is unlawful. Similarly a school that insisted that all girls wear skirts might appear even handed but the policy could be deemed discriminatory by some minority ethnic groups for whom skirts would not be regarded as an appropriate mode of dress.

> ## Planning and the Race Relations Act
>
> School 'A' has a scheme of work for personal, social and health education (PSHE)/citizenship and religious education (RE) which maps out how the school will approach these areas over a two-year cycle. The plan identifies the current focus as 'Our Culture' and the next focus as 'Other Cultures'.
>
> Is there a problem with this plan in light of the Race Relations (Amendment) Act 2000?

The Race Relations (Amendment) Act 2000 places an onus upon schools to work actively not only towards the elimination of racial discrimination but also towards the *promotion* of equal opportunities and positive relations between staff, pupils and parents of different racial groups (NASUWT, 2002). For example, staff may need to be alert to instances where disproportionate numbers of ethnic minority children are located in lower ability groups and to look for ways to tackle this underachievement. At the same time, every parent needs to be able to understand school documents (e.g. handbooks, letters, signs, displays, records and reports) and consequently information may need to be available in languages other than English.

Although the Act seeks to end racial discrimination it does provide for the particular needs of certain groups in society to be met; ending discrimination should not be equated with treating every child as identical. Dietary and clothing requirements need to be respected, as do religious holidays and festivals. Assemblies provide a valuable opportunity to impart anti-racist values to young children, as do projects and topics such as 'Ourselves' which offer opportunities to raise children's awareness of diversity in society. Resources such as reading and reference books ought to be chosen carefully so as to avoid racist stereotyping.

> ## Developing a multicultural/anti-racist approach in the nursery/classroom
>
> - Spell and pronounce children's names properly.
> - Help children to recognize and challenge discriminatory practices and behaviour.
> - Help children to begin to understand ideas such as fairness, justice and diversity.
> - Guide children in the adoption and use of non-discriminatory language.
> - Praise and reinforce non-discriminatory behaviour in children.
> - Provide resources that actively and positively promote diversity in terms of culture, class, gender and ability.

- Deal promptly and efficiently with biased or discriminatory attitudes and actions. Operate a policy of **zero tolerance** and make sure that when such incidents occur pupils are encouraged to confront their assumptions, actions and the consequences of those actions.
- Help children to identify the similarities, as well as the differences, that exist between them and their classmates. Help them to understand the differences, to behave in a considerate manner and to appreciate each other's strengths.
- Demonstrate that you value and respect diversity and individual differences by using pupils' first language where possible and by showing respect for traditions, cultures and protocols.
- Acquire and share knowledge about the historical, cultural and spiritual backgrounds in the local community.
- Enable children to take part in the everyday activities of their local community.

Gender

Schools and nurseries must provide an entitlement curriculum for both boys and girls. In part this will concern access; for example, girls have an equal entitlement to experience with the computers and construction kits. However, promoting equality of opportunity for both boys and girls also means addressing the expectations and attitudes that some pupils have acquired. Young children can form strong opinions about *boys'* things and *girls'* things at a very early age and as they get older these attitudes often are linked to job aspirations and life choices in a very limiting way.

Encountering stereotypical attitudes

- A newly qualified teacher working with a class of Y2 children had planned a simple design and technology activity involving textiles in which the children would be asked to design and make some clothes for a doll. During a discussion about resources for the activity the headteacher cautioned her that some of the boys were likely to be extremely hostile to the idea of any work involving dolls, textiles and sewing, as this would be seen as a girls' activity. After discussing strategies with the headteacher the NQT asked the children to make *papier mâché* models of themselves. The children were then asked to make clothes for these figures. The boys did not perceive their models as dolls and were enthusiastic about working with the textiles and sewing materials.
- John and Helen (Y1) were asked to produce a piece of writing on the computer. The teacher noticed that John had occupied the seat in front of the keyboard and was monopolizing the activity. The teacher intervened and informed John that it was a joint task and that Helen needed to have a go on the computer too. The teacher then moved on to work with another group of children. John meanwhile sat back in his seat with his arms folded. Helen had to reach across him to get to the keyboard. Before long Helen's exclusion was re-imposed.

Work in Australia on boys' and girls' choices of play areas has shown how there is a tendency on the part of some boys to challenge or deny access to some types of activity such as construction play on male terms. A number of teacher strategies for dealing with this phenomenon were categorized and analysed (see below) and it was found that none of them survived for long once the teacher had moved on to another area or group as previously established patterns of behaviour soon re-established themselves. The conclusion drawn was that young children are trying hard to be 'normal'; therefore to counter these types of attitudes and behaviours practitioners need to broaden children's ideas of what is normal for boys and girls (MacNaughton, 1997).

Teacher strategies for dealing with stereotypical behaviour

Sparking the girls' interest:

- Feminization (luring girls into non-traditional areas with *girls'* things)
- Separatism (*girls only* time).

Managing the unacceptable behaviour of boys:

- Fusion (combining *boys'* with *girls'* areas)
- Policing (adult intervention and mediation in the interests of equity).

(MacNaughton, 1997)

Promoting equality of opportunity for boys and girls in the nursery/classroom

- Give frequent, positive and encouraging feedback to both boys and girls across the curriculum.
- Have high expectations of both girls and boys across the curriculum.
- Teach the children that certain subjects and areas of learning are not the preserve of one sex.
- Encourage the use of non-sexist language and procedures. Do *sensible* girls always clear up? Do *big strong* boys always do the lifting and carrying?
- Provide a variety of learning materials and ensure that girls and boys have opportunities to develop their skills and confidence in using these materials through hands-on experience.
- Be aware of how boys and girls interact in lessons and where necessary tackle the behaviour of some children. Such behaviour could include boys calling out while girls put their hands up, ridiculing wrong answers, groaning at correct answers, playing in an aggressive manner, and pushing other pupils, including girls, out of reach of certain equipment and resources.
- Challenge gender stereotypes of the sort sometimes found in books and other resources by promoting positive images of women and men.

$\Rightarrow$

- Evaluate and reflect upon your teacher–pupil interactions. Do you give equal amounts of time to boys and girls? Do you respond to boys and girls differently? Are boys challenged and girls helped?
- Seek to raise and broaden parental expectations of both boys and girls.

Including children with special educational needs (SEN): Removing Barriers to Achievement

Education is a key factor in enabling children to have better futures and this means all children including those with special educational needs (SEN). Teachers are expected to respond positively to children's special educational needs; these are considered to exist in circumstances where special provision has to be made for a child because:

- he/she is affected by a disability which precludes or hampers his/her efforts to avail himself/herself of the educational facilities on offer;
- he/she is experiencing learning difficulties (in the context of SEN this implies a significantly greater difficulty in learning than that experienced by the majority of children of the same age);
- he/she is gifted or talented.

The trend has been to move away from segregation of pupils with SEN, to integration and more recently to inclusion as part of the Every Child Matters agenda and the determination to remove barriers to achievement (DfES, 2004d). Pupils with SEN are still more likely to experience such barriers even though notions that children with special educational needs are not able to take a full part in the curriculum because of access difficulties or that child-centred approaches are unimportant in comparison to mastering basic skills have been increasingly challenged.

Research, policies, legislation and trends relating to special educational needs

- Warnock Report (1978)
- Education Act (1981)
- International convention on the rights of the child (1989)
- The Children's Act (1989)
- Code of practice for children with SEN (2001)
- Disability Discrimination Act (1995)
- Removing Barriers to Achievement (2004).

- **Segregation**: provision for pupils with SEN is separate from the rest of the nursery/school population.
- **Locational integration**: pupils with SEN share a site with the rest of the nursery/school population.
- **Social integration**: pupils with SEN share out-of-class activities with the rest of the nursery/school population.
- **Functional integration**: pupils with SEN participate in some of the nursery/classroom activities with the rest of the nursery/school population.
- **Inclusion**: pupils with SEN have equal rights and experience full participation in all nursery/classroom activities with the rest of the nursery/school population.

Recent national education policy therefore has sought to remove barriers to achievement for children with SEN by taking action in four areas. The first objective is to ensure **early intervention** by improving communication between professionals, increasing the levels of resources available to nurseries and schools and by cutting back on bureaucracy. The second goal is to **remove barriers to learning in the classroom** by helping schools to improve their indigenous capacity to support learners with SEN, by extending access to external specialist knowledge and skills and by integrating the activities of mainstream and special schools more fully. The third policy objective is to **raise expectations** of pupils, parents and practitioners alike as well as levels of pupil achievement. Some of the keys to achieving this goal are believed to include personalized learning (see pp. 8–10), better training for practitioners and enhanced information for parents and families. The fourth and final area focuses on the need for **improved partnership arrangements** between the various groups involved in the care and education of children. This includes effective communication and liaison between local education, health and social care professionals in CYPS and between these professionals, pupils and their parents (DfES, 2004d).

Although individual teachers can do little to influence national policy they can tackle some of these issues in their own classrooms. First, they can set suitable learning challenges. Second, they can respond to pupils' diverse needs, and third, they can remove any impediments to learning and assessment that exist in the classroom itself (QCA, 1999). The aim is to keep children on task as much as possible in part through establishing a clear structure in which pupils with SEN are encouraged to review previous work and learning, while new skills and concepts are presented in clear unambiguous ways, and are sometimes modelled by the teacher. Modelling and **guided pupil practice** will help to ensure higher success rates as well as offering more opportunities for positive feedback to individual children. Teachers also need to find ways to facilitate independent pupil practice for children with SEN whereby they have the chance to apply their new knowledge and skills appropriately (Westwood, 1997).

For inclusion to work properly schools and staff have to be suitably prepared, trained and resourced. The management in nurseries and schools has to ensure that staff are pedagogically knowledgeable about working with SEN pupils and also that the philosophical rationale underpinning for such practice has been accepted. It is also important for nurseries and schools to have access to sufficient levels of support, both external and internal, in the form of expert advice and additional staffing in the nursery/classroom to properly meet the needs of children with SEN (see pp. 17–21). In addition, staff in schools sometimes have to maintain their commitment to inclusive practice in the face of competing policy pressures such as preoccupations with SATs scores and league tables. If these preconditions are met then there can be benefits for all in an inclusive approach to teaching and learning; however, if they are not then the experience for children, their families and practitioners could be unsatisfactory.

Intended benefits of inclusion

For children with SEN and their families

Children:

- are spared stereotyping and the negative images caused by segregation;
- may experience certain competences being modelled (i.e. by their peers);
- acquire realistic life experiences;
- have opportunities to develop friendships with peers without SEN.

Families:

- feel less isolated;
- can develop relationships with parents of children without SEN and the wider community.

For children without SEN, their families and society as a whole

Children:

- have a chance to acquire realistic views of, and positive attitudes towards, their peers with SEN;
- can learn and practise caring and supportive behaviours;
- are presented with positive role models of individuals achieving in the face of adversity.

Families:

- have opportunities to develop relationships with parents of children with SEN and their offspring;
- can transmit positive attitudes about SEN to their children.

Society:

- can make more efficient use of limited educational resources.

The range of SEN

There are numerous **physical disabilities** and **medical needs** that teachers may encounter in nursery and primary schools. In some cases the condition itself can hamper children's efforts to engage with the curriculum on offer, for example a child with a visual impairment or a child with cerebral palsy. In other cases it is the consequences of the condition such as hospitalization and absences from nursery/school that may impede children's educational progress (Dewis, 2007).

Some children experience **learning difficulties** that can range from mild to severe and from specific to complex. In some cases these learning difficulties are cognitive in nature and often result in problems with core elements in the curriculum, such as English and mathematics. Children who are experiencing learning difficulties of this sort may:

- find it hard to understand the language used;
- have a limited concentration span and engage in time-wasting or work avoidance;
- experience problems in transferring and applying knowledge and skills;
- exhibit poor general knowledge;
- find following instructions difficult;
- display a lack of care and attention when working.

In other cases, however, learning difficulties are actually rooted elsewhere, such as in **social and emotional problems** (Kay, 2007). SEN in one area can be intimately connected to SEN in another area. Language acquisition, for example, is both a precursor and co-requisite for learning in most, if not all, areas of the curriculum, and an inability therefore to make oneself understood is likely to result in considerable frustration and could lead to aberrant behaviour such as withdrawal or aggression.

Some children with SEN are described as **gifted** and **talented**. All teachers encounter pupils who are bright, but current UK government guidance suggests that gifted and talented children have abilities or aptitudes that are *significantly* ahead of those of their peers (DfES, 2006a). Exact definitions of what constitutes giftedness or talentedness are hard to produce; some, for example, apply the term gifted to children whose enhanced abilities extend across a number of areas while talented is applied to children who display advanced abilities in one just one area. However, for the DfES (now the Department for Children, Schools and Families (DCSF)) *gifted* refers to children who excel in traditional academic subjects such as mathematics or history while *talented* children excel in the more practical curriculum domains such as art, PE or music (DfES, 2006a).

Special educational needs in 3–8 settings

Physical disabilities/Medical needs

- Hearing impairment
- Visual impairment
- Arthritis
- Asthma
- Diabetes
- Epilepsy
- Eczema
- Cerebral palsy
- Cystic fibrosis
- Spina bifida
- Muscular dystrophy
- Attention-Deficit (Hyperactivity) Disorder (AD(H)D)

Learning difficulties/Behavioural difficulties

- Autism
- Aphasia
- Dyslexia
- Dyspraxia
- Emotional, social and behavioural difficulties (EBD)

Gifted and talented pupils

Following the Code of Practice for Special Educational Needs

Irrespective of the SEN in question, all teachers must be aware of the procedures laid down in the Code of Practice for Special Educational Needs (DfES, 2001b). Needs may be identified when a child starts school or nursery and concern over a child's progress can be registered at this point by teachers, parents, other carers or external agencies. Concerns may also arise at any time during the nursery and school years. Whenever there appears to be cause for concern, the nursery/school SEN Coordinator (SENCO) needs to be involved, as do the parents or carers (Fitzgerald, 2007).

The class teacher will take the lead in gathering information and evidence and completing an initial cause for concern sheet. Depending on the nature of the cause for concern, teaching staff may also need to seek information from others. For example, when a teacher suspects that a child has behavioural problems, she/he may need to establish a more accurate picture by talking to parents, carers or lunchtime supervisors. Following the initial cause for concern, teachers are required to monitor the child over a period of time and maintain a record of progress at intervals. Notes and observations need to be carefully collated and dated since they will be shared with and communicated to parents, carers, the SENCO and possibly external agencies.

If, after a term of monitoring, the child seems not to have made any progress, the school has to draw up an Individual Education Plan (IEP), which must be reviewed at least twice a year and preferably termly. The IEP will describe the nature of the child's difficulties and will outline the action(s) to be taken. In some cases the action will involve special provision and may include learning support either from outside agencies or from SEN staff employed by the nursery/school (see pp. 17–21). The expectation is that for the majority of children, early identification coupled with timely and appropriate intervention will result in them successfully overcoming their difficulties.

However, where the IEP does not result in (sufficient) progress formal assistance can be sought from external support services, which may result in a revised IEP for the child containing new targets and fresh strategies for supporting her/his progress (Roffey, 2001). Having involved the external agencies it may become apparent that the existing provision available to the child is inappropriate or insufficient to help her/him overcome the difficulties, in which case the decision will be made to request a statutory assessment of the child's needs from the local CYPS. This results in a formal Statement of Special Educational Needs, at which point CYPS takes responsibility for overseeing and managing the task of addressing the child's needs, albeit still in consultation and collaboration with parents and the nursery/school. The issuing of a Statement of Special Educational Needs carries with it the mandatory requirement to conduct an annual review. Children on the special needs register are entitled by law to even greater levels of special provision. For example, children with severe physical and learning difficulties could have support workers who accompany them throughout the school day. Chapter 3 contains further information on the adaptation of teaching and learning to promote the inclusion of pupils with SEN.

Working with the Code of Practice

John, a Y1 pupil, was deemed to have moderate learning difficulties under the Code of Practice. It was suspected that he was struggling with an attention deficiency disorder. He was easily distracted during lessons. His poor concentration and attention resulted in him wandering off task and interfering with other children which often resulted in squabbles. He also had unrealistic expectations of his abilities, leading to frustration and a tendency to give up quickly. His teacher therefore tried to plan work for John that was short and focused. In addition she made sure that John understood the purposes of the sessions and the likely outcomes and made sure too that he received plenty of praise and recognition for his efforts. During literacy hour sessions, John would work with a special needs support teacher who provided short, focused tasks on phonics and reading. John was encouraged to reflect and comment on his own learning and progress as a way of raising his self-esteem and modifying his behaviour by promoting his ability to persevere.

Ensuring the welfare, health and safety of young children

All teachers have a common law duty to take good care of their pupils and this is particularly fundamental for teachers of younger (3–8) pupils. While children are in the nursery/school their teachers take on parental responsibilities. They have a duty to use their knowledge of young children's development to prevent them from causing harm to themselves or others. Teachers are also responsible for ensuring that the physical learning environment is inherently safe for children as well as working with child protection agencies to provide whatever information and support they can to keep pupils safe in the community and the home.

✔ Audit

By the end of this section you should:

- know about the importance of managing transition periods sensitively for young children;
- know about being in *loco parentis*;
- know about teachers' duties in relation to health and safety legislation;
- know about policies and practices in cases of suspected child abuse.

Helping children to cope with transition periods

Transition to, within and between homes, nurseries and schools, and from one class or teacher to another, can be a very stressful time for both children and their parents. Frequently the transition involves a change of culture, personnel and location and where children are moving between nursery (FS1) and reception (FS2) and between reception and Key Stage 1, transition can also mean a change of curriculum as children move from the Foundation Stage early learning goals to National Curriculum Programmes of Study, plus the National Literacy and Numeracy Strategies. There are a number of significant transition events for pupils between nursery and Key Stage 2, as well as the lesser ones that occur at the start of every year when many children move to new classes in the same school.

Children's ability to make a successful transition from home to nursery, or from nursery to school (becoming happy and successful learners in the process) can have a profound impact on their future development and attainment. Any transition has the potential to make young children feel insecure and nervous. For many 3–5-year-old children, for example, starting in the Foundation Stage for the first time can be a particularly stressful experience; for some it will be their first experience away from their home. Parents are often referred to in school documentation as key players in supporting the children during these periods. It is worth remembering that parents too may be experiencing feelings of anxiety and teachers can play a part in reducing this. Parents may well seek out teachers to air their concerns or ask for information or advice. Teachers can facilitate the process of building partnerships by recognizing, taking seriously and addressing parental concerns.

Nursery and school transition policies seek to offer advice to staff on ways of easing the concerns and anxieties that families may have about transition. The priority for all teachers, whatever the transition, is to help the children to become secure and confident in their new environment as soon as possible, and to establish positive and productive relationships with both pupils and parents.

Helping children and parents to cope with transition events

- Provide written information for parents on the curriculum that the children will encounter in their new class. Talk to parents before and during the transition period. If parents are reassured they can communicate that reassurance to their children. They can also offer valuable information that you can use to help make children feel more secure.
- Talk to the children's current teacher prior to receiving a new group. He/She can offer good advice on likes and dislikes, learning dispositions, curriculum strengths and weaknesses and can also help you to identify those children most likely to be adversely affected by the changes taking place.
- Try to visit your new class in their present setting. What sort of learning environment are they used to? What sort of conventions and routines are they used to? Can you use similar conventions and routines to minimize their sense of disruption?
- Offer to swap places with your new class's current teacher, so that the children can get used to seeing you as their teacher.
- Help your pupils who are moving on to their next class to produce mini-portfolios of work that they can give to their new teacher.
- Make sure you speak positively about the new setting or class that your children will be going to. Do not reinforce or magnify their concerns and worries.
- Where children are moving schools rather than classes involve older children in the induction process (e.g. provide buddies in the playground).

In loco parentis

Being in *loco parentis* must rank very highly on a teacher's list of priorities. As child experts, teachers are presumed to be familiar with the likely actions of their pupils in a given situation and are expected to be able to exercise a degree of foresight. Teachers who fail to prevent injury or harm to a child in their care when the risks could be reasonably foreseen are themselves in danger of being deemed negligent. Unfortunately, exact definitions of what constitutes reasonable do not exist and instead, where accusations of negligence arise, the final judgements are likely to be made on the facts of the case. Teachers of young children therefore need to make every effort to ensure their children's safety and not to expose pupils to unnecessary hazards.

A major problem for teachers trying to exercise this foresight is that no environment, and certainly no 3–8 setting, can be made entirely risk free. Young children will always fall over, bump their heads, or trap their fingers from time to time. The only way to prevent all these accidents in schools and nurseries would be to close them. This is clearly a nonsense; indeed, risk management and risk awareness are important skills for children to acquire given that they cannot be supervised 24 hours a day. Consequently teachers need to reduce the risks to acceptable levels by organizing and maintaining a safe learning environment within the nursery/classroom and by thinking carefully about the children in their care before taking them beyond the nursery/school environment.

Thinking about the children

- Are they mature enough and dexterous enough to handle certain tools and materials?
- Are they strong enough to move certain objects?
- To what extent can they take responsibility for themselves and their actions?
- Do they have any physical disabilities that might put them at risk?
- Are nursery/school rules and conventions (e.g. no running) clearly understood?

Health and safety legislation

In addition to teachers' common law duty to care for their pupils, they are also bound by the provisions of the Health and Safety at Work Act 1974. Under the provisions of this Act all employees, including teachers of young children, must not meddle or interfere with anything provided for the purpose of ensuring people's health and safety. They must also have a care for their own safety at work and the safety of others who might be affected either by their actions or by their failure to act. Teachers are required to cooperate with others who have duties under the Act such as the school/nursery health and safety representative and the first aid specialist; failure to do this could lead to disciplinary action or even dismissal. Schools and nurseries have health and safety policies, often based on local CYPS policies, and staff are expected to be familiar with them.

Health and safety in 3–8 settings

Responsibilities of the headteacher

- The headteacher must ensure that all staff receive instruction in their duties regarding health and safety matters.
- The headteacher must ensure that all staff are adequately trained to carry out their duties.
- The headteacher must be familiar with the school's fire drill procedures.
- The headteacher must check the nursery/school on a regular basis for health and safety problems.
- The headteacher must ensure completion of statutory CRB checks for all staff.

Responsibilities of teaching and non-teaching staff

- All staff, teaching and non-teaching, must be familiar with the school's health and safety policy, the implications of that policy and any procedures, arrangements and practices relating to it.
- All employees, pupils and others must receive appropriate instruction to enable them to operate in a safe and efficient manner (e.g. fire drills).
- All staff must report to the headteacher any problems, defects or hazards that are brought to their attention.

Responsibilities of the caretaker

- The caretaker is responsible for ensuring that cleaning staff are adequately informed, instructed and trained in the safe use and storage of equipment, cleaning substances and other materials.
- The caretaker must not use, or allow cleaning staff to use, unsafe equipment.

Children's welfare

Under the 1989 Children Act, schools are required to assist their local CYPS when those departments are investigating allegations of child abuse. Individual teachers in schools are expected to do what is reasonable in the circumstances to safeguard and promote the welfare of their pupils. As with teachers' common law duty of care, there is no exact definition of what constitutes *reasonable*. More recently, Circular 10/95 Protecting Children from Abuse attempted to assist teachers in fulfilling their responsibilities to their pupils under the provisions of the 1989 Act by clarifying what was expected (DfEE, 1995). The main points arising from Circular 10/95 are as outlined below.

- All staff should be alert to signs of abuse and know to whom they should report any concerns or suspicions.
- All schools and colleges should have a designated member of staff responsible for coordination of action within the institution and liaison with other agencies including the Local Safeguarding Children Boards.

- All schools and colleges should be aware of the child protection procedures established by the CYPS.
- All schools and colleges should have procedures (of which all staff should be aware) for handling suspected cases of abuse of pupils or students, including procedures to be followed if a member of staff is accused of abuse.
- Staff with designated responsibility for child protection should receive appropriate training.
- Schools should develop a child protection policy and make it known to parents.
- In every CYPS there should be a senior officer with responsibility for coordinating action on child protection across the authority.

The main point arising from the 1989 Act and Circular 10/95 for students on 3–8 teacher training courses and newly qualified teachers is that should they suspect a child is being abused, then they must alert the designated member of staff in the school whose role it is to liaise with the various child protection agencies. Students and teachers can obtain a copy of the full circular through the Department for Children, Schools and Families website (www.dfes.gov.uk).

Identifying abuse

Abuse may take a number of forms:

- **Physical abuse**: a child may suffer injuries as a result of the violent actions of others. The results can include tell-tale marks such as cuts, bruises and burns.
- **Physical neglect**: a child's suffering is the result of inaction and a failure to protect, care properly and attend to physical needs.
- **Sexual abuse**: children are exploited sexually by adults. This is a particularly emotive subject and may result in children being noticeably withdrawn or, paradoxically, highly precocious.
- **Emotional abuse**: this abuse is not physical in nature and may not leave any visible marks, but it is no less harmful to a young child. Emotional abuse can result in children being persistently ill-treated or rejected by those whose duty it is to care for them. It can produce profoundly damaging and long term effects on the emotional and behavioural development of the child, resulting in excessive 'clinginess' or aggression in the nursery/school.

(Kay, 2003)

Simply because a young child is behaving aggressively or appears withdrawn does not constitute evidence of abuse or neglect of any kind. However, it could be an indicator and teachers of young children need to be alert for the signs, and if necessary try to elicit some information from a child who has made a disclosure of some kind in a tactful, sympathetic and non-leading fashion. Any such discussion must be handled very carefully. Under no circumstances should trainee teachers initiate such a discussion without first referring to their class teacher or mentor. Newly qualified teachers, too, would be well advised to seek the support and advice of experienced colleagues before becoming involved in any case of suspected abuse. Where a child has initiated such a discussion, the main aim for the teacher is to give the child the opportunity to talk and then to listen to what he/she has to say. Open-ended questions are the best way to proceed in order to get the truest picture possible and avoid prejudicing any possible future legal actions.

A worrying development

Paul was painting in the nursery. His teacher noticed that he had only used red and black paint and that the picture had a somewhat visceral quality to it. She told Paul that his painting was very interesting and asked him if he would like her to write anything under his picture for him. Paul thought for a moment and then said, 'The daddy hits the mummy with a pan, the mummy stabs the daddy.'

If such discussions between a teacher and a young child do take place, the teacher must note down the conversation, giving details of the date, time, place, any other people present and what the child said. This written evidence could form part of court proceedings at a future date and so it is important to be accurate. Once such a note has been compiled, the teacher must forward the information to the member of staff with responsibility for dealing with suspected cases of abuse or neglect. This designated teacher will then take the process forward with other agencies and individuals such as Education Welfare Officers (EWOs), the local CYPS and child protection officers. If there is to be any investigation, it must be conducted by the proper authorities. Individual class teachers and even designated teachers are not trained in investigation techniques; meddling of any kind is likely to cause more harm than good and could result in parents and carers being wrongly accused or someone guilty of abuse escaping the consequences of their actions. The primary role of the teacher therefore is to *be alert for the signs* and to *inform the proper authorities.*

Abuse by staff in the nursery/school

Physical contact is bound to take place continually between staff and children in 3–8 settings. It is not only inevitable, but also it is desirable for young children to know that they are valued and cared for by staff who are not cold, distant or aloof. However, early years teachers and teacher training students must take care at all times to ensure that the inevitable physical contact between themselves and their children is appropriate in nature and could not be misconstrued as in any way abusive or indecent. Should staff encounter children who are clearly uneasy about physical contact, they would be well advised to avoid any potentially compromising situations, and may wish to place their concerns on record.

In a situation where a young child makes a disclosure suggesting that he/she has been the subject of abuse by a member of staff the teacher must initially follow the same procedure as that outlined above. The child must be listened to, and the conversation must be noted down. However, at this stage the allegation and the notes must be reported directly and immediately to the headteacher. Where the subject of the allegation is the headteacher, the teacher has a duty to inform the governors. In cases where allegations are made against members of staff, the headteacher and/or the governors are initially responsible for determining what action to take.

> ### Possible action arising from allegations of abuse against staff
>
> The headteacher and/or governors may conclude that the allegation is sufficiently serious to warrant its forwarding to the child protection agencies. This would be because the allegation suggests that harm may have befallen a child, a criminal offence may have been committed and/or the member of staff concerned is alleged to have behaved in an unsuitable manner with children.
>
> The headteacher and/or governors could decide that the allegation arose from a lack of judgement or a degree of naivety on the part of the member of staff concerned, and that the matter would be better dealt with through normal internal disciplinary procedures. However, the headteacher/governors will still need to inform the CYPS designated officer of the complaint. This officer has the job of liaising between schools and other interested agencies such as social services or the police in order to have such allegations dealt with fairly and appropriately as soon as possible.
>
> (DfES, 2005)

Any teacher who is the subject of an allegation of abuse has the right to be informed that the allegation has been made and what action the headteacher and governing body propose to take as a result. The only exception to this rule occurs where an objection is made by the child protection agencies such as the police who may not wish the person accused to be informed before they can be formally interviewed. Teachers accused of abuse should seek advice from their union and are entitled to have a union representative present at any subsequent meeting to discuss and investigate the allegation.

Promoting positive values and maintaining good order

Schools and nurseries play an important role in helping pupils to grow into responsible adults. In part this is achieved through successfully inculcating a set of values in young children, and promoting the *spiritual, cultural, mental and physical development of pupils* (QCA, 1999). Such values include respect for one another, self-respect, honesty, trust, fairness and self-discipline. Everyone involved in the working of nurseries and schools has a part to play in promoting good behaviour and discipline, as without good order, teaching and learning will be greatly impaired.

✔ **Audit**

By the end of this section you should:

- know about some of the techniques to use to project your presence and an image of professional competence when in school;
- understand some of the factors that can contribute to poor behaviour in 3–8 settings;
- know about some of the options open to teachers for responding effectively to poor behaviour;
- know about the legislation relating to the use of force by teachers;
- know about some of the strategies for tackling bullying with children and their families.

Establishing a positive presence in the classroom

Looking like, and acting the part of, a teacher is an important element in forging professional relationships and maintaining good order. Parents, children and colleagues will make assumptions about students or newly qualified teachers based in part on their actions and appearance; children in particular are quite likely to work on the assumption that if it looks like a duck, walks like a duck and quacks like a duck, it must be a duck. Fitting the profile by looking and acting like a teacher is all part of *developing your presence in the classroom*.

Many of the day-to-day actions of teachers are fundamental in underpinning their attempts to foster good behaviour and discipline among the children. The use of praise and recognition promotes consideration and responsibility on the part of the children as well as offering encouragement for good work and behaviour.

Offering praise and recognition

- Spot on
- What a good try
- I'm impressed
- Very imaginative
- Well remembered
- Quick thinking
- I like that
- Keep on trying
- You have great ideas
- Good problem solving
- One more go and you'll be there
- You've done better than ever
- Your work is really improving.

Providing tasks that are well matched to the children's needs and abilities, and organizing sessions and lessons which start and end on time and where interruptions and diversions are minimized or dealt with efficiently, also helps to create a positive learning atmosphere where praise and recognition are attainable by all pupils. Getting to know the children enables teachers to plan ahead and anticipate where and with whom problems might arise in order to develop strategies to reduce the risk. At the same time, giving clear instructions and using language appropriate to young children, helps to avoid confusion and disruptive behaviour (see Chapter 3).

Ambiguous instruction

A group of loitering Y1 children were being ushered good naturedly from the classroom at lunchtime by their teacher, who uttered the words 'Go on, hop it you lot.' So they did!

Developing your presence as a teacher

- Show consistency in your expectations and actions.
- Radiate a sense of confidence by not hesitating or rushing your speech, by making eye contact, and by adopting appropriate body postures and tones of voice.
- Exhibit firm, though gentle, insistence when necessary.
- Avoid being overly and inappropriately friendly, especially in the early stages of the year or with older pupils.
- Establish a clear and simple set of rules or conventions within which the activities of the class will take place.

Understanding why young children sometimes do what they do

With some young children inappropriate or undesirable behaviour may be as a result of their having not yet learned what is and is not acceptable behaviour in the nursery/school context. It could be because they are still maturing and developing their awareness of what is expected alongside the skills of patience and self-control, which are necessary to avoid resorting to tantrums, sulks and verbal or physical aggression. There may also be learning, social and environmental factors feeding poor behaviour. Children who are not coping with the curriculum and the learning environment, or who are experiencing considerable distress and disruption at home, may feel frustrated, angry and upset and these feelings could well surface in their behaviour in the nursery/classroom.

The management in nurseries and schools (governing bodies and headteachers) will take the lead in drawing up the policy on behaviour. It is crucial, wherever possible, for schools to draw upon the backing of parents and other carers as they are the most influential people in the lives of young children. Parents are expected to lend their support to the efforts of the nursery/school to maintain good order. Individual teachers meanwhile are especially important in translating behaviour policies into reality through their efficiency and professionalism. Good behaviour and discipline are founded on good organization and a professional approach to the task of teaching. Teachers of 3–8 pupils must achieve a balanced approach which takes into consideration the nurture required by young children, while at the same time recognizing the importance of imparting positive social behaviour. It is important to remember that the efforts of individual teachers to promote positive behaviour and to deal effectively with inappropriate behaviour are greatly enhanced when they are in line with policies and procedures agreed and adhered to by staff across the setting. The remainder of this chapter and sections of Chapter 3 address these procedures and practices.

Things to do when it all goes wrong

Establishing your presence in the classroom and setting a good example to the children will help to reduce the incidence of unwanted behaviour but these and other strategies will not eliminate such conduct totally. Teachers who are alert and mobile may spot a situation that is about to deteriorate and may be able to use early intervention, humour or a diversion of some kind to keep children on task and to nip unwanted behaviour in the bud. However, the teacher cannot be everywhere at once and all teachers experience instances where children's behaviour will be deemed unacceptable and action of some sort will be required. Where necessary, schools and nurseries have the authority to impose punishment that is reasonable and as before, the term reasonable is subject to interpretation. Teachers need to keep in mind that any such actions need to be underpinned by their duty to:

- try to educate children about what constitutes positive behaviour;
- make it clear that they are displeased with the behaviour rather than the person;
- help children to practise and hone positive behaviours for the future.

With the three principles above in mind, teachers of young children have a number of options open to them when trying to deal with unwanted behaviour which include administering punishment, withdrawing pleasurable activities and ignoring unwanted behaviour (Robertson, 1989).

Strategies for dealing with unwanted behaviour

- Administering punishments might involve the use of reprimands or, in more serious instances, the imposition of sanctions.
- Withdrawing pleasurable activities could include the removal of attention such as not listening to and encouraging tale-tellers, or the removal of activities. Teachers need to be careful about always picking games and practical creative activities, as this can carry hidden messages about what aspects of learning are enjoyable and what are not.
- Ignoring unwanted behaviour could include rewarding desirable behaviour and denying attention for unwanted behaviour. This can be effective, but it can also be a risky strategy if applied inappropriately. In some situations, for example, other children may provide the desired attention and some actions by children such as racist or sexist abuse simply cannot be ignored. One possible refinement for teachers wishing to utilize this technique is to distinguish between ignoring something completely and deciding against any verbal rebuke or punishment, restricting themselves instead to a slightly shocked look or a raised and very disapproving eyebrow.

Ways to discipline effectively

- **Be as constructive as you can be** if you want to make progress in the longer term. Remind children about your/the school's expectations of pupil behaviour; be ready to offer (or get others to offer) one-to-one or small-group support for those activities and situations that you know from previous experience can trigger difficult behaviour in certain children; try to maintain your composure and offer a way out of tense situations: 'All right! Let's all just calm down for a minute. Now let's see what this is all about and how we can sort it out.'
- **Appropriateness is crucial** with young children, where you are engaged in the care and nurture of pupils as well as in their education. Performance and motivation can be damaged by too severe a punishment or reprimand. Where young children experience unstable care arrangements, where they have been encouraged to adopt conflict resolution strategies based on *might is right*, where adult expectations have been inconsistent with behaviour ignored one day and punished the next, or who have learned that bad behaviour gains adult attention, teachers will need to accept that changing a child's behaviour is likely to take time. Knowing the children helps teachers to make judgements about appropriateness, for example appreciating the age and maturity of children and knowing something about the possible causes of the behaviour.
- **Timing is important.** If you spot a situation developing then pre-empt misbehaviour: you can use humour or a distraction of some sort; you can direct a child to another area/activity; or you can provide a gentle but firm reminder about classroom rules and conventions. If you do not see it coming then make sure you respond promptly once it has started. Success in doing this is a powerful statement of your control and awareness. In addition, the immediacy of your actions is much more meaningful and relevant to young children, for whom an incident the day before can be ancient history.

$\Rightarrow$

- **Consistency and determination have to be maintained.** Every time a rule is broken without comment or penalty makes it harder to enforce that rule in future. Inconsistency on your part will be regarded as unfair by the children and rightly so, and failure to be as good as your word will make you look weak and ineffectual.
- **Simplicity is essential.** You should keep any rules or conventions simple unless you want to spend all your time explaining and enforcing them.
- **Fairness matters.** You should never victimize a whole group for the actions of one individual.
- **Respect is everything.** When you do have to reprimand or punish behaviour, focus on the act rather than the perpetrator. Personalizing matters and humiliating a young child does nothing for that child's self-image, it is degrading for them, constitutes a no-value statement on your part, and in some cases risks open rebellion on the part of the child concerned. Children are far more likely to respond positively to someone they respect and who obviously respects them.

A punishment fitting a crime?

A student teacher encountered a Y1 child sitting outside the headteacher's office at break time. She enquired as to why he was there. He replied that he was not allowed out to play for six months because he had been 'naughty in the playground'.

While reprimands and punishment play a small role in establishing good order in the classroom when compared to positive discipline and the principles of good classroom management and teaching, it is still a very important role. The examples below represent the more common sorts of behaviour which may require intervention on the part of the 3–8 teacher in order to maintain good order; they range from the very minor to the rather more serious.

Examples of unwanted behaviour in 3–8 settings

How would you deal with these situations?

- During a class discussion two girls begin to plait one another's hair. In so doing they opt out of the activity and begin to distract other children, who start to join in. An outbreak of hairdressing is about to occur.
- You're reading a story to the class. Matthew is next to you. When you next look Matthew has miraculously materialized in a completely different part of the room and is prodding another child.
- You have taken register, explained the morning's tasks and started the children off. It rapidly becomes apparent that chaos is ensuing about your person.
- There is a 'phantom whistler' somewhere in the room.
- Mrs Jones, the peripatetic piano player, is with you in the hall for singing and dancing. Paul and Wayne are pulling faces and objecting loudly at the prospect of having to dance with the girls.
- While moving around the classroom you overhear one individual make a racist remark directly to another child.
- A child comes to you after playtime and claims to have been struck by a child in another class.
- A parent tells you that his/her child is being bullied at school by a classmate.
- Your class is travelling to the local woods on the bus. Two burly gentlemen, one sporting a rather striking mohican haircut, board the bus and come upstairs to where the children are sitting. Unable to contain herself, and broadcasting on full volume, one of the children shouts out 'Miss! Look at the state of his hair!'
- John and Ali are marched into your classroom at lunchtime by an incandescent lunchtime supervisor after they had suggested that she try something anatomically impossible.
- A child approaches you in the playground and tells you that David has been showing his willie to the girls.
- During the previous week in the nursery Sarah slapped two other children across the face in two separate incidents and was reprimanded. While sitting with a group at the creative table on Monday morning you notice Sarah approach another girl, slap her hard across the face and then scuttle swiftly into the role-play area well away from the now screaming victim.
- Your class are discussing their activities over the weekend with you on Monday morning. Emily puts her hand up and when asked, tells the class that she has seen a film called 'George' at the weekend and it was really good. When you ask her to tell the class about the film she says that it was all about a huge fish called a shark that went around eating people. The other children start to laugh and catcall.
- The headteacher is reading to the school in assembly. It is a part of the story that is full of dramatic pauses and hushed tones, generating quiet excitement and expectation on the part of the children. Suddenly there is a noise in the midst of your class followed by much sniggering, theatrical wafting of hands, clutching of throats and holding of noses.

The use of force by a teacher

Corporal punishment of any kind is illegal; however, in extreme circumstances it may be necessary for a teacher to physically restrain a pupil in order to preserve good order in the classroom or to protect the health and safety of other children. It is hard to imagine a situation in most 3–8 settings where considerable force would need to be employed but all trainee and newly qualified teachers need to be familiar with the legislation and guidance.

> ### Need for restraint
>
> Simon (Year 2) experienced emotional and behavioural difficulties. Simon's teacher had alerted her student teacher to this fact and had made recommendations about how lessons should be organized and managed, particularly in terms of pacing and timing and what could be expected of Simon and his ability to stay on task. During an afternoon lesson on the Vikings Simon presented himself to the student teacher and made it clear that he had had enough. The student did not realize what was about to happen and instead of trying to divert the impending crisis or offering additional support, he told Simon that he would be the judge of when Simon had had enough. A few seconds later chairs started to fly around the room as children scattered for cover. The student teacher realizing his mistake held onto Simon's arms and tried to calm him down by talking to him. He then told Simon that he was going to stop holding Simon's hands and that he wanted him to take deep breath and then they could talk about how he could help Simon. He let go and Simon grabbed a pair of scissors from the desk and lunged at the student's face.
>
> (O'Hara and O'Hara, 2001)

The 1997 Education Act (Section 4) sets out the circumstances when the use of force may be appropriate to prevent a child from:

- committing a criminal offence (or in the case of very young children behaving in a way that would be criminal if they were above the age of criminal responsibility);
- injuring themselves or others;
- causing damage to property; or
- behaving in such a way as to undermine good order and discipline in the school/nursery.

In such situations, a teacher may use reasonable force. Once again, the term reasonable is open to interpretation and requires teachers to exercise their professional judgement. In making this judgement about whether or not to use force on very young children and how much force to use, teachers must weigh up what they think the circumstances warrant. In an effort to clarify for teachers what sorts of incidents might justify the use of reasonable force, the DfEE published Circular 10/98, which stated clearly that any individual has the right to defend themselves against an attack, providing they do not use a 'disproportionate degree of force to do so'. The circular also made it quite clear that any teacher is entitled to intervene where pupils are risking their own or others' safety. Circular 10/98 divides the types of incident where force might be necessary into three categories:

1 where action is necessary in self-defence or because there is an imminent risk of injury;
2 where there is a developing risk of injury, or significant damage to property;
3 where a pupil is behaving in a way that is compromising good order and discipline.

(DfEE, 1998a)

Examples to illustrate the categories of incident outlined above include:

- attacks by pupils on members of staff;
- attacks by pupils on other pupils;
- fights between pupils;
- pupils who are deliberately damaging or vandalizing property (or are about to);
- pupils causing or risking accidents through rough play or misuse of equipment and materials;
- pupils running through school in such a way as to risk injury to themselves or others;
- pupils who leave or try to leave the school premises where those pupils could be at risk if not kept in the school;
- pupils persistently refusing to obey an order to leave the classroom; and
- pupils behaving in a way that seriously disrupts a lesson.

(DfEE, 1998a)

Having tried to clarify what circumstances might warrant force being used, Circular 10/98 then attempts to assist teachers in interpreting the concept of reasonable, which it acknowledges will always ultimately depend upon all the circumstances of a case.

Teachers **can:**

- physically block a pupil or get between pupils;
- hold or restrain a pupil;
- lead pupils away.

Teachers **cannot:**

- use neck holds of any description;
- punch, kick or slap a pupil;
- twist limbs and/or joints;
- trip pupils up;
- pull hair or ears;
- hold pupils face down.

Trainee and newly qualified teachers need to be aware that any use of force is illegal if the circumstances do not warrant it, for example using force to prevent very minor incidents. They also need to maintain a sense of proportion as to the amount of force to be used; the guidance calls for the *minimum needed to achieve the desired result* and for teachers to take into account factors such as age, understanding and sex of pupils. Teachers are expected to adopt an essentially constructive and positive approach; the application of force should be the last resort, not the norm. In a situation where a teacher has concluded that force may be necessary, the teacher must tell the pupil concerned to desist from whatever it is he/she is doing and make clear what will happen if he/she does not. When force is used it should be *as well as* communication, not *instead of*. Teachers need to stay as calm as possible and inform the child that restraint or force will cease to be used once the behaviour that caused it has also ceased. In those rare instances (for nursery/infant teachers) where the pupil is particularly large or in other ways is capable of injuring the teacher, then that teacher should clear other pupils from the immediate area to remove them from risk and call or send for assistance. While waiting for this to arrive the teacher should continue to try to resolve the situation verbally, or at least to stop it from escalating. Trainee and newly qualified teachers especially should not be afraid to seek and accept help from more experienced colleagues; it is not a sign of weakness but a sign of good sense.

A no-fuss, effective procedure

A student teacher was making a preliminary visit to her teaching practice school. The school contained a number of children who were capable of becoming extremely disruptive, and in some cases violent, during lessons. The deputy headteacher introduced her to the school's procedures for dealing with these difficult situations when they occurred. The procedures included a card system which all staff used. In the event of disruption or violence in the classroom, the teacher concerned could send a responsible child to the deputy's room with a card. A yellow card meant 'Please come to my classroom when you have a few minutes as I need some assistance.' A red card meant 'I need your assistance immediately.'

There are other situations where, due to a lack of maturity on the part of pupils, teachers have to react instantly and use physical restraint in order to avoid harm befalling either other people or, particularly, younger children. On these occasions there may be no time to explain or issue a warning, and action must be immediate; for example, a reception teacher on an out-of-school visit when one of the children suddenly jumps into the road and has to be pulled back quickly; or when a young child is about to throw a heavy object at another child in the class without thinking about the likely consequences of this action. In all cases, force should only be used to protect children and others, not to punish.

Don't dither

A class of Y1 children were taken on a local walk by their teacher as part of a topic on 'Our School'. The school was situated near a block of flats and the group went up a few floors to give the children a bird's-eye view of their school and its surroundings. Suddenly the teacher noticed one of the children holding a large glass marble over the parapet with the apparent intention of dropping it. She immediately dived forward, grabbed the child's hand, drew him away from the parapet, took the marble away from him and spoke firmly to him about how dangerous such an act could be for passers-by.

The use of force always carries with it the possibility of complaints, and teachers need to act professionally at all times. Where a serious incident has occurred in which a teacher has had to use force of some description, this should be reported verbally and in writing to the headteacher. The written report should include details of date, time, names, the nature of the incident, a rationale for the use of force in the circumstances, the pupil's response and any information on injury or damage suffered.

Bullying

Of all the behaviours likely to undermine your efforts to promote positive values and maintain good order in the classroom bullying is potentially one of the most corrosive and insidious. The experience is traumatic for the victims and their families; children that feel threatened and vulnerable are not best placed to learn and achieve. Furthermore, allowing it to go unchecked will not serve the bullies well in the longer term either. Before considering what a positive response to the problem of bullying might look like it is important to note that the term is not always used accurately and is sometimes associated with behaviour that may be inconsiderate, boisterous or anxiety provoking but that is not bullying. While all allegations of bullying should be taken seriously and checked, practitioners need to be careful not to jump to conclusions prematurely. A useful set of guidelines on how practitioners can respond to allegations of bullying can be found on pp. 31–32. It can be briefly summed up as:

- Always check any allegation of bullying.
- Listen to what *everyone* has to say; sometimes all is not as it seems.
- Try to adopt a constructive approach aimed at removing any *opportunity and inclination* to bully.
- Recognize that stopping bullying is a process not an event; do not forget to monitor the situation over a period of time to make sure there is no repetition.
- If the bully will not cease bullying then the school may have no choice but to take punitive measures such as exclusion from groups, withdrawal of pleasurable activities and even, in serious cases, removal from school.

Two arenas in which class teachers are well placed to support school anti-bullying policies are through the classroom ethos and by working closely with parents (NSPCC, 2007). The learning environment in the nursery/classroom can be enhanced by the introduction of activities into the curriculum that promote understanding in children about the harm that bullying can cause and equip them with simple strategies for handling relationships with their peers constructively. Stories, poems and video/DVD materials all provide a potential stimulus for discussions.

Stories that can be used to start discussions about bullying

Cave K. (2000) *Something Else*, Puffin
Dodd L. (2003) *Scarface Claw*, Puffin
Durrant A. (2000) *Big Bad Bunny*, Orchard
Green J. (1999) *I Feel Bullied*, Hodder Wayland
Hegarty J. (2006) *Crabbit Comes to Stay*, Starlet Publishing
McKee D. (1989) *Elmer*, Andersen Press
Rosen M. (2003) *Little Rabbit Foo Foo*, Walker Books
Ross T. (2004) *Is It Because?*, Andersen Press
Thomas J. (2003) *Can I Play?*, Egmont
Wilson J. (2002) *Monster Eyeballs*, Egmont Children's Books

(Anti-Bullying Alliance, 2007)

Involvement in collaborative group work, games and problem-solving activities can give children valuable experience of working positively with others and help them to value the skills and qualities that different children have. To be successful in these activities children have to learn to share, to cooperate and to help others. Circle time is another common feature of 3–8 settings (see pp. 161–3). The knowledge gained of feelings and relationships coupled with the communication skills and techniques practised during circle time activities are intended to be used by children at other times during the school day albeit sometimes with help and guidance from practitioners. Learning to listen to others and to take turns are two such important skills. Being listened to meanwhile can boost feelings of confidence and self-esteem in children, make them more resilient and encourage a greater willingness to report any worries that they may have.

With younger children it is quite possible that an allegation of bullying will not be made to the teacher by the child but by her/his parents instead. Parental approval or disapproval can be powerful factors in modifying children's behaviour and schools often look to parents to support school policies and staff efforts to tackle instances of bullying. Class teachers may be able to help parents to remain calm in the interests of finding an equitable solution to whatever the problem is. Given the powerful parental emotions unleashed by the possibility of bullying there may be occasions where parents' first response is to encourage their child to retaliate against those accused of bullying. Such reactions are understandable but are unlikely to improve matters, partly because such approaches may be asking the *bullied* child to do the impossible and partly because such strategies will almost certainly run counter to school policies and if acted on could bring the *bullied* child and his/her parents into conflict with the school.

Parents' initial concerns need to elicit an understanding response from practitioners; yet given the emotionally charged nature of their concerns parents may be quite agitated; practitioners must therefore remain calm, explain the school policy on such complaints and reassure parents that the complaint will be investigated. Reporting back promptly, if possible by the end of the day with a simple update, helps to reinforce the seriousness with which the school is taking the complaint. Teachers may wish to note down some details and should report the matter to the headteacher or a senior member of staff and seek advice on the next step(s). It is possible that the matter can be resolved at this stage and that staff can report to the parents that measures will be taken to prevent further problems. If so it is important to check with parents in the coming weeks that these measures have been effective. However, it is also possible that the complaint has brought to light events that require teachers to talk to other parents.

If being told that your child is being bullied at school is an emotional experience then being told that your child is bullying other children at school is an equally emotional experience. Parents in this situation may feel that they are *in the dock* and are somehow being viewed as responsible; in such situations a natural response may be to become defensive. If early discussions with parents of children accused of bullying are not handled sensitively then this could result in little more than claim and counter-claim accompanied by the withdrawal of parents' support for the school's efforts to resolve matters. Schools therefore need to work carefully to defuse such situations.

Approaching the difficult subject of bullying with sensitivity

Put yourself in the position of Nigel Smith's mum below; which of the following statements would you respond more positively to?

1 'Oh, Mrs Smith thank you for coming in. I'm afraid Nigel seems to have been bullying Ben.'
2 'Oh, Mrs Smith I'm glad I've caught you. I wanted to talk to you about Nigel and Ben; they seem to have been falling out a bit in class lately and I wondered whether Nigel had said anything to you about it?'

Further sources of information

Personalized learning

- DfES (2001) *Special Educational Needs Code of Practice*. London: DfES.
- DfES (2003) *Aiming High: Raising the Achievement of Ethnic Minority Pupils*. London: DfES.
- DfES (2004) *Removing Barriers to Achievement: The Government's Strategy for SEN*. Nottingham: DfES.
- DfES (2007) *The Early Years Foundation Stage. Setting the Standards for Learning, Development and Care for Children from Birth to Five*. Nottingham: DfES.
- The Every Child Matters website contains advice and guidance for schools, parents, children and young people: www.everychildmatters.gov.uk

Partnership with parents

- The Every Child Matters website contains advice and guidance for schools concerning workforce reform and partnerships with parents: www.everychildmatters.gov.uk
- Fitzgerald D. (2004) *Parent Partnership in the Early Years*. London: Continuum.

Being inspected

- Ofsted (2005) *Every Child Matters: Framework for the Inspection of Schools in England from September 2005*. http://www.ofsted.gov.uk/publications/

The School Teacher's Pay and Conditions Act 1991

- Student teachers and NQTs wishing to find out more about the GTC should visit the Council's website: www.gtce.org.uk
- Trainee and newly qualified teachers can obtain information on conditions of service from the DCSF Teachernet website: www.teachernet.gov.uk
- Teacher unions also provide their members with information and advice on conditions of service which can be accessed through the internet. Useful websites for both trainee and newly qualified teachers include:
  - National Association of Schoolmasters Union of Women Teachers (NASUWT): www.nasuwt.org.uk/
  - National Union of Teachers (NUT): www.teachers.org.uk

Promoting equality of opportunity and inclusion

- Trainee and newly qualified teachers wishing to explore issues surrounding racial and sexual equality may wish to visit:
  - the Equality and Human Rights Commission: www.equalityhumanrights.com/
- Some Local Authorities (LAs) have resources such as Development Education Centres which can be excellent sources of multicultural and anti-racist resources covering the whole curriculum. Although the facilities and materials available at such centres can vary due to differences in

funding, trainee and newly qualified teachers would be well advised to find out if such a resource exists in their region and to contact it for teaching materials and/or advice. The national Development Education Association website can be located at: www.dea.org.uk

- DfES (2001b) *Special Educational Needs Code of Practice*. London: DfES.

Ensuring the welfare, health and safety of young children

- Baldock P., Fitzgerald D. and Kay J. (2005) *Understanding Early Years Policy*. London: Paul Chapman.

- DfEE (1995) Circular 10/95. *Protecting Children from Abuse: The Role of the Education Service*. London: HMSO.

- Kay J. (2003, 2nd Edition) *Protecting Children*. London: Continuum.

- National Society for the Prevention of Cruelty to Children (NSPCC): www.nspcc.org.uk

Promoting positive values and maintaining good order

- Anti-Bullying Alliance: www.anti-bullyingalliance.org.uk

- ChildLine: www.childline.org.uk

- Cowley S. (2006, 3rd Edition) *Getting the Buggers to Behave*. London: Continuum.

- DfE (1994) *The Education of Children with Emotional and Behavioural Difficulties* (Circular 9/94). London: HMSO.

- DfEE (1998) Circular 10/98. *Section 550A of the Education Act 1996: The Use of Force to Control or Restrain Pupils*. London: DfEE.

- Kay J. (2006) *Managing Behaviour in the Early Years*. London: Continuum.

- National Society for the Prevention of Cruelty to Children (NSPCC): www.nspcc.org.uk

- Roffey S. and O'Reirdan T. (2001) *Young Children and Classroom Behaviour: Needs, Perspectives and Strategies*. London: David Fulton.

Professional Knowledge and Understanding

2

Introduction

This chapter deals with the knowledge and understanding expected of trainee and newly qualified 3–8 teachers. The chapter will consider some of the theories concerning young children's development and the impact that such theories have on teaching and learning before outlining the aims and structure of the Early Years Foundation Stage and primary National Curriculum. The chapter concludes by examining the various areas of learning/subjects that make up the 3–8 curricula. The chapter uses the six areas of learning and development set out in the Early Years Foundation Stage to structure the review. Comments concerning National Curriculum subjects, the National Literacy and Numeracy framework, PSHE and citizenship are dealt with under these headings.

> ✔ **Audit**
>
> By the end of this chapter you should:
>
> - understand how children's development can affect their learning;
> - know about the aims, principles and structure of the Early Years Foundation Stage and the National Curriculum for Key Stages 1 and 2;
> - know about the curriculum for PSED, PSHE and citizenship;
> - know about the curriculum for Communication, Language and Literacy/English;
> - know about the curriculum for Problem Solving, Reasoning and Numeracy/mathematics;
> - know about the curriculum for Knowledge and Understanding of the World/science, design and technology, geography, history, RE and information and communications technology (ICT);
> - know about the curriculum for Physical Development/Physical Education;
> - know about the curriculum for Creative Development/art and music.

Children as learners

Various schools of thought have emerged which attempt to understand and explain children's development, and this section deals with the work of psychologists and researchers such as Piaget, Athey, Bruner, Vygotsky, Isaacs and others. The work of these constructivists and social-interactionists has had a significant impact upon current practice in 3–8 settings and is characterized by the idea that children learn best and *construct meaning* for themselves when they are interacting with their environment, with their peers and with adults (Bruce, 1997).

> ✔ **Audit**
>
> By the end of this section you should:
>
> - have developed some understanding of how pupils' learning is affected by their intellectual, emotional and social development;
> - understand the reasoning behind the need for first-hand experience, high quality adult intervention, cooperation, play and talk in 3–8 settings.

Constructivist theories of learning

The Swiss psychologist Jean Piaget made a major contribution to our understanding of how children think and learn. Through his research he hoped to understand and explain how young children come to make sense of the world around them and to develop ways of operating effectively in it. A key element in Piaget's theories was the idea that children are not passive learners soaking up the wisdom of adults. Instead, for Piaget, children were actively constructing meaning and ideas about how the world works as a result of interacting with it.

Piaget used the concepts of assimilation, disequilibrium and accommodation to explain the process of learning. A child would **assimilate** knowledge as a result of first-hand experience. Subsequent experience would force the child to re-evaluate his/her original ideas in the light of new situations and observations in order to **accommodate** to the new reality. The lack of equilibrium or **disequilibrium** caused by encountering a situation which did not conform to the child's old model (**schema**) of the world was resolved as the child incorporated the new knowledge and experience into his/her existing mental models, thus improving and enhancing them.

As a result of his observations and experiments Piaget postulated a series of developmental stages which children went through in regular and ordered sequence. The sequence was invariable; children could not bypass stages or make short cuts to reach more advanced stages. Nor was progression from one stage to the next envisaged by Piaget as a revolutionary, overnight affair, but was instead an evolutionary and more gradual process. He included guidance on the ages at which children go through these stages, although he acknowledged that these were only an approximation and believed that while children were travelling the same route they were not necessarily progressing at the same speed. Finally, although the idea did not originate with Piaget, a controversial element in his theories was the notion of **readiness**. If a child found a problem too difficult then this constituted evidence that the child was not yet ready to learn. In other words, the child's mental schema had not yet reached a level where restructuring was possible.

Piaget's stages

1 **Sensorimotor**: children are getting to know the world through the physical actions that they can perform (age 0–2 years).
2 **Pre-operational**: children have not yet acquired fully logical thinking (age 2–7 years).
3 **Concrete operational**: children can think logically about problems that are concrete, i.e. here and now (age 7–12 years).
4 **Formal operational**: children are able to think rationally about abstract or hypothetical problems (age 12 onwards).

Schema

Piaget's work on schema has since been refined and expanded upon by researchers such as Athey and others who have argued that some children, as they make sense of the world through interacting with it, appear to exhibit patterns of repeatable behaviour (Athey, 1990; Nutbrown, 1996). Through her research Athey was able to identify a number of different schema and suggested four ways in which they might manifest themselves. The first is through motor actions (i.e. physical movement). The second is through symbolic functioning (i.e. pretending or representing something through drawings or letters). The third way is through functional dependency relationships (i.e. 'I've done x so that y can happen') and the fourth and final way is through thought.

Evidence of schema

- A young child is observed running in circles during outdoor play.
- During painting activities the same child likes to paint circles regularly.
- The child appears fascinated by artefacts and objects that are circular in shape.
- This child may be showing evidence of a schema associated with rotation. She appears to be establishing connections in relation to circles.

Her teacher takes her on a circle walk round the classroom, provides different shapes to be sorted into categories such as *circles* and *not circles*, talks about properties of circles and looks at books with circles in with the child.

Research has suggested that not all children show evidence of exploring schema, and those that do, do not necessarily follow a set pattern. Furthermore, some children may explore more than one schema at a time. It may also be the case that focusing on schema will not necessarily provide much insight into a child's physical, social or emotional development. That said, knowing about the concept of schema can provide teachers with valuable insights into young children's learning and may also help practitioners to plan future activities likely to enthuse, interest and excite pupils.

Schema: some categories and examples

Title	Explanation	Examples
Enveloping/ enclosure	Going round/through boundaries Containing/wrapping/covering	Covering self with face cloth Wrapping 'presents' Covering dolls/teddies in blankets Dressing up in hats, scarves, cloaks, etc. Putting things in bags/boxes/other containers
Rotation	Dynamic circular/rotation Semi-circularity Radial (i.e. fascination with wheels, spokes) Orientation (i.e. looking at things from different viewpoints, e.g. upside down)	Observing washing machines Interest in trucks/cars/other vehicles with wheels Repeatedly drawing circles Enthusiasm for toys/games with rotating parts, e.g. tops/kaleidoscopes/Lego wheels
Trajectory	Dynamic: • vertical/up and down lines • horizontal/back and forth/side to side lines Trajectory (travelling/moving) Diagonality (i.e. curiosity about diagonal lines)	Deliberately dropping things Playing with running tap water Climbing up/jumping off furniture/apparatus Drawing/painting lines Playing with toy vehicles Making 'trains', i.e. lining up objects bricks/chalks/stickers/figures Throwing and catching balls Engaging in certain household chores, e.g. mopping/sweeping
Transporting	Climbing over/under/on top of objects Taking objects from one place to another Positioning objects in specific/particular places	Role-play involving moving people or objects Becoming drivers/pilots taking other children on a journey Moving/carrying play materials and other equipment in the indoor and outdoor areas
Connection	Joining things Dismantling things	Using string/cord to tie things together Undoing shoe laces Fascination with zips, buttons, velcro, glue, staplers, sticky tape and other means of joining things together Playing with construction kits, e.g. Lego
Others	Orientation Ordering Transforming Correspondence	Changing position to look at things from different perspectives. Turning things around. Sequencing things by height, width, etc. Changing colours/shapes/properties using malleable materials, paints or foodstuffs Matching objects, e.g. 1 cube in each pot

Social-interactionist/social-constructivist theories of learning

Like Piaget, Athey and others, Bruner made an important contribution to understanding children's cognitive development. He was particularly interested in the part played by experience in cognitive development, concluding that carefully guiding a child to new ways of coping with a new problem could aid the process of maturation (Keenan, 2002). Bruner's research suggested that children were capable of intellectual achievements at an earlier point than that predicted by Piaget as a result of instruction and carefully structured environments. This challenged the idea of readiness. For Bruner, passively waiting for children to become ready to learn might necessitate a very long wait indeed. As a result, the concept of readiness could actually lead to a lowering of educational standards and teacher expectations. While teachers of young children do need to be sensitive to a child's needs, abilities and development, they also need to be prepared to intervene through questioning, guiding and instructing in an effort to extend and challenge thinking.

Bruner's stages

1 **Enactive stage**: understanding through first-hand experience.
2 **Iconic stage**: understanding through images.
3 **Symbolic stage**: children are able to express ideas through words and numbers and have acquired the concept of conservation.

Bruner was suggesting that there is a social dimension to cognitive development, whereby a child's learning is also influenced and affected by those experiences involving interaction with others, both children and adults. In Bruner's model therefore communication and language play a crucial role in learning and cognitive development. Facilitating pupils' progress through the use of appropriate support materials and intervention provides children with **scaffolding** upon which they can construct increasingly advanced ways of thinking and understanding the world (Wood, 1998). Bruner also advocated a spiral curriculum for children in which they would revisit topics at regular intervals thus advancing their learning towards higher levels of understanding.

A spiral curriculum

Knowledge and Understanding of the World/history

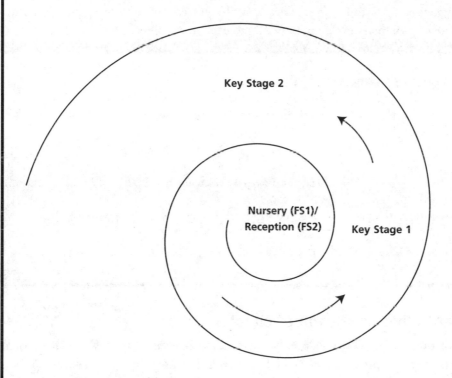

Nursery (FS1)/Reception (FS2)

30–50 months: Remember and talk about significant events in their own experience. Show interest in the lives of people familiar to them. Talk about past and future events. Develop an understanding of growth, decay and changes over time (DfES, 2007d, pp. 83–4).

40–60 months: Begin to differentiate between past and present. Use time related words in conversation. Understand about the seasons of the year and their regularity. Make short-term future plans. Find out about past and present events in their own lives and the lives of those of their families and other people they know (DfES, 2007d, p. 84).

Key Stage 1: Learn about changes in their own lives and the way of life of their family or others around them (QCA, 1999, p. 104).

Key Stage 2: Learn about how an aspect in the local area has changed over a long period of time *or* how the locality was affected by a significant national *or* local event *or* development *or* by the work of a significant individual. (QCA, 1999, p. 106).

Vygotsky, too, recognized communication and language as centrally important to children's cognitive development (Wood, 1998; Keenan, 2002). In addition, for those taking a Vygotskian perspective, readiness is not simply a question of a child's existing knowledge or schema; it is also influenced by a child's capacity to learn. Like Bruner, Vygotsky advocated the use of scaffolding to advance children's learning and developed the notion of a **zone of proximal development (ZPD)** to explain his ideas.

Vygotsky's concept of ZPD

What someone (a child) can do unaided

Zone of proximal development

What someone (a child) can achieve with help from someone more skilful/knowledgeable

The affective dimension of childhood

Any explanatory model of childhood needs to make reference to the whole child. Many researchers have pointed out that children are *made up of far more than cognitive capacities* (Zigler in Hyson, 1994, p. ix). Just as there is a relationship between thought and action, so too is there a reciprocal relationship between thought and feeling. Issacs' inclusion of an affective dimension to the nature of childhood helped to ensure that young children were seen as more than just cognitive beings. Her work helped to provide a rational theoretical underpinning for the importance of personal, social and emotional development and the need for children to exercise responsibility and choice in order to develop independence, autonomy and self-control (Isaacs, 1951).

This idea that children are not simply cognitive beings but are also emotional and social beings, and that furthermore there is a connection between growth and development in the first area and growth and development in the second area is significant (Goleman, 1995). Anyone involved in teaching young children ought not to underestimate the power of emotions (some subconscious) to motivate behaviour and learning. The idea of an affective dimension to learning is a feature of the rationale behind the current drive to match *excellence* with *enjoyment* (DfES, 2004a). Memory and learning, for example, may well be enhanced in settings that heighten interest and happiness, enabling greater tolerance of frustration, and promoting perseverance. The principles contained within the Early Years Foundation Stage acknowledge the emotional–cognitive link and the positive emotional bases of children's self-initiated learning such as:

- satisfied curiosity;
- pleasure in finding out;
- the intrinsic reward of mastery;
- identification with adults and teachers;
- the impact of adult praise, recognition, confidence and trust.

This connection between the affective dimension of children's development and their success in school is reiterated and reinforced in the primary curriculum through the National Strategy, which highlights children's Personal, Social and Emotional Development as a key precursor for learning. Under the strategy teachers are expected to foster and encourage pupils to develop a range of interrelated affective skills and qualities without which children are unlikely to make good progress at school.

Why the affective dimension of childhood matters

- Becoming more self-aware may make children better able to reflect on such things as their strengths, weaknesses, achievements and behaviour.
- Developing empathy will enable children to understand and learn from others.
- Learning to manage their feelings will help children to regulate their own behaviour and stay focused.
- Becoming self-motivated as learners will help children to exercise perseverance, determination and resilience in the face of difficulties.
- Improving children's social skills will help them to work effectively with their peers and support them in *learning how to learn* itself.

(DfES, 2004a)

Multiple intelligences and learning styles

More recently some researchers and psychologists have suggested that people may possess a range of intelligences; others meanwhile have suggested that we may all have preferred learning styles (Gardner, 2003; Teachernet, 2007).

Intelligences and learning styles

Gardner's original multiple intelligences

- **Linguistic**: the ability to use words (orally or in writing) effectively.
- **Mathematical** (logical): the ability to use reason and numbers effectively.
- **Visual** (spatial): the ability to visualize the world around you accurately, to represent things visually and to manipulate images mentally.
- **Musical**: the ability to identify clearly, change and express music.
- **Bodily** (kinaesthetic): the ability to use your body and/or hands to express ideas and make or change objects.
- **Interpersonal**: the ability to be sensitive to the emotions and thoughts of other people.
- **Intrapersonal**: the ability to be reflective and understand one's own strengths and weaknesses.

Possible preferred learning styles

- **Visual** (*show me*): learning through pictures, photographs, diagrams, charts, film/video, demonstrations, signs and symbols.
- **Auditory** (*tell me*): learning through noises, sounds and words, listening to explanations or taking part in discussions.
- **Kinaesthetic** (*let me have a go*): learning through *hands-on* experience, doing, touching, practical/physical activity, movement or role-play.

These theories have been controversial and may be hard to prove; however, awareness of multiple intelligence theories and learning styles does not mean that children should only be taught using one style or in response to a single intelligence type. Rather the theories provide a useful stimulus for teachers when weighing up the best ways to grab children's attention and to capitalize on their strengths in order to help them to learn more effectively across the curriculum; they offer a valuable reminder of the need to maintain and utilize a variety of interesting approaches.

Introducing a sociological perspective

Questions remain over the universal applicability of theories on young children's development prevalent in western societies. Isaacs, for example, identified a series of factors in the 1920s and 1930s that could play a role in determining individual differences, including inborn ability, temperament and character, and home and social background (Isaacs, 1951). Over-standardized models of childhood that advocate stages and ages of developmental change could result in a determined and determining conformity that might underestimate the impact of social, emotional and environmental factors on young children's development (Christensen and James, 2000). The childhoods experienced by children in different areas of the UK, or from different family backgrounds, are not necessarily the same (David, 1998).

Others have argued convincingly that by taking a more holistic view of childhood it is still possible to discern a period of infancy in which children do have some needs in common and, in spite of the qualifications added to developmental theories from the social sciences, the work of constructivist and social-interactionist psychologists can be seen to have informed current practice in 3–8 settings (Blenkin and Kelly, 2000). Children's development does appear to be broadly sequential in nature with things happening in a particular order, an order that to all intents and purposes is the same for all children. As such it is possible to set out principles of good early years practice provided that practitioners remember that children are individuals and as such are likely to be at different points in their development and learning. While children share a common biology and appear to follow broadly similar developmental paths, their social experiences and relative competences must always be seen as contextualized, rather than determined, by the processes of physiological and psychological change (Christensen and James, 2000). Teachers have to bear in mind that the rate of children's development can vary widely as a result of a range of factors that include environmental, social, cultural, personal, biological and economic elements; while some of these factors may enhance and promote a child's development, others might hinder and inhibit it (QCA, 2000).

The Early Years Foundation Stage: provision for nursery and reception pupils

High quality early years education can do much to lay the foundations for children's future successes in learning but the rationale behind such provision concerns more than just preparation for future educational experiences. Effective early years education requires not only a relevant curriculum and practitioners capable of implementing it but also practitioners who understand young children and their rapid development. The education of 3- to 5-year-old children should be recognized as a distinctive stage in the continuum of learning and be valued in its own right. The broad aims for early years education are very similar to those for the over-fives, with an additional emphasis on the considerable amount of care that very young children require, care which is intrinsically linked to their education (DfEE, 1997).

✔ **Audit**

By the end of this section you should:

- know about the principles underlying the Early Years Foundation Stage;
- have an overview of the six areas of learning contained within the Curriculum Guidance for the Foundation Stage.

The principles behind the Foundation Stage

During the past decade there has been a plethora of reforms aimed at extending and enhancing early childhood services in the UK including educational provision. The development of an early years curriculum is part of this much wider context, which includes the launch of the Sure Start programme and the Every Child Matters agenda; Birth to Three Matters; the establishment of Education Action Zones, Early Years Development and Childcare Partnerships (EYDCPs), Early Excellence Centres; and developments in the training of teachers and others intending to work with young children as part of Children's Workforce Reform. The developments in staff training have been paralleled by developments in the early years curriculum resulting in the publication of the Curriculum Guidance for the Foundation Stage in 2000, which set out the desired learning outcomes (early learning goals) for children upon completion of their Foundation 2/reception year (QCA, 2000). This document was superseded in 2007 by the Early Years Foundation Stage framework, which brought previously separate developments such as Birth to Three Matters, the National Day Care Standards and the Curriculum Guidance together into a more coherent and unified framework covering the birth to five age range (DfES, 2007d). The statutory framework set out in the Foundation Stage documentation and the areas of learning and development contained in it will apply to all schools and early years providers in Ofsted registered settings from September 2008 onwards. The Early Years Foundation Stage is based on a series of themes and related principles that underpin children's welfare and teaching and learning across the curriculum.

The underlying themes and principles of the Early Years Foundation Stage

The **Unique Child** theme incorporates knowledge and understanding about child development, inclusive practice, and children's safety, health and well-being. Children should be regarded as competent learners from birth who can be resilient, capable, confident and self-assured.

The **Positive Relationships** theme focuses on practitioners' abilities to develop partnerships and demonstrate respect for children, parents, other key people in children's lives and each other as well as being supportive of learning in the nursery/classroom. Children learn to be strong and independent from a base of loving and secure relationships with parents and/or key people.

The **Enabling Environments** theme addresses teachers' abilities to observe and assess children's development and needs, to plan appropriate activities and to support the learning of every child. Teachers need to be able to create stimulating and challenging learning environments and to draw on resources and expertise in the wider community where appropriate.

The **Learning and Development** theme emphasizes the importance of play, exploration and active learning as well as chances for children to be creative and engage in critical thinking. Children need opportunities to learn and develop in different ways and at different rates. Parity of esteem is given to the various interconnected aspects or Areas of Learning and Development.

(DfES, 2007d)

Teachers are reminded that the rate of children's development is different and uneven and that some children will have had a wide range of experiences before they enter an educational setting of any kind while others will not. Children are not all on the same start line when they enter nursery (FS1) or reception (FS2) classes. They will display a range of predispositions and some will have special educational needs (SEN), be they physical, emotional, behavioural or cognitive, while others may be gifted or talented in some way. To provide an appropriate curriculum, therefore, early years practitioners need first to bear in mind the children's abilities and experiences to date.

The structure of the Foundation Stage curriculum

The development of a curriculum for the under-fives has also been influenced by a desire to ensure breadth and balance and a wish to achieve a measure of continuity with the National Curriculum. The Early Years Foundation Stage organizes the early learning goals into six areas of learning and development which, while frequently corresponding to, do not replicate the subjects in the National Curriculum.

The six areas of learning and development

1 Personal, Social and Emotional Development

- Dispositions and attitudes
- Self-confidence and self-esteem
- Making relationships
- Behaviour and self-control
- Self-care
- Sense of community.

2 Communication, Language and Literacy

- Language for communication
- Language for thinking
- Linking sounds and letters
- Reading
- Writing
- Handwriting.

3 Problem Solving, Reasoning and Numeracy

- Numbers as labels and for counting
- Calculating
- Shape, space and measures.

---

4 **Knowledge and Understanding of the World**

- Exploration and investigation
- Designing and making
- ICT
- Time
- Place
- Communities.

5 **Physical Development**

- Movement and space
- Health and bodily awareness
- Using equipment and materials.

6 **Creative Development**

- Being creative: responding to experiences, expressing and communicating ideas
- Exploring media and materials
- Creating music and dance
- Developing imagination and imaginative play.

The Foundation Stage early learning goals represent what most children are expected to achieve by the end of their time in reception (FS2) classes. They are preceded by a series of developmental markers which set out a model of progression in terms of the knowledge, skills, attitudes and behaviours that practitioners can look for when gauging children's learning and development. The revised documentation also contains advice for teachers on effective practice as well as planning and resourcing matters alongside these developmental markers (DfES, 2007d). Progression through the markers is age related in the EYFS but indicative; they overlap and some children will progress faster in some areas and others will progress more slowly in others.

Examples of the early learning goals

Creative Development: developing imagination and imaginative play

- **Birth–11 months**: smile with pleasure at recognisable playthings.
- **8–20 months**: enjoy making noises or movements spontaneously.
- **16–26 months**: pretend that one object represents another, especially when objects have characteristics in common.
- **22–36 months**: begin to make-believe by pretending.
- **30–50 months**: notice what adults do, imitating what is observed and then doing it spontaneously when the adult is not there. Use available resources to create props to support role-play. Develop a repertoire of actions by putting a sequence of movements together. Engage in imaginative play and role-play based on own first-hand experiences.
- **40–60 months**: introduce a storyline or narrative into their play. Play alongside other children who are engaged in the same theme. Play cooperatively as part of a group to act out a narrative.
- **Early learning goals**: use their imagination in art and design, music, dance, imaginative and role-play and stories.

(DfES, 2007d, pp. 113–14)

Although one aim of the Early Years Foundation Stage is to foster continuity with the National Curriculum it remains the case that the structure, organization and delivery of the curriculum in the early years is often different to that in primary schools. This difference is based in large part on social-interactionist and constructivist understandings of how younger pupils learn and is viewed as the best way of addressing the particular needs of 3–5 year olds during this crucial period of their development (QCA, 1998b). Young children do not necessarily make the same subject distinctions with which adults seek to organize teaching and learning. In the Foundation Stage the term curriculum is interpreted in a holistic and inclusive manner and is sometimes rejected in favour of alternative descriptions, such as *framework*, that are felt to be more in keeping with an approach to learning that is not structured using National Curriculum subject boundaries. The Foundation Stage encompasses not just the six areas of learning but includes all aspects of young children's experiences. The early years curriculum is *everything children do, see, hear or feel in their setting, both planned and unplanned*; in nursery and reception classes activities can offer starting points for learning across a number of areas (Drake, 2001).

The National Curriculum for 5–8 year olds (Years 1, 2 and 3)

The National Curriculum sets out a broad and balanced curriculum that should be offered to pupils at both Key Stage 1 (children 5–7 years of age) and Key Stage 2 (children 7–11 years of age), and that should be relevant to the needs of the pupils taking it. The curriculum comprises the National Curriculum subjects (core and foundation), Religious Education for all children over 5, and a series of cross-curricular elements.

✔ Audit

By the end of this section you should:

- know about the structure of the National Curriculum and its underlying principles;
- know about the Primary National Strategy, Excellence and Enjoyment and the place of literacy and numeracy hours within the primary curriculum;
- know about the cross-curricular elements.

The principles behind the National Curriculum

The underlying principles of the National Curriculum are based on the Education Reform Act (1988) and the Education Act (1996) and are set out in the current documentation (QCA, 1999) in the form of two interrelated aims and four main purposes. Aims of the National Curriculum state that:

1 the National Curriculum is a curriculum for all; all children, irrespective of their social, ethnic, or cultural background or their ability, need to be helped to learn and to achieve;

2 the National Curriculum concerns the development of the whole child not just their academic progress; education must contribute to children's moral, spiritual, social and cultural development as a means of preparing them for the *opportunities, responsibilities and experiences of adult life.*

(QCA, 1999, p. 11)

Meanwhile the purposes of the National Curriculum are:

1 to establish an entitlement to a range of subjects, and to develop a range of skills and attitudes essential for academic achievement, self-fulfilment and socially responsible behaviour;

2 to establish standards by making expectations clear to all those involved in teaching and learning (children, teachers, parents, governors, society) and to use these standards to measure attainment and set improvement targets;

3 to promote continuity and coherence, to ensure progression in children's learning and to facilitate transition into, within and beyond educational settings;

4 to promote public understanding and thereby confidence in the performance of compulsory education and to facilitate and inform debates within society about educational matters.

(QCA, 1999, pp. 12–13)

The structure of the National Curriculum

Currently the National Curriculum comprises ten subjects, plus RE, plus a number of non-statutory cross-curricular elements.

National Curriculum subjects

Core subjects	Foundation subjects
English	design and technology
mathematics	history
science	geography
information and communications technology (ICT)	music
	art
	physical education

(QCA, 1999)

Each subject in the National Curriculum has a Programme of Study (PoS) for Key Stages 1 and 2, which is intended to help teachers plan and organize the curriculum. Each PoS sets out the curriculum content under the headings of **Knowledge, skills and understanding** and **Breadth of study**. In the case of the core curriculum subjects (English, mathematics and science) this content is further divided into discrete sub-sections.

Programme of Study (PoS) for science

Sc1 Scientific enquiry

Sc2 Life processes and living things

Sc3 Materials and their properties

Sc4 Physical processes.

(QCA, 1999, pp. 78–82)

Each subject in the National Curriculum also has a set of Attainment Targets (ATs), broken down into level descriptions, intended to help teachers assess and make judgements about children's learning and achievements. Teachers are expected to use a *best fit* approach when deciding the level that most closely corresponds to a child's abilities.

Programme of Study for music at Key Stage 1

Knowledge, skills and understanding

- Controlling sounds through singing and playing – performing skills (1a–1c)
- Creating and developing musical ideas – composing skills (2a–2b)
- Responding and reviewing – appraising skills (3a–3b)
- Listening, and applying knowledge and understanding (4a–4d).

Breadth of study – Pupils should be taught the knowledge, skills and understanding through:

- a range of musical activities that integrate performing, composing and appraising (5a);
- responding to a range of musical and non-musical starting points (5b);
- working on their own, in groups of different sizes and as a class (5c);
- a range of live and recorded music from different times and cultures (5d).

(QCA, 1999, pp. 124–125)

To be considered at Level 1 for attainment in music, children have to show that they can:

- recognize and explore how sounds can be made and changed;
- use their voices in different ways;
- repeat short rhythmic and melodic patterns;
- create and choose sounds in response to given starting points;
- respond to different moods in music;
- recognize well-defined changes in sounds;
- identify simple repeated patterns;
- take account of musical instructions.

(QCA, 1999, p. 35)

Since its inception in 1989 the National Curriculum for Key Stages 1 and 2 has been subject to a number of refinements and modifications, for example the introduction in 1995 (DFE) and then again in 1999 (QCA) of revised documentation with more compact Programmes of Study (PoS) to make it more manageable. In addition, information and communications technology (ICT) first appeared in the National Curriculum distributed among the various other subjects and was particularly prominent in the Programme of Study for design and technology. During the 1995 revisions it was subsequently brought together into what amounted to a *de facto* additional subject in the documentation, with its own Programme of Study and Attainment Targets, while still retaining a high degree of relevance for most of the other subjects. Since then ICT has continued to assume increasing importance in the curriculum; other subjects have remained constant throughout the various revisions.

The introduction of the National Curriculum carried with it an inherent tension between the desire to offer pupils a broad and balanced curriculum and the desire to raise standards, particularly in subjects like English and mathematics. This tension was further exacerbated by developments such as the introduction of targets for SATs results and of literacy and numeracy hours for pupils in Key Stages 1 and 2. The consequences of this initial tension (and subsequent developments) have included pressure on the amount of time available for delivering the foundation subjects necessary for a broad and balanced curriculum and fears about *teaching to the test*. The QCA (1998a) offered guidance to practitioners in an attempt to retain the commitment to breadth and balance by developing more flexible approaches to the teaching of subjects other than English and mathematics. This was followed by the launch of *Excellence and Enjoyment*, which sought to ensure high standards of pupil achievement in subjects such as English and mathematics in parallel with and through a curriculum that was *rich, varied and exciting* (DfES, 2004a). The strategy proposed more freedom for schools to develop the curriculum on offer to children, the chance for schools to set targets for themselves, greater emphasis on teacher assessments and encouragement for schools to share good practice. The wider curriculum could now expect similar levels of support and resources that had previously been the preserve of literacy and numeracy strategies. The literacy and numeracy strategies themselves remained under the overall Primary Strategy but were revised into a new framework in response to the principles underlying the Excellence and Enjoyment documentation. The Primary Strategy itself set out to:

- support teachers in understanding some of the developmental factors that underpin children's learning such as self-awareness and motivation;
- offer guidance to teachers on establishing stimulating learning environments;
- enhance teachers' abilities to use assessment *for* learning.

Further information relating to all of these elements can be found in the remainder of this chapter and in Chapter 3.

The cross-curricular elements

The cross-curricular elements were originally envisaged as important areas of learning with relevance across the National Curriculum as a whole and addressed the broader development of children, key skills and metacognitive skills (learning how to learn). They were not restricted to any one subject area; their purpose was to pull together the broad education of the individual and augment the basic curriculum as set out in the core and foundation subjects (NCC, 1990).

Since their original appearance some of these cross-curricular elements have assumed increasing prominence in education. ICT has evolved into a National Curriculum subject in its own right. Personal, social and health education (PSHE) and citizenship have a non-statutory Programme of Study attached to them within the revised National Curriculum, while literacy and numeracy hours now dominate the activities of many, if not most, primary classrooms for nearly half of every day (DfEE, 1998b, 1999; QCA, 1999). Other cross-curricular elements, however, have retained a status that is lower profile; teachers, perhaps understandably, prioritize areas such as statutory subjects (e.g. English and mathematics) where public accountability is greatest.

Learning across the National Curriculum in the revised documentation

- Promoting spiritual, moral, social and cultural development
- Promoting personal, social and health education (PSHE) and citizenship
- Promoting key skills across the National Curriculum:
  - Communication
  - Application of number
  - Information technology
  - Working with others
  - Improving own learning and performance
  - Problem solving
- Thinking skills:
  - Information processing skills
  - Reasoning skills
  - Enquiry skills
  - Creative thinking skills
  - Evaluation skills
- Financial capability
- Enterprise Education
- Education for sustainable development

(QCA, 1999, pp. 19–23)

Personal, Social and Emotional Development (PSED)

Nurseries and schools seek to help young children develop their understanding of social and personal values. Actively promoting children's personal, social and emotional development in this way benefits teachers in 3–8 settings by encouraging good behaviour and achievement on the part of the pupils. Teachers of young children are often building on the work of the family, starting from and continuing the good work done by most parents and carers, and ameliorating the worst effects of the minority (Kay, 2006).

✔ **Audit**

By the end of this section you should:

- know about provision for Personal, Social and Emotional Development (PSED) in the Early Years Foundation Stage (DfES, 2007d, pp. 22–38);
- know about the teaching of personal, social and health education (PSHE) and citizenship in the primary curriculum (QCA, 1999, pp. 19–23, 136–141).

PSED in the Foundation Stage

A child's personal, social and emotional development will affect the way he/she relates to peers and adults. At the same time, it provides children with strategies for reconciling social and emotional conflicts and offers opportunities for them to establish good interpersonal relationships. These experiences will be of use to them during their continuing education and later as adults.

Developmental skills

- **Social development**: the ability to interact positively with peers, practitioners and others.
- **Moral development**: an increasing awareness of right and wrong and why things are right or wrong.
- **Emotional development**: the ability to control impulses and express feelings in increasingly mature and responsible ways, the ability to understand why one feels a particular emotion coupled with awareness and understanding of the feelings of others.
- **Personal development**: the growth of self-esteem and the acquisition of a set of positive qualities and dispositions including determination, industriousness, creativity, enthusiasm, independence and patience.

While most children's social and emotional development, their self-confidence and their understanding of right and wrong begins through the support of their families, for some, their development in this area is impeded by stressful home circumstances. There may have been a failure to meet children's basic need for affection and security, or conflict in the home could lead to their frustration, tension, anger and anxiety. In the case of parental separation, some children may actually feel guilty and somehow responsible for events. Other children will find it difficult to express their emotions or to understand the feelings of others having experienced abusive behaviour on the part of adults. Faced with such experiences practitioners need to be consistent and reliable, for example doing what you said you would do, when you said you would do it and within a time-frame that is meaningful to young children. Practitioners can also model positive emotional management by staying calm and being willing to talk about their own feelings and the feelings of others.

Adults can model desired behaviours by:

- playing/working cooperatively;
- sharing and taking turns;
- dealing positively with conflicts that arise;
- caring about others;
- making decisions and forming opinions;
- demonstrating independence, confidence and self-reliance.

By the time children reach nursery and reception settings between the ages of 3 and 5, most will be able to cope with more than one regular carer provided there is at least some consistency, predictability and regularity. Having a special relationship with one adult can be an important source of security and stability for children and can greatly aid teachers' attempts to promote children's Personal, Social and Emotional Development. In reception and Key Stage 1 settings stability and continuity are provided in part by the class teacher system. Many nurseries meanwhile operate a key worker/person system whereby all practitioners (teaching and learning support staff) have responsibility for certain children, although the teacher retains overall responsibility for the children's well-being and education. Such systems also support teachers' efforts to monitor and assess children's continuing development over time.

Monitoring young children's Personal, Social and Emotional Development

Nursery	Reception
Will approach/participate in some activities and move around without adult intervention	Will participate and persevere in activities of their choice for 5–10 minutes
Is becoming aware of routines and session organization	Is becoming aware of school routines and organization as regards each session and each day
Is able to locate own coat and some equipment with help	Is able to locate equipment necessary for a specific task
Can follow simple instructions with guidance	Can follow simple instructions with guidance Can follow simple instructions
Will confidently pursue activities they enjoy at the start of the session	Settles in the classroom confidently each morning with minimum staff support
Plays confidently in all areas	Has a positive self-image
Is naturally curious about the learning environment	Is developing his/her natural curiosity and questioning skills
Can concentrate on teacher directed activity with adult support for 5 minutes	Can concentrate for ten minutes with small amounts of adult support
Is able to listen and respond in specific situations, e.g. action songs	Can listen and respond appropriately to questions in a group
Is beginning to share and take turns and has an awareness of others	Shows simple cooperative play
Is easily motivated and shows interest in nursery activities	Is well motivated and interested
Is beginning to make links between activities and their own experiences	Is beginning to make links and will find something seen or discussed on their own
Pays attention and is able to focus in a one-to-one situation	Pays attention and is able to focus with support or in a small group

Although established patterns of behaviour with others will be in evidence when children start in FS1 and FS2 settings, teachers play a big part in influencing the continuing PSED of young pupils. For children to learn and develop positively and to their full potential they need to feel secure, cared about, valued and successful. Self-esteem is an important contributory factor in children's social and emotional development, which in turn underpins their progress elsewhere in the curriculum. Children with low self-esteem and impaired social or emotional development may struggle in their relationships with others, may find it harder to work in groups, may be less willing to try new things as a result of a fear of failure, may find it much harder to pay attention becoming easily disheartened and may even find praise and recognition hard to accept having become convinced that they are *rubbish* at everything. In contrast children with greater self-esteem are more likely to:

- attempt to acquire new skills;
- experiment/try things out/be prepared to make mistakes;
- take criticism without feeling emotionally crushed;
- feel good about joining in with others;
- cope with losing/not always getting their own way;
- be enthusiastic and willing to persevere if at first things do not go as they would like.

Practitioners need to let the children know that they like and respect them by listening to them; by offering opportunities for them to exercise choice and decision-making skills; by offering opportunities for success, mastery and achievement; and by offering praise and recognition. Even occasional disapproval of children's actions does not detract from this acceptance and valuing of them as individuals. Practitioners also need to be willing to mediate between children to ensure that discriminatory or anti-social behaviour on the part of peers does not undermine their sense of worth.

Promoting pupils' Personal, Social and Emotional Development

Aims

Help children to develop an understanding of their position and role within their family context.

Strategies

Encourage children to develop an awareness of their position in the family:

- name family members;
- describe family roles and responsibilities;
- seek information and clarification about family members;
- develop family trees/maps;

Help children to become increasingly aware that they are part of a larger community.

Help children to learn about their local community:

- elicit children's knowledge and understanding of where they live;
- ask children to identify and describe features of their neighbourhood;
- discuss community rules relating to road safety, littering, signs and symbols;
- talk to the children about people from/in other parts of the country/world.

Encourage children to develop positive relationships outside the family context in nursery/school enabling them to participate as members of a group.

Teach children that cooperating, taking turns, waiting and becoming less egocentric are all valued behaviours. Encourage them to:

- help and look after others (parents, peers, pets);
- take turns;
- line up and move sensibly as a group/class;
- listen to other children and adults;
- share with others;
- talk about fair and unfair behaviour;
- show consideration to others in the group;
- show respect for others in their class and in their surroundings.

Increase and extend children's self-awareness and independence.

Encourage children to take increasing responsibilities, to develop increasingly realistic expectations of themselves and to exercise increasing control over their own learning experiences, their environment and their resources. Encourage them to:

- exercise choice over activities or food;
- dress themselves after dance/movement;
- go to the toilet independently;
- look after their possessions properly, e.g. hanging up their coats after outdoor play;
- resolve disagreements amicably and independently;
- express themselves confidently;
- try new things and have a go;
- tidy up after themselves;
- tell the truth;
- look for alternative/independent solutions to problems.

Personal, social and health education (PSHE) and citizenship in the National Curriculum

Education, PSHE and citizenship

Dear Teacher,

    I am a survivor of a concentration camp.

    My eyes saw what no man should witness:

- Gas chambers built by learned engineers;
- Children poisoned by educated physicians;
- Infants killed by trained nurses;
- Women and babies shot and burned by high school and college graduates.

So I am suspicious of education.

My request is:

- Help your students to become human;
- Your efforts must never produce learned monsters, skilled psychopaths, educated Eichmanns;
- Reading, writing and arithmetic are important only if they serve to make our children more human.

(Pike and Selby, 1988)

Personal, social and health education (PSHE) and citizenship were revised in 1999 to form part of the non-statutory guidance accompanying the National Curriculum for Key Stages 1 and 2 (QCA, 1999, pp. 136–41). They are not subjects but are important cross-curricular themes with their own non-statutory Programme of Study (PoS), and formalize the work done in fostering responsibility, care and concern in children, building on the work done in PSED. However, PSHE and citizenship also provide a framework within which children can be introduced to topics such as sex and drugs education as well as some of the systems and institutions of the society within which they live.

Health education topics

- Exercise
- Diet
- Family life/relationships
- Substance abuse (drugs/household chemicals)
- Personal hygiene
- The environment and human health
- Disease (spread and control)
- Safety (road safety, personal safety)
- People who help us to stay safe and healthy (fire service, police, doctors, nurses and other health professionals).

Work on PSHE and citizenship in primary settings is intended to ensure that children:

- understand the nature of community (different communities, organization, the family, serving the community, public services, pluralism, multicultural Britain);
- know about democratic approaches to society (reconciling competing needs and ideas, diversity and interdependence among groups in society, politics);
- understand their rights and responsibilities in society (social and moral aspects of behaviour, law, work and leisure).

The inclusion of PSHE and citizenship in the non-statutory guidance for the National Curriculum does not mean that subjects such as politics, economics, sociology, human biology, environmental sciences or law have to be added to the primary curriculum. Instead teachers are expected to look for opportunities to help children to learn about these things as part of their everyday work in school. For example, a visit to a local industrial museum would offer opportunities to discuss people's working conditions in the past and introduce notions of fairness, right and wrong and social justice with children as part of the history curriculum. Similarly work in geography on distant locations offers children the chance to think about and discuss comparisons, diversity and interdependence today, while work in design and technology offers opportunities to consider issues such as sustainable (e.g. wind farm) versus consumptive (e.g. coal fired power station) technologies. In addition to the integration of PSHE and citizenship themes into existing activities, the scheme of work to accompany the non-statutory Programme of Study also offers ideas for interesting activities on discrete topics such as 'Making choices', 'Taking part', 'People who help us' and 'Animals and us' (www.standards.dfes.gov.uk).

Communication, Language and Literacy

This area of learning forms a huge part of the 3–8 curricula. Not only do Communication, Language and Literacy in the Foundation Stage and English in the primary phase have a distinct identity of their own, they are involved in some way in almost every other activity that takes place in nursery or school. There can be few aspects of the 3–8 curricula more important for children's future educational achievements and opportunities in life.

✔ **Audit**

By the end of this section you should:

- know about the teaching of Communication, Language and literacy in the Early Years Foundation Stage (DfES, 2007d, pp. 39–60);
- know about the teaching of English in the National Curriculum (QCA, 1999, pp. 42–58);
- know about the revised national literacy framework and its relationship with English in the National Curriculum (DfEE, 1998b);
- be familiar with some of the strategies that can support the learning of children with English as an additional language (EAL).

Speaking and listening

Teachers recognize the fundamental importance of language development, for both the children's future adult prospects and their educational achievements. Oral language is the basis for literacy, and as a result teachers give significant consideration to both the quantity and quality of talk. Adults are constantly putting young children into situations where they need to pay attention. Listening carefully (individually, and in group and class situations) is an essential learning skill, albeit one that can prove a challenge for some young children. Many children entering nursery or reception classes are relatively skilled in speaking and listening, having had experience of listening to stories, learning rhymes or singing along with songs on the radio or television at home. At the same time, some of their peers are lacking in confidence and can be reluctant to communicate. They may have difficulty in listening attentively for even the shortest of periods, and may also have only a very limited vocabulary. Other children may be fluent speakers and listeners, but not in English. This wide range of ability results in a great deal of time spent in providing opportunities designed to promote speaking and listening (Burnett and Myers, 2004).

Dealing with a reluctant speaker

When Matthew joined the reception class he was very reluctant to contribute verbally in front of his peers and others, so much so, that he would approach the teacher and whisper any questions or requests in her ear. His teacher realized that she would need to make Matthew feel secure and raise his confidence through patience, praise and quiet encouragement. The process took a great deal of time but by the end of the year Matthew felt able to join in group discussions and answer questions with support.

The ethos and environment in 3–8 settings play a crucial part in fostering children's speaking and listening skills. It is vital that young children have the confidence to talk. Conversations with peers and adults can improve children's abilities to describe, to remember, and to develop and clarify their thoughts and ideas. Offering less threatening opportunities for children to express themselves verbally such as daily chats and discussions with small groups and individuals can be particularly rewarding for children who find talking in large groups or whole-class situations difficult and who may therefore be reluctant to contribute. Familiar topics for discussion may further bolster children's confidence and skills, such as experiences in the home, activities in the nursery/school, and observations and events in the local environment. Puppets, telephones and masks can also be introduced to help some children overcome their anxieties about speaking in front of others. Listening to stories meanwhile can be a powerful way to introduce new vocabulary and to extend the children's familiarity with the rhythms, patterns and structures of language.

Speaking and listening: the benefits of stories and story telling

Listening to and telling stories can help children to:

- absorb patterned and rhythmic language and to broaden their repertoire of language use;
- become active listeners by joining in refrains, making sound effects and speculating on characters, places and outcomes;
- experience sustained speech and to develop an awareness of how to structure speech to capture and retain an audience's interest;
- practise their creativity during the act of telling or retelling and embellishing.

(Burnett and Myers, 2004)

Questioning by teachers is valuable in promoting good dialogue and interaction with pupils, and children need to be allowed the opportunity to ask questions as well as to answer them. Questions that are open-ended can provide opportunities for children to talk at length on a topic. Such questions offer more children the chance to respond and can be a good way of challenging the more able pupils. Closed questions meanwhile (where there is one correct answer and what is being sought is more clearly defined) can offer greater security for some children. Having asked a question, teachers should not be tempted to cut off the reply through impatience. Those teaching the 3–8 age range have to be prepared to wait and avoid jumping in too quickly to answer their own questions. Prompting can be helpful when children are making an effort to express themselves verbally, but if done too often or too quickly it can be frustrating for children who know the word(s) they need but just want a second or two to remember and arrange them. At the same time, teachers need to be sensitive to children who are genuinely struggling and be ready to support them when necessary.

Increasing pupil confidence in speaking and listening

- Encourage children to ask and answer questions; seek information and clarification; retell and share personal experiences; participate in group discussions; and to work cooperatively and collaboratively with their peers, in pairs and groups, during activities such as circle time.
- Establish speaking and listening conventions such as *hands-up* and reward appropriate behaviour with praise and recognition.
- Read stories to the children; look at and talk about books, including non-fiction titles.
- Issue simple instructions to encourage children to demonstrate attentiveness and respond appropriately to the speaker, for example when getting changed for dance and movement, washing hands before lunch, or putting on aprons before painting. These routines and procedures, while being effective as class management strategies, are also an important part of the learning process.

- Introduce musical activities, nursery rhymes, action games and songs (e.g. 'Simon/Susan Says') to provide listening skills practice.
- Create role-/pretend play areas in the classroom where children can use their verbal communication skills through participation in imaginary play, acting out a variety of roles and make-believe situations, and organizing and planning scenes using various props (e.g. telephones/mobiles) or small-world figures.
- Look for opportunities to develop speaking and listening skills across the whole curriculum (e.g. using tape recorders to record science investigations or history/geography field trips).

Reading and writing

Reading and writing are interdependent areas of learning. As with speaking and listening the range of ability in 3–8 settings can be very wide. Some children upon entering nursery are able to recognize their own names in print and to engage in mark-making on paper which closely resembles writing. A few may even be able to read and write simple words such as their own names. By the time children move on to Key Stage 1 they should have improved their understanding of the functions of print, be experimenting with it, be using books and a variety of texts for pleasure and information, and be actively seeking and engaging in literary experiences.

Below is a broad brush model of the stages that young children go through in becoming readers and writers. Trainee and newly qualified teachers will need to refer to the further sources of information (p. 154) in order to appreciate more fully this area of children's learning.

Emerging readers/writers, while taking part in shared activities with the teacher, are beginning to realize that writing and drawing are different means of communication, and that speech can be recorded in print and that print can be turned back into speech. They are beginning to learn some of the letter shapes, to write their name and to recognize familiar logos and signs in their local environment. They can move on to identify a handful of the more common words encountered in books such as 'is', 'and', 'the', and are also learning to recognize these words in isolation. Establishing attractive and stimulating reading and mark-making areas are important strategies in fostering a positive approach to reading and writing at this stage of children's development.

**Emergent writing
(Isobel)**

(Aged 3 years, 9 months)

Beginning readers/writers are able to write their own name plus a small number of common words. They are also learning to recognize an increasing number of these common words such as 'in', 'my', 'her'. They are starting to join in much more with reading and discussion of stories, are beginning to blend sounds into words, can play I-Spy games, and can match a range of words and letters by sight.

Developing readers/writers are beginning to read and write independently. They are able to use the context of a text and initial letters in their efforts to establish meaning, can read and write individual letters as well as an increasing range of words, for example 'dog', 'cat', 'red'. As the children progress they become increasingly adept at using the context of a text to predict meaning and to work out more complicated phonic blends. They can read and write words with consonant blends (st, fr, sk and sl), consonant (ch, sh, th) and vowel (ea, oi) digraphs and are aware of the silent 'e' (like, come). They have a more extensive and increasing sight vocabulary. Although children's reading and writing development are interrelated it is worth remembering that developing readers and writers may be able to read more complex words than they can spell.

Fluent readers/writers have successfully achieved the basic competences. They can select books on the basis of interest and need. They can read and write words involving silent letters, longer word endings and polysyllabic words, and they can self-correct in reading.

Recent developments in the teaching of reading and writing

Learning to read and write means learning a set of grammatical rules, understanding the context, recognizing words and symbols and decoding and encoding those words and symbols. Children need to be helped to develop word recognition and language comprehension in parallels but with young children in particular acquiring and improving their word recognition skills is a crucial precursor for success in reading and writing overall. Increasingly therefore educational policy on the teaching of reading and writing has identified the teaching of phonics as an important contributory factor in this process. The approach currently advocated (although it is not yet prescribed) is that of synthetic phonics (DfES, 2006b). Children are taught to recognize a series of phonemes (i.e. sounds in words) and their accompanying graphemes (i.e. the letters that make up those sounds) in order to decode the meaning of words. Some sounds can be represented using more than one letter or combination of letters and some letters can be used to make more than one sound. Children are also taught to *blend* and *segment*. Blending requires them to recognize graphemes and to merge the individual phonemes together to pronounce a word; this is decoding. Segmenting means being able to divide words up into their individual phonemes and to select the correct grapheme in order to spell them; this is encoding.

Graphemes

	1st grapheme	2nd grapheme	3rd grapheme
	c	ar	
	pl	ay	
	sl	eigh	
	d	o	g
	ch	ur	ch
	sw	ee	t

Certainly teaching synthetic phonics can offer children potentially useful techniques to help them to learn to read and write. However, English is not always regular or consistent and it is also possible that the approach will not suit all learners; some children may need extended opportunities for speaking and listening before being taught a prescribed list of phonemes and graphemes. Other children may be much further on with their reading and writing and might find the process constraining and lacking in challenge. It is likely therefore that teachers will need to use a range of techniques rather than relying solely on a single approach. The Primary National Strategy has published the document *Letters and Sounds* on phonics as part of its revisions to the Primary Framework for Literacy (www.dfes.gov.uk); the reader is advised to consult this document for details of the six phase programme for teaching phonetics to Foundation and Key Stage 1 pupils (DfES; 2007e).

Promoting reading and writing in 3–8 settings

- Set up a reading area in the nursery/classroom. Offer a wide range of texts to appeal to the widest possible audience and extend pupils' experience (e.g. fiction, picture books, touch-and-feel books, books with flaps, dual language texts, poems and rhymes, reference and non-fiction books, books that the children have written themselves). Display the books attractively to encourage children to select them (e.g. using book boxes to present front covers rather than spines). Provide comfortable seating and carpeting to encourage children to spend time in the area. Include audio materials and ICT equipment such as story tapes and talking books.
- Provide opportunities for children to select books for individual needs and interests, and to request favourite stories in order to help them to become increasingly enthusiastic about using books for pleasure and information.
- Encourage children to read and reread simple texts that are known/familiar to them.
- When trying to help children to become increasingly knowledgeable about the functions of print, provide opportunities for them to see that written language has meaning, for example by reading familiar signs, labels and names.
- Encourage children to seek information about the meaning of print, attempt their own writing and share texts.
- Set up a writing or mark-making area in the nursery/classroom. Give the children a wide range of good quality mark-making resources to encourage their involvement and to demonstrate the status such activities have in the teacher's mind (offer a wide variety of pencils, pens and crayons, and good quality paper). Provide a range of real-life writing materials and artefacts (e.g. printed stationery, envelopes, labels, greetings cards, forms, tags, stamps and a post-box) to help pupils see that writing has a purpose. Include scissors, tape, paper clips, stapler, noticeboard and marker pens. Give children access to a computer or other word processing equipment (e.g. the concept keyboard).
- Take care not to rush the youngest children prematurely into formal approaches to reading and writing. In many nurseries, for example, reading and mark-making areas are set up to encourage children to engage in and enjoy the earliest stages of reading and writing in more informal settings. Socio-dramatic role-play areas such as the travel agents or the post office also offer opportunities to foster purposeful reading and writing activities as well as the obvious potential for speaking and listening.
- Model purposeful reading and writing for the children (e.g. signing your name, writing a list/birthday card/letter, looking for information in a reference text). Young children often get some of their earliest ideas about reading and writing from watching and copying the adults around them whom they see reading and writing themselves.

The Revised National Literacy Framework

In 1998 a National Literacy Strategy (NLS) was introduced in England and Wales in response to perceived shortcomings in literacy levels among pupils in compulsory education, although the rationale was hotly contested both at the time and since (DfEE, 1998b; Burnett and Myers, 2004). The NLS has subsequently been revised as part of the Primary National Strategy and schools are now working with a renewed literacy framework available online (The Standards Site, 2007). The framework is not compulsory and schools retain the right to introduce their own literacy programmes, however the majority use the national framework. Nor is the literacy framework an entire scheme of work for English in the National Curriculum; other work on reading, writing, speaking and listening will take place beyond any dedicated literacy sessions. As a result schools are expected to conduct teaching and learning in English in addition to that undertaken as part of the national literacy framework.

A stated intention of the revised framework is to give teachers greater flexibility in literacy lessons. This is an effort to move away from the previous prescriptive format of the literacy 'hour' in which teachers and pupils were expected to spend set amounts of time on the three interrelated strands of word, sentence and text level work incorporating direct, whole class teaching as well as a range of independent/individual work and guided group tasks. The timescale of one hour was quite tight, and many primary teachers raised concerns about issues such as children being repeatedly unable to complete written work in the 20 minutes allocated and the difficulties in trying to carry out guided reading activities in dynamic, busy and sometimes noisy classroom settings. Concern was also expressed over the lack of responsiveness of the system when children found particular elements difficult to grasp and yet the teaching programme for the term had already been mapped out. In addition in some Year 2 and Year 6 classes in particular the old NLS could also evolve at certain times of the year into preparation sessions for the Standard Assessment Tasks and tests.

The revised framework therefore sets out programmes of work across the primary age range but is intended to provide greater scope for practitioners to develop the curriculum in response to their assessments of the needs of their pupils in an effort to introduce greater personalization of learning. The learning objectives contained within the framework are organized around a set of 12 strands of learning and are intended to help teachers identify progression through these strands. Four of the strands focus on the need for children to be able to speak and listen for a wide range of purposes in different contexts, they are:

- Speaking
- Listening and responding
- Group discussion and interaction
- Drama.

The remaining strands centre on the need for children to become increasingly proficient at reading and writing for a range of purposes on paper and on screen, they include:

- Word recognition: decoding (reading) and encoding (spelling)
- Word structure and spelling
- Understanding and interpreting texts
- Engaging and responding to texts
- Creating and shaping texts
- Text structure and organization
- Sentence structure and punctuation
- Presentation.

The reader is advised to refer to the Letters and Sounds document in the 'Further sources of information' section of this chapter and to visit the DCSF Standards Site at the URL below in order to look at the full details of the different strands, their accompanying objectives and supporting guidance on the effective teaching of literacy.

- www.standards.dfes.gov.uk/primaryframeworks/literacy

Children with English as an additional language (EAL)

Many schools and nurseries have pupils for whom English is an additional language (EAL). These children are far from being part of a homogeneous group. Such pupils may be bilingual or even multilingual; alternatively, they may be at the very earliest stages of English acquisition. They may have very diverse backgrounds linguistically, socially and culturally and may well have different levels of language competence both in their home language(s) and in English. Failure to appreciate this diversity could result in teachers concluding, wrongly, that children have behavioural problems of some kind, or are less motivated or less intelligent than their English-speaking peers. Many bilingual pupils are capable of achievement as high as, or higher than, their monolingual peers even before fluency in English has been mastered, particularly in subjects such as mathematics or art where an incomplete grasp of English is less of a barrier to accessing the curriculum (DfES, 2003b). Bilingual children learn English best in mainstream settings in which they are supported in the acquisition of English across the whole curriculum and alongside English speaking peers. In this way bilingual children encounter English in subject specific and meaningful contexts which speeds up their access to the curriculum (DfES, 2003b; Burnett and Myers, 2004).

Supporting the Communication, Language and Literacy skills of EAL pupils

- Provide a learning environment in which children feel able to utilize the full range of their linguistic repertoire and feel confident that their first language has a legitimacy in the classroom (Barratt-Pugh, 1994). Bilingual support staff can be particularly effective in helping teachers to achieve this; such support can help children overcome feelings of isolation and frustration where much of what goes on in the nursery/classroom may pass them by.

$\Rightarrow$

- Learn key words and phrases in order to be able to meet and greet parents and children using their first language.
- Provide resources including books, posters and ICT software that are free from cultural bias and negative, stereotypical images.•Use dual-language books and tapes to give parity of esteem to other languages.
- Provide play equipment such as clothing, construction kits and artefacts that reflect a wide range of cultural experiences.
- Use a range of teaching techniques and devices to assist bilingual children in reading and writing, for example introducing writing frames or providing collaborative reading experiences.
- Ensure that displays, labelling and written communication with children and their families reflect the diversity and variety of young children's languages. Once again bilingual support staff can be an invaluable resource enabling schools and nurseries to do this.

Problem Solving, Reasoning and Numeracy

Children's mathematical development occurs as they seek patterns, make connections and recognize relationships through finding out about and working with numbers and counting, with sorting and matching and with shape, space and measures.

(DfES, 2007d, p. 61)

Mathematics is a powerful means of communication with importance and application across the curriculum. The inclusion of mathematics in the 3–8 curricula provides opportunities to improve children's abilities to think logically, calculate, represent, explain and predict, as well as developing their spatial awareness. Many day-to-day nursery and school experiences, including play, provide opportunities for children to learn mathematical concepts and ideas including:

- recognizing and using numbers;
- comparing and recognizing relationships;
- ordering and sequencing;
- sorting and classifying;
- establishing invariant properties;
- using mathematical language;
- using mathematical knowledge to carry out simple number operations and solve practical problems.

✔ **Audit**

By the end of this section you should:

- know about the teaching of Problem Solving, Reasoning and Numeracy in the Early Years Foundation Stage (DfES, 2007d, pp. 61–74);
- know about the teaching of mathematics in the primary curriculum (QCA, 1999, pp. 60–74);
- know about the revised National Numeracy framework and its relationship with mathematics in the National Curriculum (DfEE, 1999).

Number

From birth children are surrounded by ideas in number form. Number concepts which develop in the early years are the result of both teaching and informal experiences. Children come to attach meaning to number names as a result of frequent use in different contexts, such as sorting activities with beads and cotton reels, matching activities with collections of natural objects, counting games, and songs and rhymes involving numbers. Much early number work concerns correspondence and conservation, while using number names encourages the beginnings of understanding cardinal, ordinal and nominal numbers.

Cardinal, nominal and ordinal numbers

- **Cardinal numbers** are used to count or indicate quantity: 'There are 5 apples'.
- **Nominal numbers** are used to name or identify things: 'I'm catching the number 63 into town'.
- **Ordinal numbers** are used to signify ranking, order or position: 'He's 3rd in line to the throne'.

Teachers of younger pupils need to appreciate the importance of children understanding number, and avoid confusing this with formal number operations and recording. There may be a discrepancy between children's use of symbols in the classroom and their ability to apply them elsewhere and so time is needed for children to relate their concrete understanding of number to the abstract written symbols (Hughes, 1986).

Early number activities

- Make number collections
- Thread coloured beads following a sequence card
- Number rhymes and songs
- Count on/back
- Number jumps
- One more than/less than
- Number patterns
- Simple number bonds: 1–5 leading to 5–10
- Number trails inside/outside the nursery/classroom
- Collecting groups of objects: 4 bricks, 3 leaves, 5 cars
- Counting to 5, counting to 10.

Helping children with number

- Offer pupils activities leading to counting. Without the ability to count, progress in children's general mathematical development will be severely limited.
- Take advantage of the myriad of counting opportunities that present themselves during the course of any day in a nursery or classroom, such as 'How many …?'; 'Who is second/third?'; 'Who has the most/least?'; 'Is it the same as/more than/less than?'
- Assist children to develop their skills in mental number work and provide opportunities to develop their understanding and skills still further through practical work. Encourage children to try out their own mental strategies. Many strategies can lead to the 'right answer'.
- Emphasize the importance of thinking mathematically (understanding, interpreting and communicating solutions) as well as standard calculation procedures.
- View computational skills as tools. Children need not only the ability to perform a particular numerical operation, but also knowledge of when it should be employed. Many teachers will be familiar with questions such as 'Is it an add, Miss?' as some children struggle to make sense of written symbols, particularly operator signs such as + and −.
- Offer children opportunities to record number activities in a variety of ways.

Providing practical experience of mathematics

Although mathematical operations such as addition and subtraction are crucially important, real and relevant contexts within which children have to exercise their mathematical skills are equally valuable. Practical mathematical experiences can include work on shape and space, measurement, number work and logic.

Practical mathematics tasks

- Find and match bricks in the construction kits that are the same
- Compare (two objects to begin with)
- Work with foodstuffs, follow simple recipes
- Look for *big/large* leaves and *little/small* leaves in the park
- Pass the parcel *quickly* and *slowly*
- Run on the spot in PE for a *long* time and a *short* time
- 'Which is the biggest/smallest?'
- 'Which container holds the most sand or water?'
- Position and reposition play figures (e.g. behind, in front of, on top of)
- Sort and classify objects according to type (e.g. sort toy animals or cars as part of small-scale structured play activities)
- Sort and classify objects according to shape (e.g. two-dimensional card cut outs, three-dimensional construction bricks)
- Sort and classify objects according to colour (e.g. beads, bobbins)
- Sort and classify objects according to size (e.g. containers in sand and water play)
- Sort/group each other (e.g. 'Who's got laces on their shoes?' 'Who's got brown hair?')

Many everyday activities in 3–8 classes provide real-life contexts to think logically and solve practical problems using mathematics, for example sharing out biscuits at milk time. The skills of prediction, classification and sequencing can be encouraged through questions such as 'What will happen?' and 'Why do you think?' during structured play activities. Furthermore, everyday sorting and classifying activities can be useful in developing early logic. Children's logical thinking and reasoning begins to develop as they start to distinguish differences and similarities in things, making comparisons and arranging them systematically.

Providing a practical dimension to mathematics

Offer children activities which require them to:

- make direct comparisons (e.g. small and large, long and short);
- sequence more than two objects;
- measure (e.g. mix and combine materials such as foodstuffs or paint);
- utilize their estimation skills when measuring and/or comparing;
- move and handle a range of equipment and objects as a way of improving their spatial awareness (e.g. estimating distances using floor robots) and developing an appreciation of patterns and relationships in shape and number;
- engage in structured play activities, including outdoor play and work with construction kits, to develop their awareness of shape and space.

Mathematics and the wider curriculum

Linking mathematics with other curriculum areas provides further opportunities for skills to be used in practical and meaningful situations, for example measuring and marking out in design and technology, or using simple charts to record scientific observations. Teachers need to be adept at drawing mathematical experiences out of activities that are ostensibly creative, scientific or physical in nature.

Opportunities for mathematical learning across the curriculum

- Matching objects in collections (e.g. leaves, seeds)
- Making sets of up to 10 objects (e.g. 6 cars, 10 bricks)
- Sorting clothes in the home corner (e.g. hats, coats, gloves)
- Counting out objects (e.g. plates and cups in the home corner, sweets or biscuits at snack time)
- Creating different structures/shapes with the same number of Lego bricks
- Practising songs and rhymes which involve counting by rote (e.g. 'Currant Buns in The Baker's Shop')
- Using mathematics in socio-dramatic role-play (e.g. setting up the Three Bears' House in the home corner)
- Providing games which have the potential to reinforce mathematical learning (e.g. rolling dice, playing cards, completing jigsaws, matching shape games, lotto and snap)
- Baking and measuring out ingredients for simple recipes
- Practising positional and directional language using small-world play equipment or programmable vehicles and floor robots (e.g. the Beebot, the Pixie or the Roamer).

Establishing links with Communication, Language and Literacy/English is of prime importance. A great many stories, poems and songs support mathematical ideas, knowledge and understanding, for example 'There Were Ten in the Bed'. The relationship between language and mathematics is particularly important. If children fail to understand what is being asked of them they are unlikely to be able to complete the activity they have been given. Adult–pupil talk provides numerous opportunities to encourage young children to think mathematically about:

- number: 'Have we got enough?'
- measurement: 'Which is longer?'
- logic: 'Why did that happen?'
- spatial awareness: 'Which brick will fit in there?'
- mathematical language: 'Whose is the tallest/heaviest?'; 'Who's got the most/least?'

> ### Promoting mathematical knowledge, skills and understanding in 3–8 settings
>
> - Set up a maths table or area in the nursery/classroom. The resources could include:
>   - counting materials (e.g. beads, buttons, number lines);
>   - blocks, shapes, sorting games and jigsaws;
>   - measuring equipment (e.g. rulers, metre sticks, scales and balances, clocks and timers);
>   - maths books and stories with a mathematical theme;
>   - writing and drawing materials.
> - Observe and talk about numerals around the classroom (e.g. using the clock, handling coins, work on number lines, imagining telephone numbers in the role-play area, or talking about page numbers in books). Accompany the children on maths trails and visits to look at number in the local environment (e.g. on houses, cars, buses and signs) or to buy items in a shop.
> - Provide opportunities for young children to engage in discussions on mathematical topics as a means of improving their understanding.
> - Offer counting and number games to provide opportunities for children to engage in skills practice and for you to explain mathematical ideas.
> - Use the medium of structured play with a wide range of equipment such as sand, water, construction kits and toys to provide investigative, measuring and problem-solving mathematical experiences.
> - Remember the importance of opportunities for consolidation and reinforcement, rather than rushing to insist on formal recording too quickly, especially with younger children.

The Revised National Mathematics Framework

As with the National Literacy Strategy, in 1999 a National Numeracy Strategy (NNS) was introduced in England and Wales to tackle perceived underachievement, this time in relation to mathematics (DfEE, 1999), although the term numeracy 'hour' was always something of a misnomer, particularly in Reception and Key Stage 1. Like the NLS before it teachers raised concerns about the advisability of mapping out a set amount of content to be covered at a set pace when many children were struggling to grasp the concepts or skills being taught in the time available. These concerns were only partly addressed by dividing NNS objectives into plain and bold text with teachers expected to prioritize those in bold. Consequently, as with literacy, the NNS 'hour' has been revised as part of the Primary National Strategy and schools are now working with a renewed mathematics framework available on line (The Standards Site, 2007). Schools can opt out of the framework by introducing their own mathematics programmes if they wish, however the majority use the national framework. Unlike the literacy framework the mathematics framework does form a scheme of work for mathematics in the National Curriculum, covering as it does all aspects of the National Curriculum Programmes of Study (QCA, 1999). The new framework is also intended to support younger children in progressing towards the Early Learning Goals (DfES, 2007d).

The learning objectives contained within the mathematics framework are organized around a set of seven strands of learning and are intended to help teachers identify progression through these strands. It is important to note that although they are interconnected the strands are not equally weighted. There was a strong emphasis in the previous NNS on mental calculation and while number facts and calculation are still important the revised framework represents a shift of emphasis with using and applying mathematics coming increasingly to the fore. The seven strands therefore are:

- Using and applying mathematics
- Counting and understanding numbers
- Knowing and using number facts
- Calculating
- Understanding shape
- Measuring
- Handling data.

The revised mathematics framework sets out programmes of work for pupils from Foundation Stage to Year 6 and provides teachers with guidance on lessons and assessment. As before, it is expected that schools will engage in direct mathematics teaching and in interactive oral work with classes, groups and individuals. However the intention is to facilitate teachers' efforts to interpret the curriculum in the best interests of their children by personalizing the learning. The revised framework encourages teachers to move away from the idea of one lesson meaning one learning objective, and to try to make links and connections between the different objectives and strands to help children make more sense of their learning.

The reader is advised to visit the DCSF Standards Site at the URL below in order to look at the full details of the different strands, their accompanying objectives and supporting guidance on the effective teaching of mathematics.

- www.standards.dfes.gov.uk/primaryframeworks/mathematics

Knowledge and Understanding of the World

Young children are fascinated by the natural surroundings, phenomena, manufactured objects, customs and traditions that they see around them on a daily basis. By introducing practical activities which enable children to use their senses, nursery/reception teachers can help to lay some of the foundations for understanding in geography, history, ICT, technology, science and RE which their primary colleagues can build on as the children enter Key Stage 1 and 2. Pupils need opportunities to:

- identify the features of living things, objects, materials and events in the natural and made world, including looking closely at similarities, differences, patterns and change;
- gain information about why things happen and how things work;
- talk and think critically and creatively about their observations and begin to record them with adult support;
- select and use materials and equipment, and take turns and cooperate when using equipment;
- use technology to support their learning;
- find out about some of the different religious beliefs and traditions in society.

✔ **Audit**

By the end of this section you should:

- know about the teaching of Knowledge and Understanding of the World in the Early Years Foundation Stage (DfES, 2007d, pp. 75–89);
- know about the teaching of science, design and technology, ICT, history and geography in the National Curriculum (QCA, 1999, pp. 76–89, 90–95, 96–101, 102–107, 108–115);
- know about the teaching of Religious Education (RE).

Science

First-hand experiences and observations of the world around them provide children with opportunities to foster positive attitudes towards investigation and experimentation, such as curiosity and perseverance (Farmery, 2002). This can relate to a range of topics including materials and their properties, similarities and differences, patterns and changes, living things and forces. At the same time first-hand experiences present opportunities for younger children to acquire a range of skills and experiences useful in their future National Curriculum science work, including:

- critical thinking (asking and answering questions about why and how things happen, predicting);
- problem solving and investigating;
- observational skills;
- measuring, sorting and classifying;
- hypothesizing (talking about their observations, identifying cause and effect).

A taste of science

A class of Y1/2 children had been doing work on the theme of 'Ourselves'. They had been investigating the five senses. The children had a small selection of plastic pots each of which held a similar-looking white material – sugar, salt, icing sugar, self-raising flour and cornflour – to be identified by smell, touch and taste. They described what the substances smelled and felt like and one of the children said that the salt and sugar were 'all crunchy'. The teacher asked the children to look very closely at the different materials to see if they were really that similar. During the subsequent discussion the teacher introduced the words powder and crystal. The children then compared the taste. Some were easily identified (salt and sugar), others (flour and cornflour) were unknown to the children. One child then asked what would happen if they mixed in some water. The teacher seized the opportunity to extend the children's learning further in the area of materials and their properties. They were asked to predict what would happen and then she added some water to the pots and stirred the mixtures. The children noticed that some of the substances seemed to disappear. The teacher asked the children to taste the liquids and the children observed that they could still taste the sugar and salt even though they had apparently disappeared. The teacher then introduced the word *dissolve*.

Terms such as investigation, enquiry or experimentation can suggest a more formal approach that may not be particularly appropriate for children at the younger end of the 3–8 age range. Younger children are unlikely to plan fair tests, take standard measurements or form scientific hypotheses. The term *exploration* may therefore offer teachers a better description of early science activities in which the Foundation Stage teacher's role is to encourage imitation, to broaden the children's knowledge of the physical world around them and to challenge their thinking and ideas. **Guided exploration** can be child initiated or adult initiated with the adult intervening to question/suggest ways forward. **Structured exploration** is adult initiated with the adult deliberately scaffolding concepts, skills and attitudes (Davies and Howe, 2003).

When engaged in science activities, children should be encouraged to become increasingly responsible for handling equipment and resources safely and sensibly. This could include selecting and collecting objects to see if they will float or sink, putting magnets back where they came from with their keepers attached, and keeping their work area reasonably tidy. When children are making these choices and exercising their decision-making abilities, they need to do so in an environment that is inherently safe.

Using equipment safely

- Do not allow children access to hot materials or sharp tools without close adult supervision.
- Remind children about the hazards of tasting or smelling strange materials and liquids.
- Use plastic containers not glass ones.
- Use water based glues not solvents.
- Warn children of the dangers of mains electricity.

Teachers should also strive for variety and appropriateness when it comes to children recording their science work; written accounts are not always the most suitable method. Some investigative work with young children may not warrant a permanent record and in such cases children could be encouraged to talk about their work and their observations. Many young children will be emerging writers and to produce written accounts at the end of every science task could well reduce their interest in and enthusiasm for the activity. Some investigations could be recorded in an ongoing rather than a summative form, such as keeping a daily record of the weather or the growth of cress seeds. Where a written account is appropriate, teachers can act as scribes for those children who need this level of support. Other options for recording science work in ways that best suit the task include pre-prepared charts and simple tables, diagrams, pictures, photographs, tape recordings and cooperative or group reports.

Science activities provide a wealth of cross-curricular learning opportunities. PSHE and elements of citizenship can be fostered by studying health related or environmental themes, as well as encouraging young children to work harmoniously and sensibly with their peers. Praise and recognition can make children aware that listening to others, offering ideas and observations, carefully following instructions, and considerately sharing tasks are all valued behaviours. At the same time, encouraging and assisting children in recording science activities provides opportunities to foster the development of their mathematical and literacy skills, as well as providing teachers with concrete evidence with which to support the assessment, recording and reporting of children's learning.

More 3–8 science activities

Sound and music

- Make shakers using rice and peas, or 'guitars' using boxes and elastic bands.
- Make and play with string telephones.
- Introduce a sound quiz; identify recorded sounds on a tape.

Electricity and magnets

- Which materials are attracted to magnets?
- Can the children move objects with a magnet at a distance (e.g. through the tabletop, through a sheet of paper)?
- Make simple circuits using batteries, bulbs, buzzers and switches.

Investigating soaps and detergents

- Make bubbles and get things clean.

Light and colour

- Observe the movement of the sun by looking at shadows changing.
- Make shadows using torches.
- Mix powder paints.
- Test a range of fluorescent and luminous materials in a range of light conditions as part of a road safety project.
- Conduct a science walk around the school/nursery looking at the use of colour in the local environment (e.g. shop fronts, road signs and traffic lights).

Materials and their properties

- Introduce children to different sorts of paper (writing paper, newsprint, cards, wallpapers and gift wrap), and encourage them to describe the different properties such as texture, colour and pattern.
- Test a range of fabrics to find the most waterproof.
- Investigate and compare the properties of other solids and liquids.
- Change the shape/properties of materials by bending, stretching, twisting, squashing, heating and cooling them (e.g. baking bread, thawing ice/evaporating water).

Living things

- Visit a local park and collect objects such as autumn fruits and leaves. Talk about the impact of weather and seasons.
- Use books and/or a database with children to find out about animals as part of a project on pets.
- Observe the appearance and behaviour of minibeasts using magnifying glasses and/or microscopes.
- Grow seeds and discuss the needs of living things.
- Observe, catalogue and name human features (e.g. eye colour) and body parts. Make comparisons with other creatures.

$\Rightarrow$

- Test different senses (i.e. tasting for sweet and sour; identifying objects in a 'feely box' through touch alone).

Patterns and changes

- Keep a daily weather chart.

Forces

- Explore the concept of friction by rolling toy cars down a ramp at various angles and measure the distances travelled over different surfaces.
- Test objects to see which ones float and which ones sink. Make floaters sink and sinkers float.

Design and technology

There are many links between science and design and technology but they are not one and the same thing (Davies, 1997). Young children need opportunities to develop their technological skills and knowledge by designing and making, as well as developing their scientific understanding by observing, investigating and exploring the physical world around them. Local walks and visits provide opportunities for children to observe the wider *built* or *made* environment, including such things as street furniture, machines and buildings. Story, imaginative and investigative play can be also be used to develop children's interest in the technological products they see around them (Hope, 2004). Much design in the early stages of a child's education is changeable, based on trial and error; it often runs concurrently with making and the products themselves can be ephemeral in nature, such as sand structures. Although even quite young children are able to engage in planning their work orally, using simple pictures, or by listing the materials they will need, designing in more traditional ways such as through drawing can prove more of a challenge. Children's drawing skills may be insufficient for the task, their knowledge and understanding of the tools and materials may lead to unrealistic proposals and some children find it hard to appreciate the purpose of two-dimensional design work (Fleer, 2000).

Evolution of a child's idea

During a nursery placement Judy, a student teacher, was asked to work with children engaged in a construction activity using junk materials and paint. She asked one child about his model and he replied that it was a fire engine. Later in the session Judy praised the child's construction (a series of cardboard boxes glued together and painted bright red). 'That's a fantastic fire engine you've made.' 'It's not a fire engine,' the child replied indignantly, 'it's a lighthouse.'

A good range of low-cost and no-cost materials (e.g. cardboard boxes, yogurt pots, lolly sticks) are invaluable in giving children opportunities to select and make decisions. At the same time, augmenting such materials with more sophisticated, commercially produced resources such as construction kits gives children a chance to model with an accuracy that would otherwise be far beyond them.

Setting up a design and technology area in the nursery/classroom

Textile equipment

- Large needles (some pre-threaded)
- Variety of threads, silks and wool
- Hessian and binka fabrics, felt, patterned offcuts
- Scissors (for textile use only, paper blunts scissors quickly)
- Miscellaneous materials (ribbon, elastic, buttons, feathers, beads and sequins)
- Baskets for storage.

Work with food

- Utensils (knives, mixing bowls, wooden spoons, whisks)
- Crockery and cutlery
- Foodstuffs (flour, fat, milk, vegetables, fruit, salt, yeast, sugar, eggs)
- Heat source/microwave
- Cold storage (fridge)
- Hygienic work surfaces/chopping boards.

Work with more resistant materials

- Tools (scissors, hole punchers, staplers, pliers, vices, hammers, bench hooks, glass paper and/or hobby sanders, saws, drills and glue guns for use under supervision only)
- Joining materials (good quality PVA adhesive, sticky tape, masking tape, string, paper fasteners, elastic bands, nails)
- More resistant materials (dowelling, soft timber, balsa, wooden wheels).

Work with less resistant materials

- Range of paper and card
- Plastics and acetates (drinking straws, cotton bobbins, plastic bottles and containers)
- Junk and purchased materials (cardboard boxes, card wheels, lolly sticks)
- Clay and other malleable materials (plasticine, play dough)
- Rolling pins, moulds, stamps
- Drawing/colouring materials
- Scissors.

Construction equipment

- Large-scale kits (Bau Spiel, Tac-Tic, block play materials)
- Small-scale kits (Lego, Duplo-Toolo)
- Instruction/example sheets (remove for free play; include for more directed tasks)
- Extension materials for small-scale play activities (plastic figures, floor maps)
- Extension materials for large-scale play activities (role-play materials).

Work with textiles and food can be particularly useful as it allows young children to design and make with materials that are accessible, exciting, easily worked and that offer a wide range of possible outcomes. Introducing textile and food activities can also provide opportunities to introduce a multicultural dimension to the 3–8 curricula but teachers should familiarize themselves with the food rules of different cultures and faith communities in order to do this properly.

Some ideas for food activities

- Taste different breads and fillings and then make sandwiches.
- Taste a variety of breads then bake bread. Add different ingredients and flavourings to the dough.
- Make a green salad or fruit salad.
- Make butter.
- Make fruit yogurt by adding fruit to a plain yogurt base.
- Cook eggs in different ways.
- Make vegetable soup.
- Make a pizza.
- Make drinks (e.g. tea, coffee, cocoa, fruit juice, milkshakes).
- Make festive foods and food presents.
- Add beans, salad ingredients and dressings to rice, bulghur wheat or cous-cous.
- Make baked potatoes with different fillings.
- Make a Teddy Bears' Picnic meal.
- Make different coloured peppermint creams.

Health and safety in design and technology

- Trainee and newly qualified teachers should consult the nursery/school health and safety guidelines when planning design and technology activities.
- Children should be shown how to handle tools properly.
- Certain tools and equipment should only be used under adult supervision. Young children can use knives but only under close supervision. All such tools must be stored out of reach when not needed.
- Some tools should only ever be used by the teacher or another responsible adult (e.g. craft knives).
- When working with food, discuss healthy eating and make sure that surfaces are clean, hands have been washed and that pupils with allergies (e.g. nut allergies) have been identified.
- When using heat sources children should not move hot liquids. Microwave ovens provide opportunities to make some dishes more safely, easily and quickly.

Some health and safety limits

Establishing clear boundaries

The woodwork bench in the nursery had a range of soft timber offcuts, two pots of nails, two hammers, two saws and two vices. Teaching and learning support staff taught the children how to hold and use the saws properly and safely, how to put timber in a vice and how to use a hammer to drive a nail into wood. When an adult was present in the area, children could opt to experiment with the tools and materials. When no adult was there, a thick blanket was placed over the whole bench and children knew that the activity was off-limits.

Avoiding unnecessary risks

A reception teacher was setting up a structured play area in her classroom. The theme was 'The launderette' and the children were constructing some of the artefacts to go into the area, gaining experience of handling tools and materials in the process. One group was making a washing machine from a large cardboard box. They drew round a plastic plate to show where the door needed to go but the card was too thick for scissors, so the teacher did the cutting for them using a craft knife which was always kept securely locked away. The children were not allowed to use it, even under supervision.

As with early science work, work in design and technology can contribute to children's learning in other areas. Children can begin to hone their abilities in reasoning and thinking logically as well as their interpersonal skills such as cooperation, sharing and negotiation. Children's aesthetic awareness can be promoted by encouraging them to make things which are artistically appealing as well as purely functional. Similarly, designing and making activities can give children the chance to apply knowledge and skills gained in

English and mathematics, for example measuring before cutting, buying materials with budgets, and discussing their plans. Design and technology can also be used to support children's learning in science, for example collecting moving toys (such as battery powered, mechanically powered using clockwork motors, or stored energy in springs) and investigating what makes them work.

Information and communications technology (ICT)

ICT does not form a separate area of learning within the Early Years Foundation Stage but ICT is given a more discrete form within the National Curriculum. ICT incorporates any technology related to information, control and communication, including television, radio, audio tape, video, programmable toys, mobiles, photocopiers or faxes (O'Hara, 2004). Although the Foundation Stage documentation contains explicit references to the use of ICT in nursery and reception classrooms, ICT itself has had a less than well-developed identity in many 3–5 settings in the past (O'Hara, 2004). Critics of ICT in early years education have described it as alien and inherently unsuitable because of its inability to meet what are widely accepted as the needs of young children including first-hand experience, play and talk. Computers, in particular, have been singled out by critics as inappropriate tools that risk stunting children's intelligence and social skills and of damaging their health (Alliance for Childhood, 2004). For commentators such as these ICT offers only virtual and passive experiences and not the first-hand and physical experiences that children need to grow and develop properly (*Telegraph*, 2006; BBC, 2004).

While viewing ICT as a panacea to all education's problems is certainly a mistake, some of its critics seem overly preoccupied with PCs, conflating the acronym with that of ICT as a whole. Some also appear to lay responsibility for inappropriate practice with ICT at the feet of the technology rather than at the feet of those using it. An over-preoccupation with computers could result in a failure to recognize that a myriad of other forms of ICT exist, some of which are already widely used in early years settings and others still with the potential to fit well with a variety of teaching and learning approaches. As the example overleaf indicates, ICT can involve much more than just the computer.

Nursery: Autumn term

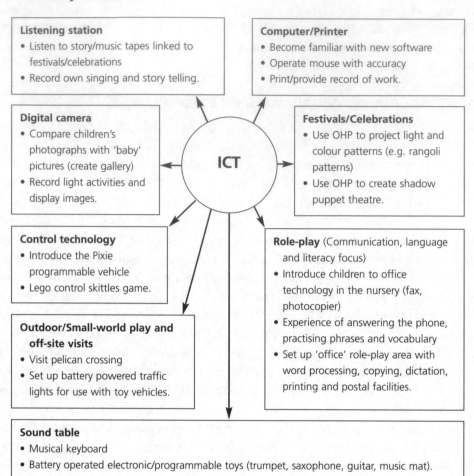

Listening station
- Listen to story/music tapes linked to festivals/celebrations
- Record own singing and story telling.

Computer/Printer
- Become familiar with new software
- Operate mouse with accuracy
- Print/provide record of work.

Digital camera
- Compare children's photographs with 'baby' pictures (create gallery)
- Record light activities and display images.

Festivals/Celebrations
- Use OHP to project light and colour patterns (e.g. rangoli patterns)
- Use OHP to create shadow puppet theatre.

ICT

Control technology
- Introduce the Pixie programmable vehicle
- Lego control skittles game.

Role-play (Communication, language and literacy focus)
- Introduce children to office technology in the nursery (fax, photocopier)
- Experience of answering the phone, practising phrases and vocabulary
- Set up 'office' role-play area with word processing, copying, dictation, printing and postal facilities.

Outdoor/Small-world play and off-site visits
- Visit pelican crossing
- Set up battery powered traffic lights for use with toy vehicles.

Sound table
- Musical keyboard
- Battery operated electronic/programmable toys (trumpet, saxophone, guitar, music mat).

(O'Hara, 2004)

An alternative view of ICT is that it might offer a range of potentially valuable pedagogic tools if properly utilized and may even support the development of some positive learning dispositions (e.g. perseverance, creativity, collaboration) if used appropriately. ICT may have the potential to enhance learning, to foster problem solving, to promote higher order thinking and generally contribute to the development of children's physical and mental development. It can be *interactive* offering immediate, dynamic and patient feedback coupled with opportunities to learn through trial and error about decision-making, consequences and forward planning. ICT has *capacity* and offers enormous potential for storing, organizing, manipulating, sending and presenting data at speed and following instructions. It can also extend and enhance children's access to *knowledge and information*, for example by presenting data and images in dynamic and varied ways including the use of animation and graphics to facilitate understanding. Finally ICT can support *modelling and provisionality* by enabling the user to test out theories and hypothesises as well as improving outcomes by promoting the scope for editing and trial and error (Loveless, 2003).

In some UK settings nursery and reception practitioners have embraced the use of ICT based on their understanding of the needs and characteristics of young children (Ager and Kendall, 2003). In these settings ICT is categorized as a new tool that could and should be incorporated into existing early years practice in developmentally appropriate ways, supplementing, not replacing, other important first-hand experiences and interactions (Anderson, 2000). In addition play, that ever-present feature of good quality Foundation Stage practice, can actually be expanded and enhanced by the introduction of ICT as children use equipment such as floor robots, walkie-talkies or computers. Quality adult input meanwhile is used to help children learn about and through the technology (Turbill, 2001; Sarama, 2003).

The degree to which an electronic whiteboard is interactive, or not, depends to a large extent on the way in which it is used in the nursery or classroom

- In Heath School all the nursery children are timetabled to use the ICT suite for 30 minutes every Tuesday afternoon. While there they use simple letter or number recognition software and/or a drawing package. A touch-sensitive electronic whiteboard is mounted 4–5 feet high on the front wall and staff tend to use it in a fairly didactic, *show and tell* fashion to demonstrate how to use the different software packages.
- In Park School every class has a touch-sensitive electronic whiteboard and in the nursery it is mounted 1–2 feet off the ground to enable the children to use it. The board is located in a carpeted area and staff use it with small groups as part of continuous provision. Children can come to the area for as long as they like to draw *huge* pictures, play games and to tell stories and move characters around on the screen.

If good early years education *starts from the child* then it is worth remembering that ICT (in its broadest sense) is an everyday experience for many, if not most, UK children in the home and in their local community (Kerawalla and Crook, 2002; O'Hara, 2004). Young children are increasingly enthusiastic and proficient users of information and communications technology; when they arrive in nursery and reception classes they are *informed* and have pre-existing ICT capabilities and knowledge (Marsh *et al.*, 2005).

Young children can be surprisingly knowledgeable about ICT

Chris (Aged 4): 'You want to see on the computer, I've got a *folder*!'

Adult: 'Have you? On that computer?' (Points to the nursery PC)

Chris: 'No, on my computer at home.'

Adult: 'Oh. What's in your folder?'

Chris: 'Woody.'

Adult: 'Woody?'

Chris: (Withering look) 'Woody! Buzz Lightyear! Woody!'

Diane (Aged 4) enters the nursery creative area carrying a mobile phone from the role-play area. She places it next to her on the table while she begins to paint. After a few minutes she picks up the phone and begins to press the buttons.

Adult: 'What are you doing, Diane?'

Diane: 'I'm *texting* Julie.'

Adult: 'Oh, what's your message?'

Diane: 'To see if she can pick me up from nursery.'

Diane places the phone back on the table and starts painting again. A few minutes later she stops again, places the phone to her ear and starts talking.

Diane: 'Hello, Julie, are you picking me up from nursery or is my mum?' (Pauses for the imaginary reply) 'Oh, okay.'

Diane then returns to her painting.

(O'Hara, 2004)

Organizing and managing learning and teaching involving ICT

Using ICT appropriately in 3–8 classes can therefore provide opportunities for interactive learning, the promotion of fine motor control, personal and social development and the development of reasoning skills. Using ICT in a variety of ways and contexts also helps children to become increasingly familiar with it, and increasingly confident and positive about their skills as users (Sharp *et al.*, 2002). Teachers should give children experience of as wide a range of ICT applications as possible in and out of the nursery/school, not just the computer. Off-site visits can be particularly useful as a means of drawing pupils' attention to the use of ICT in the wider world (e.g. the library, supermarket bar codes, concept keyboards in shops and fast food outlets).

Children need to be introduced to the equipment and taught how to use it properly. The use of content rich software can help to introduce children to the keyboard in a structured and systematic fashion but keyboard skills will also develop as a consequence of using the computer in a variety of purposeful contexts (e.g. using more open-ended software to write stories or draw pictures). Children can even be included in adults' day-to-day use of ICT in the nursery/school (e.g. sending faxes and e-mails, photocopying work or answering the telephone). It will take time for young children to master ICT skills and providing regular and frequent turns may be much more effective as a means of increasing competence and confidence than longer but much more infrequent turns.

Teachers also need to extend ICT use into curriculum areas previously devoid of ICT. Placing ICT equipment (e.g. listening stations, mobile phones) in the role-play area offers a means of integrating new technologies with structured play activities on different themes such as the travel agents, the bank, the ticket office or the theatre. At the same time, digital cameras, walkie-talkies, programmable toys and floor robots work well as a means of extending the learning opportunities during outdoor play (O'Hara, 2004). Increasingly, many games and simulations are available using ICT. Although some schools and nurseries remain to be convinced of the educational worth of such games, it is possible that they may, with the right teacher support, offer children the chance to:

- practise physical skills such as hand–eye coordination;
- develop their intellectual potential by demanding memory and planning;
- promote social and emotional development by encouraging children to share, take turns, cooperate, negotiate and make decisions for themselves.

Teachers should also take time to find out about and take account of children's ICT experiences beyond the nursery/school such as those in the home or the local community. Most children will have experience of a range of ICT use in the home but not all parents will be fully aware of the place of ICT within their children's education and may not appreciate its relevance.

Ways in which parents can support children's learning in ICT

- Spending time with and showing interest in the child's interactions with ICT – drawing children's attention to the use of ICT in the home (programmable washing machines, video timers) and in the world around them (pelican crossings, bar code readers in the local library).
- Listening, talking to and asking questions of the child – using technical vocabulary and expressions such as *CD, mouse, program*; explaining the relationship between the mouse and the pointer on the computer screen; reading information together from a screen; listening to taped stories and music together; stopping/pausing a video to talk about the characters or events.
- Developing children's practical skills – giving children the chance (with supervision where appropriate) to switch things on and off, change channels, play, rewind, fast forward and record, change CDs, using the mouse, clicking and double clicking.
- Encouraging the child to find out, explore, solve problems and try out new things – seeking information using CD-ROMs or the internet (see www.naeyc.org or www.ictadvice.org.uk for guidance on using the internet).
- Playing with the child – using programmable or battery operated toys, computer games, musical keyboards, taping and playing back the child's own songs.

(O'Hara, 2004)

To be effective ICT needs to be integrated appropriately into the curriculum and to qualify for the same sort of teacher involvement as any other area of the curriculum. It is easy to become complacent, blinded by the obvious enthusiasm of some pupils coupled with the presentation of the resource, to the need to monitor and ensure quality in teaching and learning. Unsupported involvement, for example, with unsuitable or undemanding drill and skill software packages is unlikely to provide much in the way of intellectual and creative challenge for children and teachers must be ready to step in and intervene if necessary (Edgington, 1998). Equally, while ICT suites can be a valuable resource for the delivery of ICT in the National Curriculum, moving whole classes of FS1 or FS2 pupils to designated ICT suites may result in experiences that are inappropriate given the ways in which young children often learn. There may be practical difficulties in terms of staffing and young children may spend far longer in front of a computer screen than is advisable from a health and safety point of view (Siraj-Blatchford and Siraj-Blatchford, 2002). The teacher is key to providing positive ICT experiences for all the children.

A computer is a tool; to get the best out of it sometimes requires a teacher

Three nursery children are sitting in front of a computer using a software package that claims to help children with number recognition. Whenever the right number is matched to the right image the children are rewarded with a flashing screen and a simple jingle.

Closer observation shows that the children are not using their knowledge of number at all and may not even be aware of the purpose of the task. Instead they are systematically matching every number to every image using a process of trial and error until they have cleared the screen of all the numbers and images.

Good problem solving perhaps but are these children really reinforcing their number recognition? Quality adult input could have helped them to make the most of the technology and to understand what was being asked of them.

Organizing and managing learning involving ICT in the classroom

- Well-targeted teacher intervention will help children to get the most out of their ICT experiences. Do not rely on the technology to do the teaching; ICT is a tool not a teacher.
- Be alert to experienced children denying access to others. The warning signs include children making unilateral decisions; children monopolizing equipment; children operating equipment too quickly for their partner(s) to follow or understand; children bossing other children, generating disagreements and squabbles; and children being excluded or ignored by their peers. Try to observe the children soon after they have started working with the equipment so that there is time to intervene at an early stage and be prepared to alter your groupings to ensure that pupils have positive collaborative experiences while working with ICT.
- Think about the different ways in which you might group children:
  - Group children of similar ability, personalities and dispositions together to generate lively and rewarding discussion, where the pace tends to be agreed and children are less likely to be excluded.
  - Use mixed ability pairs, particularly if there is a lot of reading to be done.
  - Use children with previous ICT experience as an 'expert' in groups.
  - Younger children work well in pairs in front of a computer. While threes are possible, more than three tends to lead to exclusion and lack of space to sit comfortably.
  - Ensure that children have a clear role when working together. Encourage children to have a turn in different roles to avoid individuals monopolizing control of the equipment.
  - If the ICT being used is a computer remember that the seat in front of the keyboard is where control is maintained and there are only really three roles possible when working on a PC: operating the keyboard; reading the screen; recording any information (Ellis, 1986). A change of role ought to be accompanied by a change of seat.
- When organizing computer resources make sure there is a range of generic (open-ended) as well as content rich software.

ICT and learning across the curriculum

The use of ICT in the nursery/classroom offers considerable potential for enriching and enhancing the whole curriculum (Sharp *et al.*, 2002). There is a clear correspondence between Communication, Language and Literacy/English for example and the strand of ICT associated with the communication of information. ICT can provide valuable tools for reinforcing the essential first-hand and practical mathematics experiences of young children. Children's Creative Development may be underpinned and enriched through the inclusion of an ICT dimension. ICT may also provide yet another context within which young children can progress in terms of their Personal, Social and Emotional Development through being encouraged to work collaboratively with others (Cooper and Brna, 2002).

Using ICT to support learning across the 3–8 curriculum

- Integrate ICT resources into socio-dramatic role-play areas to extend and enhance opportunities for speaking, listening, reading, writing and the application of number. For example:
  - a travel agent that contains a telephone, a mobile phone, a fax machine, a photocopier, an electronic cash register and a computer showing images of holiday destinations on a timed loop using PowerPoint;
  - a photographer's studio containing a digital camera.
- Point out examples of ICT during visits and local walks (e.g. traffic light sequences, burglar alarms, CCTV cameras, speed cameras).
- Speaking and listening can be enhanced through the use of audio-taped stories, while promoting collaborative (paired) work using ICT requires the children to contribute verbally to the completion of the task.
- Talking books can be used to support early reading as the children can hear the words on the screen. Software that involves matching objects to letters and finding the correct letters, such as 'My World', can also support reading. For older/more able pupils there is software to reinforce phonics.
- Writing can be supported through the use of ICT. Editing and redrafting benefit in particular from open-ended (generic) software. Software is also available that will demonstrate letter formation on the screen, and children can use the keyboard or a concept keyboard to produce emergent writing.
- Pupils' facility with number can be advanced through the use of simple operations software and the use of ICT in meaningful contexts, for example the electronic calculator or cash till in the role-play shop.
- Work on shape, space and measurement can be supported through the use of shape naming programs or work with floor robots and other programmable devices.
- Using drawing and painting packages offers advantages for young children in terms of the quality of the finish and the opportunity to edit their art work in a way that does not require excessive use of materials or result in messy outcomes.
- Music keyboards, music mats, toys and software exist which enable young children to play and compose tunes, and raise their appreciation and awareness of a wide range of different types of music.

Geography (place) and history (time)

Geography and history can be fascinating for young children. Although at first glance teachers may find it hard to relate their adult understanding of these subjects to their practice in 3–5 settings, a great deal of potential exists in the Foundation Stage for using geography and history to make the curriculum exciting and relevant while simultaneously laying the foundations for later learning at Key Stages 1 and 2 (Edwards and Knight, 1994; Turner-Bisset, 2002).

Geography

Geography involves more than simply memorizing and locating different places. It is a way for children to study and begin to make sense of the world around them. Geography involves knowledge and understanding about the interaction between the environment and people, as well as developing a set of enquiry based skills (Owen and Ryan, 2001). The concepts and skills developed through geography include:

- pattern;
- processes and systems;
- similarities and differences;
- asking questions;
- collecting information;
- interpreting and presenting information;
- drawing conclusions.

Activities which introduce children to ideas of place, diversity, interconnectedness, complexity, uncertainty and spatial understanding all offer opportunities to develop skills and knowledge relevant to geography on themes such as:

- Identity: 'Who am I?'; 'Who are the people around me?'; 'What is my/our "story"?'
- Place in the world: 'Where do I live/come from?'; 'What does it look like?'; 'How is it changing?'
- Physical world: 'How did this place and the wider world come to be?'
- Human world: 'What is fair/unfair?'; 'How do people deal with their differences?'

(Geographical Association, 2007)

The precise processes by which young children's spatial understanding and local awareness develop are not fully understood but children do become increasingly skilled at anchoring themselves and their ideas in space as they mature (Golbeck, 2005). Although younger children may find it hard to represent their geographical understanding and ideas using conventional means, their comprehension of place may be quite sophisticated and by introducing appropriate learning, teaching and assessment approaches children's real level of understanding may be better appreciated (Sowden *et al.*, 1995). The picture overleaf was drawn by a reception/FS2 child following a visit to another school. His developing sense of place and places is clear from the use of arrows, non-standard symbols to represent particular points on his journey as well as more formal symbols such as the compass.

Some early geography: Reception map

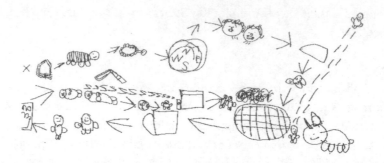

Teachers of the 3–8 age range can support children's developing sense of place by making sure that they become familiar first with the local area and subsequently with more distant locations. In doing this practitioners should remember that geography is dynamic and enquiry based. Asking questions such as 'Where are you going at the weekend?' is one way of exploring the concept of place with children. Drawing on the family also puts the curriculum into a meaningful context. Teachers might initiate discussions on different places that children have visited on holiday or maybe even lived in. Going out into the local area and discussing how it has changed and continues to change allows children to move beyond the immediate and the personal and begin to see themselves as part of a larger community. Children need to have first-hand experiences of different locations, including their own locality if they are to acquire knowledge, skills and interest in this area of the curriculum (Geographical Association, 2007).

In geography, learning can occur when you:

- talk about and examine the immediate environment, including where the children live;
- read stories about journeys or particular places such as 'The Shopping Basket';
- make three-dimensional maps in the sand tray;
- use roll-out road maps in small-world play;
- use floor robots and games to teach children about positional vocabulary and directions;
- look at photographs of local places; for example, children can zoom in on the school and their own homes using aerial digital images available by downloading Google Earth onto the class PC;
- go on local walks to introduce children to appropriate language such as semi-detached, valley, hill or church;

- visit contrasting locations to encourage enquiry skills and to introduce new concepts and language;
- look at/produce plan views of the classroom/school;
- make memory maps of how the children came to school;
- use photographs and other secondary sources to find out about more distant places;
- introduce children to maps and atlases of all kinds;
- talk to the children about more distant locations that they have visited on holiday or seen in the media.

History

If history were simply concerned with mastering a prescribed set of names, dates and past events in the correct sequence it would be hard to see what relevance it could have for young children. Fortunately history offers children a way of understanding the past, including their own past, through the introduction of key concepts and enquiry skills as well as the assimilation of particular pieces of information or facts (O'Hara and O'Hara, 2001). Historical concepts include the following ideas:

- there was a past;
- the past was different from the present;
- there was an order or sequence to the past;
- in many cases (though not all) objects and information from the past remain and can help us to make sense of what things used to be like.

Historical skills include the following activities:

- finding out about other periods, asking and answering questions;
- interpreting historical events;
- organizing and communicating historical information (Edwards and Knight, 1994).

Younger children's appreciation and understanding of the passage of time is undoubtedly underdeveloped and imperfect but this should not be used as a reason for ignoring history in the 3–8 curricula. As Alice's remark below indicates, children are not oblivious to the passage of time nor are they uninterested:

Alice: 'I can wait on the step for my mummy for a long, long time ago!' (Aged 4)

Young children often mix up letters such as *b* and *d* but not many people would suggest this was a valid reason for not teaching them to read and write. Children who are still coming to terms with concepts such as *earlier than*, *later than*, *yesterday*, *today* and *tomorrow* are not incapable of understanding the passage of time provided teachers introduce them to the idea in ways that are appropriate and manageable for them (Turner-Bisset, 2002). From the day they are born children encounter and seek to comprehend change in their circumstances and surroundings. They experience simple daily sequences and are introduced to regular temporal events ranging from birthdays to the seasons.

- Perhaps they have outgrown a favourite item of clothing: 'That's too small for me now, isn't it, Mummy?'
- Perhaps they are introduced to family photographs taken before their birth: 'Where was I, Daddy? And did I float down into Mummy's tummy?'
- Perhaps they are speculating on their future capabilities: 'And will I be able to ride my bike when I'm a big girl?'

When children first arrive in nursery their ability to communicate about and comprehend time will vary widely. For some there may be *now* and *before* and *later*. Others may possess a more extensive vocabulary and facility for dealing with time; past, present and future. Words like *yesterday* and *tomorrow* may be used although not necessarily with complete accuracy. Teachers should look for children's developing abilities to handle:

- Sequences: 'I'm using it after Alice aren't I?'
- Frequency: 'He's been two times already!'
- Rhythm: 'I go to ballet every Saturday.'
- Duration: 'That was a long time ago wasn't it, Miss?'

(Bertrand, 2006)

As children progress through the Foundation Stage they will become increasingly aware of significant personal events such as birthdays, celebrations or holidays. They should also become more adept at selecting the correct verb tenses and will make increasing, and increasingly accurate, use of words and phrases such as *day, everyday, week, next week, time, summer, in a minute, ten minutes ago*. As children make the transition into Key Stage 1 they are more likely to demonstrate improved abilities to discuss past, present and future tenses without confusion. They may also *know* (i.e. they can name) key periods such as bedtime or the time they go to school (although they are unlikely to be able to tell the time as such) and the days of the week in sequence. Children making the transition from Key Stage 1 to Key Stage 2 can usually tell the time, are becoming familiar with calendars and diaries and enjoy hearing and enquiring about past events of both family and wider historical significance. They will be capable of thinking about more complicated sequences and of travelling in time mentally, for example anticipating exciting future experiences in some detail (Bertrand, 2006).

Beginning by asking questions such as 'What did you do yesterday?' is one way of introducing the concept of time to young children and introducing a familial dimension to discussions can help to stimulate their interest. Teachers might, for example, initiate conversations on what life was like for different generations in a family. As children become older and more experienced teachers can broaden the curriculum to consider the more distant past, including periods beyond living memory, as well as national and international events.

Some early history

It was the start of the new school year in the nursery. All the children brought photographs of themselves as babies or toddlers with them and nursery staff took new pictures of the children using the digital camera. A display of the images was mounted and children were encouraged to talk about themselves and how they had grown and changed.

In history, learning can occur when you:

- talk about past and present events in the children's own lives;
- use stories, poems or songs to reinforce children's ideas about time;
- talk about time and the passage of time with the children (e.g. using clocks and watches, discussing sequences and how their activities may change at different times of the day, week or year);
- invite older relatives or other visitors to the classroom to talk about how things used to be;
- make timelines, scrapbooks and albums;
- collect and display artefacts from previous times in a class museum or on a display table (e.g. coins, stamps, posters, tickets);
- discuss, compare and sequence past and present artefacts (e.g. collecting toys that parents and grandparents may have kept from their own childhood and comparing them with toys today);
- look at and discuss old photographs or postcards showing past times and events;
- visit local historical sites and museums to consider how and why people and places have altered over time;
- use secondary sources to find out about the more distant past.

Religious education (RE)

If preparing children spiritually, morally, socially and culturally for the opportunities, responsibilities and experiences of adult life is one of the purposes of education then it is hard to see how some aspects of this could be satisfactorily addressed without the inclusion of some form of religious education (QCA, 2004). It is also the case that there is a legal obligation on schools in the maintained sector (although not nurseries) to teach RE as part of the curriculum to all the children apart from those whose parents have requested that their child be withdrawn from such teaching.

RE in the Foundation Stage guidance

Although not compulsory for nursery aged children, RE may feature as part of children's experiences in the different areas of learning. Examples could include:

- listening to and discussing religious stories (PSED);
- talking about right and wrong/fair and unfair in circle time (PSED/CLL);
- learning about important religious festivals, celebrations and events (KuW);
- looking at religious artefacts, designs or images and listening to religious songs, music or calls (KuW/CD);
- visiting religious places (KuW);
- marking/celebrating religious events and festivals in class (CD).

Note: The areas of learning suggested here (e.g. KuW, Knowledge and Understanding of the World) are indicative only; they are not intended to be definitive.

The primary RE curriculum is decided at local CYPS level, setting out what schools in that area are expected to cover, and providing guidance on how to gauge pupil attainment. These local syllabuses, however, are informed by the national framework and by legislation which states that although local syllabuses are expected to include attention to the plurality of religious beliefs and ideas they must still reflect the predominantly Christian tradition of the UK.

The primary national framework for RE

Knowledge, skills and understanding

- Learning about religion
- Learning from religion.

Breadth of study

- Different religions and beliefs (e.g. Christianity, at least one other principal religion and a local religious community/secular world view where appropriate)
- Themes (e.g. believing, story, celebrations, symbols, leaders and teachers, belonging and myself)
- Experiences and opportunities (e.g. visiting religious places, listening to religious visitors, using their senses, quiet reflection, encountering religious art and music, talking about beliefs and values, and using ICT to find out more about religion).

(QCA, 2004)

The moral dimension of RE offers considerable potential for overlap with PSHE; both are concerned with developing notions of correct and incorrect forms of behaviour. RE can provide opportunities to help children develop their understanding of what it means to be fair, considerate, courageous and truthful, through introducing stories associated with a range of religious faiths; however, it also incorporates cultural and spiritual dimensions. These aspects of RE involve both concepts (such as life after death, creation and miracles) and knowledge and understanding of the many different religions in Britain today including Christianity, Islam, Hinduism, Judaism, Buddhism and Sikhism (Edwards and Knight, 1994).

Promoting knowledge and understanding of different religions with young children

- Seek specific information on different world religions by contacting regional or national organizations direct or by accessing suitable websites (see p. 157).
- Celebrate a range of religious festivals such as Eid, Diwali and Christmas.
- Tell stories as ways to celebrate, and introduce to young children, the diversity and range of religious ideas and beliefs.
- Present religious ideas with respect if they are not to become indistinguishable from nursery rhymes and fairy stories. Unlike 'Goldilocks and the Three Bears', religious events and stories are underpinned by important articles of faith and belief.
- Invite visitors to explain what it means to live life, for example, as a Muslim or a Christian. Liaise with local representatives on clear learning objectives.
- Discuss any special books associated with different religious faiths, for example the Bible, Qur'an or Torah.
- Visit places of worship to look at the structure, architecture, designs and objects (both functional and symbolic). Encourage the children to reflect on:
  - protocols, conventions or actions upon entering a place of worship;
  - sights, sounds and smells, including signs and symbols, songs and chants, incense and perfumes, colour, pattern and design used in the construction;
  - special areas and/or artefacts such as holy books;
  - their feelings and emotions while in the place of worship.

Physical Development

Physical Development is a major part of the 3–8 curricula and is intimately connected to intellectual and academic progress. The physical education, dance, movement and play activities that young and active children enjoy in Foundation Stage settings constitute much more than ways of letting them burn off excess energy. Children who have not been able to practise using their bodies with increasing levels of skill can experience difficulties in other areas of learning as they progress through nursery and school. The inclusion of Physical Development and PE in the 3–8 curricula helps to ensure that:

- children will be encouraged to develop positive attitudes and confidence about themselves and their physical abilities;
- children are kept safe and secure both physically and emotionally;
- schools create a learning environment which allows children to develop a degree of autonomy and independence;
- progress in physical development is encouraged across a broad range of activities including gross and fine motor control, hand–eye coordination, body awareness, sensory awareness, spatial awareness, safety awareness, hygiene and healthy living.

✔ Audit

By the end of this section you should:

- know about the teaching of Physical Development in the Early Years Foundation Stage (DfES, 2007d, pp. 90–103);
- know about the teaching of Physical Education in the National Curriculum (QCA, 1999, pp. 128–33).

Physical Development in the Foundation Stage

Children's physical development involves the acquisition of gross and fine motor skills. Between the ages of 3 and 8 years children make considerable progress in their coordination, manipulation and muscular control (Woodfield, 2004). Gross motor skills include the ability to sit, walk, run, climb, balance, throw, catch, kick and pedal. Fine motor skills include the ability to grasp, hold, pick up, stick, cut and thread. By the time children enter the nursery and reception most already have an understanding and awareness of their bodies and their physical competence and many everyday activities can contribute to children's physical development and their sense of growing independence (e.g. dressing and undressing, cleaning teeth, feeding self using a knife and fork, combing hair, fastening shoes, or washing hands and faces). However, the point at which children develop many of these physical skills can vary greatly and so practitioners need to be aware of those whose development seems to be slower than others and those who have physical difficulties. A child's physical development not only has importance in and of itself but also can contribute to a sense of self-worth and emotional well-being through the sense of satisfaction gained from doing something well and with skill such as catching or hitting a ball, cycling, or creating a recognizable image with a paint brush. Growing confidence in physical abilities can promote a growing confidence and self-esteem across the curriculum.

Health, fitness and bodily awareness form a central part of Physical Development, the PE Programme of Study and the non-statutory Programme of Study for PSHE (QCA, 1999; DfES, 2007d). When promoting good health practices teachers need to help pupils to improve their understanding of how their bodies function and how to keep them healthy. Safety too is essential and teachers of young children have a legal obligation to keep them safe, an obligation that is much easier to fulfil if the children themselves are conscious of safety issues (see Chapter 1).

Promoting positive attitudes towards safety, health and fitness

- Require children to demonstrate appropriate hygiene practices such as washing their hands before going to lunch or after visiting the toilet.
- Talk to children about different foods and the food–health connection.
- Talk to children about the positive effects of exercise.
- Teach children about the need to warm up and cool down, and help them learn about appropriate posture and use of their bodies.
- Give children opportunities to discuss safety and what it means, for both themselves and their peers. Such discussions could include revisiting and restating rules and conventions that help to create a safe environment (e.g. avoiding household chemicals and medicines and crossing the road safely with an adult).
- Encourage children to exercise their judgement and be assertive enough to be able to say no to others when their safety is at risk, as well as identifying and reporting unsafe resources and situations to their teachers.
- Insist on appropriate clothing. Wearing the right clothing is one way to avoid accidents. Teachers can reinforce this idea by changing into sports clothing themselves, even if it only involves putting on a pair of trainers.
- Teach children to use, manipulate and move equipment safely (e.g. carry mats in fours).

Play can provide excellent opportunities to promote Physical Development. Many play activities involve a mixture of both gross and fine motor skills, for example construction/block play. Sand and water play offers children the chance to extend and improve fine motor control as well as being a way to introduce pupils to scientific and mathematical ideas, to foster language and creativity, to encourage cooperative learning and personal and social development. Play with apparatus in the outdoor area or hall provides opportunities to develop gross motor control, hand–eye coordination or to engage in role-play. Outdoor play meanwhile not only promotes children's Physical Development but also enhances their development across the curriculum including their Personal, Social and Emotional Development, Creative Development, and Knowledge and Understanding of the World.

Fostering Foundation Stage pupils' physical development through play

Water play

- Pouring and exploring the properties of a liquid using funnels, jugs, containers, water wheels, ice cubes, coloured water and washing-up liquid for bubbles
- Creating small-world scenarios using plastic figures or boats
- Fostering health, hygiene and safety practices with aprons, buckets, mops and cloths.

Sand play

- Building with/handling the material using a range of tools including spades and trowels, buckets, containers, spoons and rakes; using both damp and dry sand
- Setting up small-world play opportunities using plastic figures, toy vehicles and toy animals
- Encouraging health, hygiene and safety practices using aprons, sweeping brushes and dustpans.

Note: It is important to change the water or sand regularly and to ensure that equipment for clearing and cleaning up is readily to hand.

Creative play, construction play and mark-making

- Drawing and/or writing on the mark-making table
- Painting using different brushes and different kinds of paint
- Collage activities involving cutting and sticking
- Modelling with malleable materials (e.g. play dough, clay, plasticine)
- Building with bricks and other construction materials.

Musical activities

- Singing
- Dancing/moving to sounds and music
- Playing instruments.

Outdoor play

- Climbing and balancing on apparatus, crates, wooden boxes, cubes, planks and beams
- Crawling through barrels and tunnels
- Playing on see-saws, rockers and slides
- Building dens/shelters using large blocks
- Rolling on padded surfaces (mats under climbing apparatus)
- Playing games requiring adherence to simple rules such as skipping or hopscotch
- Riding on tricycles, bicycles, scooters or wagons
- Playing throwing games using balls, bats, bean bags, targets on walls, nets/hoops, quoits or rings.

Physical education (PE)

As children move through the 3–8 age range and into the primary school at the age of 5 they are introduced to more formal physical education (PE) lessons. Effective provision in PE offers children a range of indoor and outdoor activities that encourage them to respond confidently to physical challenges in a safe environment and enable them to become increasingly competent in the use of their bodies. PE can do much to increase children's ability to engage in both cooperative and independent learning, as teachers encourage children to:

- show consideration for their surroundings and peers;
- collaborate, share and negotiate with other children; and
- follow rules and play fairly.

PE involves children in planning and performing physical activities in a range of contexts, including gymnastics, games and dance. Games help children to develop their physical skills and understanding of simple tactics and rules. In dance and movement children have the chance to develop actions, appreciate concepts such as fast and slow, learn to make effective use of personal and general space, and have opportunities for creativity and composition, for example moving like an animal. In gymnastics children learn and develop actions and movements that contribute to the development of their gross motor control and hand–eye coordination as they move from floor work to apparatus work. Primary children should also be encouraged to evaluate their own and others' achievements in PE as a means of raising attainment. This can be done by asking pupils to observe, describe and copy the actions and movements of their peers; they can be encouraged to identify and comment on good work; and to compare actions and movements, suggesting modifications and improvements.

Helping primary children to become increasingly proficient at planning and performing in PE

- Show that you are enthusiastic about PE activities.
- Encourage and support children in taking calculated risks and offer praise for showing confidence and enjoyment in physical activity.
- Teach a range of physical skills and techniques.
- Be alert to children's capabilities and confidence and do not introduce tasks prematurely (e.g. forward rolls) that will undermine confidence and enthusiasm.
- Promote positive attitudes towards health and fitness and an increased awareness of safety principles.
- Promote both cooperative and independent learning.
- As pupils become more skilful, provide opportunities for them to start to link and combine actions and movements and plan more complex movements, sequences of movements and tactics in games (rolling, bouncing, throwing and catching balls).

Creative Development

Creative Development involves much more than just art or music; it has the potential to be a feature of learning across the whole of the curriculum (DfES, 2004e; 2007d). This said, young children respond well to sensory experience and the chance to experiment with tools, materials, sounds, shapes and colour. Creative work in art and music allows children to express their ideas and feelings, to make sense of the world in a very practical way, to experience making choices and decisions, and can promote independence and perseverance. Through art and music pupils can broaden their imaginations, use materials creatively and learn to appreciate beauty.

✔ Audit

By the end of this section you should:

- know about creativity across the curriculum;
- know about the teaching of Creative Development in the Early Years Foundation Stage (DfES, 2007d, pp. 104–14);
- know about the teaching of art and music in the National Curriculum (QCA, 1999, pp. 116–21, 122–27).

Creativity

Creativity can manifest itself in any area of the curriculum and fostering it in children is regarded as a crucial component in schools' efforts to develop pupils' self-esteem and motivation as well as preparing them for the opportunities, responsibilities and experiences of adult life (QCA, 2007). It is important to be wary of commonsense assumptions about the nature of creativity; these include ideas such as:

- creativity is a genetic gift granted only to an elite few;
- creativity is a purely individual activity;
- creativity *just happens*; creative ideas arrive as if by magic;
- creativity is always a good thing;
- creativity occurs largely in the realms of the arts and is something we do after our *real* work (e.g. studying English or science) is completed.

Synchronicity, being in the right place at the right time, can facilitate creative thinking and help children to make important intuitive or imaginative connections or leaps. However, creative activity can also be intellectually demanding; it often requires concentration, perseverance, collaboration and discussion as well as access to the right knowledge and skills, and a conducive learning environment and curriculum. In addition the Report of the National Advisory Committee on Creative and Cultural Education sets out a much more democratic and inclusive view of creativity in which all children have the potential to think and act creatively and where their creative endeavours are not restricted to particular subjects or areas of learning. The report also provides practitioners with a checklist which can be used to identify examples of children acting creatively (DfES, 2004e). For the advisory committee creative activity:

- involved a melding of imagination with purpose;
- was original to the child but was not necessarily original to others;
- produced worthwhile outcomes when judged on the basis of whether they worked, were useful, were ethical, were a valid solution to a problem or were aesthetically pleasing.

Democratic and inclusive approaches to creativity

Melding imagination with purpose

- Jenny was playing with two friends in the nursery role-play area. She picked up a telephone and began an imaginary conversation as part of a shared story line that she and her friends were acting out. Jenny then used and referred to the conversation to lead the play in a new direction.
- Will and James were designing packaging for a muesli-type breakfast cereal that they had made during a design technology lesson. They decided that the packaging must be attractive to look at otherwise people would not want to buy their cereal. They spent much of their time experimenting with colours and shapes to come up with a design that would make people want to buy their muesli.

Originality

- Lee's class were talking about bonfire night and after the discussion the children were given the opportunity to paint pictures of the event. The theme was common but the paintings were all unique individual interpretations of the feelings and experiences that different children had; in this sense each of the paintings was original.
- Kim's group rolled vehicles down a slope to see how far they went across different surfaces. Kim's teacher encouraged the children to come up with suggestions for different surfaces to test, for ways of ensuring a fair test and for ideas about recording the outcomes. These problems had been solved before but not by Kim and her group.

Ethical, practical or aesthetic worth or value

- When Mrs Clark went into the mark-making area she found that Evlyn and Philipa had decided to design and make a get well card for their friend Rebecca, who was off school sick that day.

The definition of creativity outlined above is a useful tool and calls for creativity to be encouraged and nurtured by teachers are certainly welcome, but turning such aspirations into reality is not entirely unproblematic (Craft, 1999; Prentice, 2000). Teachers who feel overshadowed and overwhelmed by league tables, targets and tests may be tempted to avoid creativity in their own practice and it is hard to see how the risk-averse could be effective as models of creativity. It may also be the case that children do not always find it easy to make connections between different areas of learning unaided and so may not be drawing on skills and knowledge acquired in other places and at other times in order to be creative in a particular situation. Nor can creativity be forced in a hot-house fashion and classroom practices designed to bring creativity to the fore may well take time to have an effect; creative responses that appear instantaneous and revelatory may be the exception rather than the rule. The reality could be that most creative activity is characterized by hard work and perseverance, and may be adversely affected by factors such as tiredness, health and/or emotional problems or contextual factors. Nor is creativity value free; the creators of a new industrial process might be deemed highly creative but anyone made redundant as a result of its use might feel differently. Being creative requires us to ask not only how we might do something but also whether we should do something.

Uncertainty surrounding the concept of creativity complicates the identification of any uniquely creative qualities that teachers should focus on. Creativity might result from a willingness to think the unthinkable, or from being comfortable with uncertainty, or from working with the right peers, or from the possession of an urge to play and experiment, or even from stubbornness, determination and an ability to focus and concentrate. This said, the following behaviours may be indicative of creative activity in children:

- a willingness to take (calculated) risks, to try/test things out and to respond positively and constructively to the results;
- a desire to question and sometimes challenge experiences, information, ideas and assumptions;
- the ability to reflect on previous experiences and making connections (both logical and intuitive);
- imagining and visualizing changes and alternative futures.

(QCA, 2007)

One approach to encourage such behaviours is to give recognition and praise; a second is to ensure that the curriculum gives children chances to display these qualities. Secondly hands-on, problem solving and enquiry-based activities involving collaboration provide opportunities to practise risk-taking, experimenting, explaining, discussing and imagining. Meanwhile, using a range of techniques to stimulate children's curiosity and ambition (e.g. visitors, visits, artefacts and resources, restrictions, unanticipated events) can get lessons/sessions off to a good start. Thirdly, discussion activities encourage questioning, critical thinking, reflection and making connections; while children are working get them to make their thinking explicit by asking open-ended *how* and *why* questions and speculate aloud in front of them to model your own creative thinking.

Music

Music is a universal phenomenon found in all cultures; it seems to serve a deep and possibly innate need in people and as such it is a valuable part of the 3–8 curricula (Welch and

Adams, 2004). Children's musical experiences prior to starting nursery/school are likely to be both considerable and largely informal in nature. Whether it is advertising jingles on the television, songs on the radio, listening to an older sibling's CDs or singing at a playgroup, young children are often exposed to music on a daily basis. Music is a means of communication and expression that has both cognitive and emotional dimensions and the affective impact is a common experience (QCA, 1999). Listening to or playing music can be deeply pleasurable experiences; music can calm a listener down; equally, it can be used to express or exorcize frustration, anger or sadness. Music also introduces children to aspects of different cultures past and present and offers them the opportunity for practical hands-on work. Music is particularly useful as a way of helping children to acquire the vital learning skill of listening and it should be valued for the opportunities it offers to underpin learning in other areas of the curriculum such as mathematics (time, tempo, rhythm) as well as for its inherent worth.

Most children do not start formal instrumental music instruction before they are 8 or 9 years old and most 3–8 practitioners lack the technical musical ability to provide such specialist instruction anyway. The comments that follow are therefore aimed at the majority of generalist 3–8 teachers; although there is a technical element to music, teachers who do not possess technical skills can still be effective in helping children to enjoy and gain confidence in their creative musical abilities. Children should be given opportunities to perform and compose music informally and to experiment with and learn about the different sorts of sounds made by a range of instruments (percussion, string, wind). Learning and singing rhymes and songs with accompanying actions and using their own bodies as instruments (e.g. clapping, tapping, clicking fingers) can also provide enjoyable and useful starting points for music education.

Singing songs and rhymes

- 'One, Two, Three, Four, Five, Once I Caught a Fish Alive'
- 'Pat-a-Cake, Baker's Man'
- 'Incy Wincy Spider'
- 'Row Your Boat'
- 'I'm a Little Teapot'
- 'I Hear Thunder'
- 'Ring a Ring o' Roses'
- 'If You're Happy and You Know It'
- 'The Wheels on the Bus'
- 'Head, Shoulders, Knees and Toes'
- 'Nicky, Knacky, Knocky, Noo'
- 'A Sailor Went to Sea, Sea, Sea'
- 'Oh, We Can Play on the Big Bass Drum'
- 'Hokey-Cokey'

Rehearsing, practising, copying, imitating, experimenting, improvising, creating and composing are all important musical experiences for children. Listening and responding to a range of musical expressions, including music from different cultures and periods, as well as discussing their feelings, helps to promote appreciation, knowledge and understanding, for example of the difference between *loud* and *quiet* or *fast* and *slow*. There may also be a reservoir of musical talent in the local community, whether formally trained or informally acquired, that teachers can draw on to extend children's experiences and fire their imaginations. Hearing an instrument, or instruments, played well at first hand can be an intense and even magical physical and emotional experience for children.

In 3–8 settings, a music table, trolley or area offers children first-hand experience of a range of sounds and simple percussion instruments and other musical equipment including homemade instruments. New technologies in particular (e.g. computer software packages, programmable keyboard toys, tape recorder/listening stations, CD players) can offer non-specialist teachers and children additional opportunities to experiment with sounds and tunes, and to practise, compose and listen to music. A key advantage to some of these new technologies is the potential contribution that they can make to children's efforts at musical compositions, facilitating the practical aspects of the activity and providing relatively high quality finished outcomes.

Giving children hands-on musical experiences

Provide children with access to:

- tambourines, drums, cymbals, triangles, shakers, bells, chime bars, wind instruments;
- tape recorders and blank tapes for children to record and listen to their songs and compositions;
- pre-recorded songs, tunes and rhymes on tape or CD;
- song books;
- ICT music packages and electronic keyboards;
- homemade shakers (boxes, plastic pop bottles, tins, thick paper bags, peas, beans, pasta shells, rice, buttons);
- homemade drums (ice cream containers, plastic tubs and bowls, tins);
- homemade chimes (metal objects on string such as knives and forks);
- homemade pluckers (boxes/tins with elastic bands stretched across the top).

Instruments and examples of the music made with them ought to originate from a wide variety of different cultures and locations to extend musical knowledge and understanding, particularly where social, family or peer pressure may act to narrow children's musical horizons. Teachers can help to broaden awareness and appreciation of diverse musical types, traditions and styles by introducing as wide a range of music as possible including music from films, classical music, jazz music, world music, pop and rock music. This can be done in a number of ways and not just through timetabled music *lessons*. Opportunities for the wider inclusion and incorporation of music into children's daily activities in nurseries and schools include:

- playing music during transition times (e.g. tidying-up time);
- running a lunchtime music club;
- playing music in the morning as children arrive;
- playing music to accompany children's entry/exit during assemblies;
- playing music as part of a school's wider efforts to mark significant occasions;
- playing music as a starting point for other activities such as a discussion about feelings in PSHE.

Art and design

Through art children can explore, experiment and work with two- and three dimensional materials in an imaginative manner; they can develop their abilities to handle tools and equipment safely and effectively and learn useful techniques with which to express themselves. Art with young children should value and emphasize the process as well as the product; the ability to mix the paints and understand colour and texture, for example, are important concomitants to the imaginative and expressive aspects of the subject. Art offers excellent opportunities for the development of fine motor control and knowledge and understanding about the world as children are given opportunities to observe carefully, record natural and manufactured objects from a range of cultures and locations, and express their ideas and feelings visually (Myer, 2002; Cox and Watts, 2007).

Many 3 year olds are beginning to want to draw rather than simply scribble, often trying to represent people they know; end results are often reminiscent of a 'Mr Man', appearing to float almost weightlessly, unconnected to other images.

By the ages of 5 or 6 as children get more practice and become more proficient, their drawings and paintings begin to include more detail; a person may now be shown to have a body or fingers. Children start to make decisions about what they will draw or paint prior to doing so, rather than deciding what something is as they go along or even after they have finished. Their spatial awareness is also developing and a very rudimentary sense of perspective is beginning to appear in their drawings and paintings and images will often be aligned in a horizontal (occasionally vertical) row.

By the time children are moving from Key Stage 1 to Key Stage 2 many are able to incorporate a number of different objects in their pictures and are able to organize the images along more than one dimension as they attempt to give the viewer a sense of depth with houses, trees, people or clouds in the background (Golbeck, 2005).

It is important to remember that children's abilities in art vary, just as they do in other areas. Some pupils may be adept and experienced in the use of textiles, paints or malleable materials; others will be less assured. Some pupils may be competent at drawing and thus capable of representing their observations and ideas at a level normally associated with older children. Others may have had fewer opportunities to experiment with drawing materials

age 2½

age 3

age 3½

age 4

age 5

age 6

age 7

age 8

and, therefore, their pictures may be less well crafted than those of their peers. The examples illustrate the sort of progression that can be seen in children's drawing skills but they are indicative and should not be seen as definitive.

Providing art materials and activities in 3–8 settings

Drawing materials:

- Pencils
- Coloured pencils
- Crayons
- Felt tips and pens
- Pastels
- Chalks
- Charcoal

Drawing activities:

- Wax crayon rubbings
- Tracing round hands and feet
- Making simple patterns
- Observational drawings

Painting and printing materials:

- Range of brushes
- Sponges
- Easels
- Pots and palettes
- Dry powder paints in primary colours
- Ready mix paints

Painting and printing activities:

- Splatter painting (flicking paint onto paper using a small brush)
- Blow painting (blowing runny paint around the paper using a drinking straw)
- Finger painting
- Wax paintings (drawing a picture with a white wax candle, painting over with a thin paint wash to reveal the outline)
- Vegetable printing (potatoes can by cut to create simple shapes)
- Block printing (using Styrofoam, clay, plasticine or cotton bobbins)
- Body printing (hands, feet, fingers)
- Symmetrical printing (drip paint onto one half of the paper and fold over to create the final pattern, alternatively drape painted string onto one half of the paper and then fold)
- Poster and powder paints in black, white and primary colours offer children the chance to experiment with a wide range of effects and to learn how to mix their own colours. Paints can be watered down or thickened using PVA adhesive, flour and water or wallpaper paste (avoid fungicidal pastes)

Three-dimensional materials:

- Malleable materials for exploring form (clay, plasticine, play dough. Play dough recipe: 2 parts plain flour, 1 part salt, 1 part cold water and 1 tablespoon vegetable oil)
- Boards
- Rolling pins, cutting tools, stamps
- Collage materials

Three-dimensional activities:

- Collage
- Mobiles
- Mosaics
- Greetings cards
- Folding and cutting doilies to make snow flakes
- Colour and scent play dough for variety using food colourings and essences (make sure it does not tempt young children to consume it)
- Modelling figures and containers

Imaginative play and drama

The strong desire on the part of young children to engage in imaginative play suggests an inherited base and thus an evolutionary imperative. Imaginative play may well have physical, cognitive, social and emotional benefits and provide opportunities for symbolic, creative and internal thinking (Brierley, 1994). Imaginative play offers children opportunities to work through, to make sense of and come to terms with events in the world around them such as the loss of a pet or going to the dentist. Imaginative play also offers children opportunities to experience autonomy and control over events, to become the expert or the authority albeit in an imaginary context (Rogers, 2003). Although children may start with *scripts* and repertoires of actions and sayings drawn from the world around them, imaginative play also gives them the chance to improvise and experiment with storylines. Young children can display very high levels of involvement in these kinds of activities, often being completely absorbed by the activity over an extended period of time.

Imaginary play can appear in a variety of places and guises ranging from small-world play involving puppets, miniature figures, model animals, houses, farms or cars, to block play outdoors, to socio-dramatic role-play in the nursery home corner. Imaginary play can start from recreating the children's own experiences (e.g. shopping, going to the vets or visiting a café), but it can also offer teachers and pupils the chance to create, and be part of, entirely fictitious scenarios with fantasy characters (e.g. a jungle camp, super heroes or a fairy story such as The Three Bears). Such play can be solitary or it can be truly collaborative in nature, requiring children to make use of their social and interpersonal skills as well as their creativity and imagination. Often discussion of plot lines, characters and other ideas is woven into this kind of play as children negotiate a shared understanding of the different elements involved.

Negotiating shared storylines

'Right, you be the mummy pony and you be the daddy pony and I'm the baby pony. Neighhhhh!'

Supporting imaginary play in the nursery/classroom

- Make time and space in your planning for imaginary play. This is much easier to do in Foundation Stage settings where imaginary play is recognized as an essential part of the provision for 3–5-year-old children.
- Remember that imaginary play can become very physical and the outdoor area offers an invaluable forum for activities featuring lots of running, jumping and climbing.
- Provide children with a wide range of attractive dressing-up clothes to encourage them to 'get into role'.
- Subject to common sense and health and safety regulations try, wherever possible, to provide children with 'real' props (e.g. real telephones, real coins) to increase the seriousness with which children engage in the activity.
- Set up specific areas for imaginary play in the nursery classroom such as a small-world play area and a role-play area. However, remember that children's imaginary play will not necessarily be contained or constrained by such areas; imaginary play may well spill over from one area to another. For example, picture a group of FS1 boys in the outdoor area running around being dinosaurs; after a while they may opt to come indoors and continue the dinosaur theme with the block play materials or the small-world play figures.
- Remember that imaginary play may suddenly and spontaneously burst forth in all sorts of unexpected places. For example, exploratory play in the sand or water tray may suddenly be given an imaginary storyline.
- Imaginary play creates opportunities for children to practise and reinforce learning across the curriculum, for example using number and writing for a purpose. Provide themed imaginary play provision alongside spontaneous child directed imaginary play to broaden their horizons and skills.

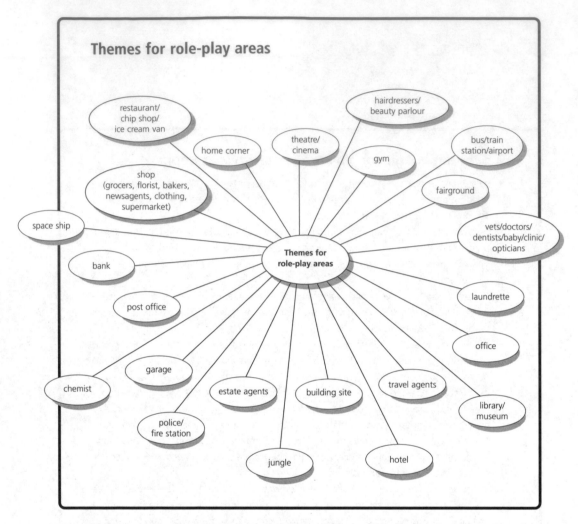

As children get older and move into the primary phase of schooling the opportunities to engage in child initiated imaginary play are frequently squeezed out of the formal curriculum becoming instead the preserve of play times and after school. In part this is a result of the pressure of having to fit a large number of National Curriculum subjects into a limited number of hours. It may also be because some practitioners regard such free play as inappropriate now that children have left the Foundation Stage. This is a shame as it seems quite likely that 6 and 7 year olds can get as much out of pretending and imagining as 3–5 year olds. However, all is not lost as the primary phase does give teachers the opportunity to introduce elements of drama into the curriculum which, while more teacher directed, do at least provide children with a place in which to continue to perform, to act out and to imagine (Burnett and Myers, 2004).

Although drama could be used in many areas of the primary curriculum it has a particular relevance for speaking and listening in English. The use of drama can provide primary children with another way to explore a wide range of scenarios and issues as well as using an enhanced range of spoken language while in role and for a range of purposes. The use of drama can also be highly engaging, motivating, exciting and stimulating for children. It is important to remember the point made earlier about creativity more widely; it does not appear by magic, children's imaginations have to be fed. If, for example, you really want your Year 3 children to deepen their understanding of, and empathy for, a Victorian child labourer through drama then they will need some preparation in order to be able to give a convincing performance. They will need material with which to work; visits to local museums, poems and stories, access to non-fiction texts and talks by outside experts could all help children to really develop their comprehension by engaging in imaginary scenarios.

Some drama techniques for use with Year 1–3 pupils

- **Teacher in role**: interacting with children *in role* gives teachers a novel way to present pupils with interesting challenges and problems, or to explore their thinking about puzzles or disputes. Teachers may choose *high status* roles, *low status* roles or *expert* roles.
- **Freeze-frames**: children create a tableaux to represent an event, an idea or a feeling.
- **Thought-tracking**: children observing a freeze-frame or a paused dramatic episode are asked to speculate on the thoughts and feelings of the participants' characters.
- **Hotseating**: children adopt a role and then have to answer questions from their peers and their teacher while in role.
- **Decision alley**: one child in role has a difficult decision to make. He/she walks between two rows of their peers (the *alley*) while their peers make suggestions about what they should do.
- **Forum theatre**: a small group of actors in a scene are *directed* and re-directed by their peers as a way of allowing children to consider events and ideas from different perspectives.
- **Role on the wall**: children suggest words to describe a character, their thoughts, feelings, actions and words. The suggestions are scribed onto an outline drawing of the character.

(Burnett and Myers, 2004, p. 39)

Further sources of information

Children as learners

- Bruce T. (Ed) (2006) *Early Childhood: A Guide for Students*. London: Paul Chapman.
- Fleetham M. (2007) *Pocket PAL: Multiple Intelligences*. London: Network Continuum.
- Keenan T. (2002) *An Introduction to Child Development*. London: Sage.

- Macintyre C. (2001) *Enhancing Learning Through Play: A Developmental Perspective for Early Years Settings*. London: David Fulton.
- May P., Ashford E. and Bottle G. (2006) *Sound Beginnings: Learning and Development in the Early Years*. London: David Fulton.
- Miller L., Cable C. and Devereux J. (2005) *Developing Early Years Practice*. London: David Fulton.
- Miller L., Drury R. and Campbell R. (Eds) (2002) *Exploring Early Years Education and Care*. London: David Fulton.
- Rogers S. (2003) *Role Play in the Foundation Stage: Role Play with Early Years Children*. London: David Fulton.

The National Curriculum for 5–8 Year Olds

- DfEE (1998b) *The National Literacy Strategy*. London: DfEE.
- DfEE (1999) *The National Numeracy Strategy*. London: DfEE.
- QCA (1999) *The National Curriculum: Handbook for Primary Teachers in England Key Stages 1 and 2*. London: QCA.
- QCA (2000) *Curriculum Guidance for the Foundation Stage*. London: QCA.

Personal, Social and Emotional Development

- Bliss T. and Tetley J. (2006, 2nd edition) *Cicle Time*. London: Paul Chapman Publishing.
- Buck M., Inman S. and Tandy M. (2003) *Enhancing Personal, Social and Health Education: Challenging Practice, Changing Worlds*. London: Routledge.
- Burrell A. and Riley J. (2007) *Promoting Children's Well-Being*. London: Continuum.
- Dowling M. (2005, 2nd Edition) *Young Children's Personal, Social and Emotional Development*. London: Paul Chapman.
- Roger R. (2004, 2nd Edition) *Planning an Appropriate Curriculum for the Under Fives: A Guide for Students, Teachers and Assistants*. London: David Fulton.
- Taylor, J. (2006) *Getting to Know Me.* London: David Fulton.

Communication, Language and Literacy

- Burnett C. and Myers J. (2004*) Teaching English 3–11*. London: Continuum.
- Campbell R. (2002) 'Exploring key literacy learning: own name and alphabet', in Miller L., Drury R. and Campbell R. (Eds) *Exploring Early Years Education and Care*. London: David Fulton.
- Coleman W. (2007) *Brave Tales: Developing Literacy Through Storytelling*. London: Network Continuum.
- DCSF (2007) *Letters and Sounds: Principles and Practice of High Quality Phonics*. London: DfSE Publications.
- DfES (2004) 'Playing with sounds: a supplement to progression in phonics'. www.standards.dfes.gov.uk/primary/publications/literacy/948809/
- Gouch K., Grainger T. and Lambirth A. (2005) *Creativity and Writing: Developing Voice and Verve in the Classroom*. London: Routledge.
- Marsh J. and Hallet E. (Eds) (1999) *Desirable Literacies: Approaches to Language and Literacy in the Early Years*. London: Chapman.

- Nutbrown C. (1996) *Threads of Thinking*. London: Sage.
- Palmer S. (2003) *How to Teach Writing Across the Curriculum at Key Stage 1*. London: David Fulton.
- Parke T. and Drury R. (2002) 'Who's listening? Who's teaching? Good circumstances for the language development of young bilinguals in early years settings', in Miller L., Drury R. and Campbell R. (Eds) *Exploring Early Years Education and Care*. London: David Fulton.
- The Phonics Website: www.standards.dfes.gov.uk/phonics/
- Primary Framework for literacy and mathematics: www.standards.dfes.gov.uk/primaryframeworks/literacy/
- Riley J. (2006) *Language and Literacy 3–7*. London: Paul Chapman.
- Selley N. (1999) *The Art of Constructivist Teaching in the Primary School: A Guide for Students and Teachers*. London: David Fulton.
- Waugh D. and Jolliffe W. (2007) *English 3–11: A Guide for Teachers*. London: David Fulton.
- Whitehead M. (1999) *Supporting Language and Literacy Development in the Early Years*. Buckingham: Open University Press.
- Wood D. (1998, 2nd Edition) *How Children Think and Learn*. Oxford: Blackwell.

Problem Solving, Reasoning and Numeracy

- Anghileri J. (2005) *Children's Mathematical Thinking in Primary Years*. London: Continuum.
- Anghileri J. (2006, 2nd Edition) *Teaching Number Sense*. London: Continuum.
- Askew M. (1998) *Teaching Primary Mathematics*. London: Hodder & Stoughton.
- Briggs M. and Davis S. (2007) *Creative Teaching: Mathematics in the Early Years and Primary Classroom*. London: David Fulton.
- Edwards, S. (1998) *Managing Effective Teaching of Mathematics 3–8*. London: Paul Chapman.
- Foster M. and Foster R. (2003) 'Sum stories: developing children's mathematical knowledge with meaning', in Cooper H. and Sixsmith C. (Eds) *Teaching Across the Early Years 3–7: Curriculum coherence and continuity*. London: RoutledgeFalmer.
- Haylock D. (2001) *Mathematics Explained for Primary Teachers*. London: Paul Chapman.
- Orton A. and Frobisher L. (1996) *Insights into Teaching Mathematics*. London: Cassell.
- Suggate J., Davis A. and Goulding M. (2006, 3rd Edition) *Mathematical Knowledge for Primary Teachers*. London: David Fulton.
- Thompson I. (Ed.) (1997) *Teaching and Learning Early Number*. Buckingham: Open University Press.

Knowledge and Understanding of the World

- Cooper H. and Sixsmith C. (Eds) (2002) *Teaching Across the Early Years 3–7: Curriculum Coherence and Continuity*. London: RoutledgeFalmer.

Science

- Farmery C. (2002) *Teaching Science 3–11: The Essential Guide*. London: Continuum.
- Howe A., Davies D., McMahon K., Towler L. and Scott T (2005) *Science 5–11: A Guide for Teachers*. London: David Fulton.

- Sixsmith C. and Melbourne L. (2003) 'Developing a scientific understanding of the world', in Cooper H. and Sixsmith C. (Eds) *Teaching Across the Early Years 3–7: Curriculum Coherence and Continuity*. London: RoutledgeFalmer.

Design and technology

- Fleer M. (2000) 'Working technologically: investigations into how young children design and make during technology education'. *International Journal of Technology and Design Education*, Vol. 10, pp. 43–59.
- Hope G. (2004) *Teaching Design and Technology 3–11*. London: Continuum.
- Ritchie R. (2001) *Primary Design and Technology*. London: David Fulton.
- Rogers G. and Wallace J. (2000) 'The wheels on the bus: children designing in an early years classroom'. *Research in Science and Technological Education*, Vol. 18, No. 1, 127–36.

Information and communications technology

- O'Hara M. (2004) *ICT in the Early Years*. London: Continuum.
- Sharp J., Potter J., Allen J. and Loveless A. (2000) *Primary ICT: Knowledge, Understanding and Practice*. Exeter: Learning Matters.
- Siraj-Blatchford J. and Siraj-Blatchford I. (2002) 'Guidance for practitioners on appropriate technology education in early childhood'. www.ioe.ac.uk/cdl/datec/
- For help in picking good quality software try visiting the websites below:
  - The British Educational Communications and Technology Agency (BECTa) offers practitioners ICT advice as well as access to an educational software database: http://schools.becta.org.uk/ **Select: Resources – Essential Websites – Evaluate**
  - Micros and Primary Education (MAPE), now merged with the National Association of Advisors for Computers in Education (NAACE), offers practitioners advice on and links to software evaluation and suggestions for using ICT not just in primary settings but also in the different areas of learning to be found in the Curriculum guidance for the Foundation Stage (QCA, 2000): www.mape.org.uk/ **Select: Curriculum Support – Reviews: Software**
  - Teachers Evaluating Educational Multimedia (TEEM) provides practitioners with access to evaluations of educational multimedia written by classroom teachers: www.teem.org.uk/ **Select: By Key Stage – Foundation**

Geography

- Cooper H., Asquith S. and Rowley C. (2006) *Geography 3–11: A Guide for Teachers*. London: David Fulton.
- The Geographical Association (GA) website contains a variety of learning and teaching materials plus guidance for early years and primary practitioners: www.geography.org.uk/eyprimary/
- Owen D. and Ryan A. (2001) *Teaching Geography 3–11: The Essential Guide*. London: Continuum.
- Palmer J. and Birch J. (2004) *Geography in the Early Years*. London: Routledge.
- Simco N. (2003) 'Developing geographical perspective within an integrated theme', in Cooper H. and Sixsmith C. (Eds) *Teaching Across the Early Years 3–7: Curriculum Coherence and Continuity*. London: RoutledgeFalmer.

History

- Cooper C. (2003) 'History: finding out about the past and the language of time', in Cooper and Sixsmith, see previous reference for details.
- The Historical Association website contains advice and suggestions for primary practitioners on the teaching of history including tackling emotive and controversial topics: www.history.org.uk/Primary.asp
- O'Hara L. and O'Hara M. (2001) *Teaching History 3–11: The Essential Guide*. London: Continuum.
- Turner-Bisset R. (2002) 'The essence of history in the early years', in Miller L., Drury R. and Campbell R. (Eds) *Exploring Early Years Education and Care*. London: David Fulton.
- Turner-Bisset R. (2005) *Creative Teaching: History in the Primary Classroom*. London: David Fulton.

RE

- The BBC's religion and ethics site provides access to extensive background information on world religions: www.bbc.co.uk/religion/
- DfES (2007) 'RE at Key Stages 1 and 2'. The Standards Site. www.standards.dfes.gov.uk
- The Multifaith website offers teachers detailed information on key tenets and features of world religions: www.multifaithnet.org/
- The REonline site provides a range of online activities and materials for teachers and students: www.reonline.org.uk/
- St Martin's College Lancaster offers a Religious Education Exchange Service for teacher training students with information on world religions, ethical issues, teaching resources and useful links: http://re-xs.ucsm.ac.uk/

Physical Development

- Bilton H. (2002, 2nd Edition) *Outdoor Play in the Early Years: Management and Innovation*. London: David Fulton.
- Bilton H., James K., Wilson A. and Woonton M. (2005) *Learning Outdoors: Improving the Quality of Young Children's Play Outdoors*. London: David Fulton.
- DfES (2007) 'PE at Key Stages 1 and 2'. The Standards Site. www.standards.dfes.gov.uk
- Doherty J. (2007) *Physical Education and Development 3–11: A Guide for Teachers*. London: David Fulton.
- Doherty J. and Bailey R. (2003) *Supporting Physical Development and Physical Education in the Early Years*. Buckingham: Open University Press.
- Garrick R. (2004) *Playing Outdoors in the Early Years*. London: Continuum.
- Lavin J. (2003) 'Physical development into physical education: is it fair play?', in Cooper H. and Sixsmith C. (Eds) *Teaching Across the Early Years 3–7: Curriculum Coherence and Continuity*. London: RoutledgeFalmer.
- Pickup I. and Lawry P. (2007) *Teaching Physical Education in the Primary School: A Developmental Approach*. London: Continuum.
- Woodfield L (2004) *Physical Development in the Early Years*. London: Continuum.

Creative Development

- Allen R. (2002) 'Drawing as a language in the early years', in Miller L., Drury R. and Campbell R. (Eds) *Exploring Early Years Education and Care*. London: David Fulton.

- Cox S. and Watts R. (Eds) (2007) *Teaching Art and Design 3–11*. London: Continuum.

- Craft A. (1999) 'Creative development in the early years: some implications of policy for practice'. *The Curriculum Journal*, Vol. 10, No. 1, 135–50.

- Glover J. and Ward S. (Eds) (1998, 2nd Edition) *Teaching Music in the Primary School*. London: Cassell.

- Klijn K. (2003) 'Music: feel the beat', in Cooper H. and Sixsmith C. (Eds) *Teaching Across the Early Years 3–7: Curriculum Coherence and Continuity*. London: RoutledgeFalmer.

- Myer C. (2002) *Not Just Pictures: Children Developing Creativity Through Art*. London: The British Association for Early Childhood Education.

- National Society for Education in Art and Design (NSEAD): www.nsead.org/home

- Prentice R. (2000) 'Creativity: a reaffirmation of its place in early childhood education'. *The Curriculum Journal*, Vol. 11, No. 2, 145–58.

- Rogers S. (2003) *Role Play in the Foundation Stage: Role Play with Early Years Children*. London: David Fulton.

- Sharp C. (2004) *Developing Young Children's Creativity: What Can We Learn from Research*. National Foundation for Educational Research (NFER). www.nfer.ac.uk/publications

- Skinner S. (2007) *Creative Activities for the Early Years*. London: Paul Chapman.

Professional Skills

3

Chapter Outline

Introduction

Chapter 2 dealt with the need for 3–8 teachers to have a good knowledge and understanding of children as learners and the curriculum. However, knowing what needs to be taught is insufficient on its own to make someone effective as a teacher. Teachers of 3–8 pupils must also be good planners, managers and communicators and they must be able to deploy a range of effective strategies in the nursery/classroom that facilitate learning and teaching. Children need opportunities to learn through play, first-hand experience and high quality interactions with adults and peers in order to foster their personal, social, emotional, physical and cognitive development. Teachers therefore need to be able to:

- offer a broad and balanced curriculum in a high quality learning environment which motivates children and supports their learning;
- plan stimulating and interesting activities at an appropriate level for young children;
- employ a range of assessment methods and use assessment information to inform future planning;
- record and report on children's progress and achievements;
- take account of and respond to children's differing needs and abilities;
- manage a class effectively.

✔ **Audit**

By the end of this chapter you should know about:

- some of the key characteristics of good quality 3–8 learning environments;
- planning and target setting with Foundation Stage and lower primary pupils;
- monitoring, assessing and reporting on pupils' learning;
- differentiating lessons and responding to the needs of individual children, including pupils with SEN;
- effective classroom organization, management and teaching strategies.

Promoting positive relationships and active learning

Young children are perceived as active learners who learn well in situations that include an element of doing and who benefit from relevant first-hand experiences coupled with opportunities to play and talk in secure and caring environments. Schools and nurseries assist pupils in making sense of the world by exploring objects, materials and feelings in meaningful situations. The children's natural curiosity is harnessed as they are encouraged to ask why and how things are as they are by practitioners who are capable of scaffolding the children's learning.

✔ **Audit**

By the end of this section you should:

- know about the importance of positive relationships in high quality learning environments;
- know about the learning benefits of some of the different types of play and talk that children need to engage in.

Building positive relationships in the nursery/classroom

Good teachers see the inculcation of certain interrelated skills, values and attitudes associated with Personal, Social and Emotional Development as a key part of their role and as crucial in determining children's progress and development across the curriculum as a whole.

> ## Interrelated skills and attitudes
> - **Self-awareness**: get children to reflect on events and on their learning, their successes, possible weaknesses, their likes and dislikes. Help them to set achievable and appropriate goals and targets for themselves.
> - **Coping with emotions**: talk about when they feel things, what they do when they feel certain emotions, what happens as a result and whether they could do things differently.
> - **Motivation**: use the curriculum to introduce children to people who have achieved things (e.g. artists, scientists), invite visitors into the nursery/classroom who have worked hard to develop particular skills or expertise, respond positively and encourage children's interests and questions.
> - **Social skills**: give children experience of working with different peers from time to time. Talk about sharing, taking turns and about being considerate, empathetic and supportive of others.

In many settings circle time is often used as one of the ways in which practitioners try to help children to focus on things like self-esteem, caring relationships and emotions. Circle time works best when used in an ongoing and proactive fashion rather than as an *ad hoc* response to unwanted incidents. Circle time activities can help children to acquire the sorts of social skills necessary to be able to live and work together in a more harmonious fashion and offer pupils the chance to experience *being trusted*; *being respected*; *being successful*; *being praised*; *being listened to*; *listening to others*; *cooperating* and *working constructively in groups* (Curry and Bromfield, 1995). Circle time can offer teachers interesting and fun ways of helping children to:

- become more self-aware;
- develop strategies for managing and dealing positively with their feelings;
- develop empathy and tolerance towards others;
- improve their social skills;
- increase their levels of self-motivation;
- cope with change;
- deal with conflict;
- solve problems.

The structured nature of these activities (they often require children to adhere to certain rules and conventions) may make them more demanding for some of the youngest (nursery) children and care should be taken not to *over-dwell* by keeping children sitting still for too long; 10–15 minutes may be sufficient at any one time for the younger children. Circle time requires children to adhere to some simple rules which themselves provide useful personal and social training, for example 'when other people are speaking we listen'. With some 3–8 children this rule may be particularly challenging and some practitioners introduce a special object such as a sea shell or teddy bear which gives the holder the right to speak. For other 3–8 children the prospect of speaking in front of a large group may be particularly daunting and one rule for circle time ought to be that 'I do not have to say anything until I am ready'. All the children have the right to decline to contribute until such time as they feel confident enough to do so. Once again some practitioners use special objects to encourage contributions, for example giving shy and reticent children a puppet or a doll which can *talk for* the child.

An example of circle time with Y2 children

Level	Purpose and activities	Example
Warm-up games	Practising/reiterating the rules and conventions (e.g. turn-taking, sharing, listening): • 'My name is . . . . . .' • 'My favourite colour/animal/food is . . . . . .' • 'My best friend is . . . . . . because . . . . . .' • 'I'm good at . . . . . .' • 'Something nice that happened to me was . . . . . .' • 'Everyone with black hair get up and change places.' • 'Everyone wearing green get up and change places.' Building confidence and trust by providing affirmation for the participants. Fostering an awareness of others, listening skills and imagination.	A group of 12 children and their teacher sit together on the carpet. The children are in a circle. There is a gap in the circle. The child on the right of the gap has to ask someone to come and sit next to him/her. (Rule: boys must pick a girl and girls must pick a boy.)
Introducing the theme	Exploring feelings, empathy, problem solving and conflict resolution • 'I feel happy when . . . . . .' • 'It makes me angry when . . . . . .' • '. . . . . . is fair/unfair because . . . . . .' • '. . . . . . is right/wrong because . . . . . .' • 'I want to try to . . . . . . today.'	The teacher tells the children that they are going to be thinking about things that make them sad and what they can do to help other people who are sad. The teacher says 'I feel sad when . . .' The child on the right tells the group what makes him/her sad and so on around the circle. (Rule: everyone must start with the phrase 'I feel sad when . . .') The teacher groups the children into threes and asks the children to think about what they could do if they see someone who is sad. The teacher spends time with each group, offering encouragement and sharing ideas.

| Plenary/ conclusion | Checking on learning and offering praise, recognition and encouragement for the future. | The children reform the original circle of 12 and the teacher chairs the feedback session in which children can report to the whole group on their ideas and suggestions. Children who are reluctant to comment in front of everyone else are not forced to do so.

A short finishing-off activity praising one or two children in the group by giving them a round of applause. Finally, recognizing the efforts of all the group by getting everyone to give themselves a pat on the back. |

Running circle time activities

- Do not make the group too large with younger infants, and do not make the task too complicated.
- Remember the age and maturity of the children. Having to sit still and passively for long periods is likely to provoke considerable disruption and undermine the purposes of the activity.
- 'Little and often' can be a useful motto for those working with younger pupils. These children are likely to benefit from more frequent, shorter sessions that encourage greater participation.
- Simple rules and conventions can be introduced to help get circle time activities up and running with the minimum of fuss, for example developing special signs and signals for gaining children's attention, or passing an object round the group which confers the right to speak on the holder.

Playing and talking as vehicles for learning

It may be possible to take the play out of learning (if one must), but it is likely to prove impossible to take the learning out of play (Edwards and Knight, 1994). Building in opportunities for play is an essential feature of teaching and learning in 3–8 settings. The Early Years Foundation Stage refers to the need for children to experience a wide variety of play opportunities in order for them to *learn at their highest level* (DfES, 2007d). Play offers children the chance to learn in contexts in which they are highly receptive.

It is much more than simply a recreational time-filler; it is a valuable approach to learning. Through play children:

- experience making choices and taking charge of their own learning;
- can test out their ideas and reinforce their learning;
- can act out and come to terms with their feelings;
- can encounter new ideas;
- learn in a very physical way using all their senses;
- can engage in extended exploration;
- can draw together all of the above to make sense of the world.

(Bruce, 1997)

For Bruner, play was a phenomenon that everyone could recognize but none could *frame* (i.e. define) (Abbott and Rodger, 1994). He suggested that play could be either exploratory and/or social in nature, while Vygotsky felt that pretend and role-play was particularly valuable in developmental terms. Play can therefore be categorized in a number of ways and it would be a mistake to think that the boundaries between the different categories are anything other than permeable (Macintyre, 2001). Spontaneous child-directed scenarios can emerge out of settings that are ostensibly teacher directed in nature. Similarly, scenarios designed to foster social or imaginative play can also provide opportunities for exploratory play at the same time; for example, some role-play areas incorporate mark-making materials, tools and equipment.

Structured play describes situations that have been planned and initiated by the teacher; these might include role and pretend play, social or exploratory play opportunities. Games and puzzles can also be used by teachers to structure children's learning by providing pupils with interesting situations in which they can hone their problem-solving skills, cooperate with others, and learn to compete in non-aggressive ways.

In contrast, **free play** is a term used to describe spontaneous play initiated by the children in which they have the chance to interact with their peers in activities that they themselves have devised and through which they can express themselves and explore things that are of special interest to them. Such play can be a powerful method of arousing and sustaining children's curiosity and motivation.

Exploratory play describes children experimenting, often purposefully, with tools, equipment and materials. This could involve sand or water play, using tricycles in the outdoor area, making dens, junk modelling, mark-marking, painting, using ICT or building with construction kits. Exploratory play provides opportunities for children to be creative, to hone their physical skills and to investigate the world around them.

Types of social play

Associative play: Children talk to one another and share materials but do not take on different roles within the same imaginary context or work towards completing a joint project. Most common form among 4 year olds.

Parallel play: A child plays *beside*, rather than *with*, other children. He/she might be using the same toys and materials but not interacting. Most common form among 2 year olds.

Onlooker behaviour: A child watches other children, but does not join in.

Unoccupied play: A child is present alongside other children but does not play with anything and instead watches whatever interests him/her.

Solitary play: A child plays by him/herself in a way which is different from those around them.

(Parten in Keenan, 2002)

Pretend/imaginary play and **role-play** (see pp. 150–3) are very effective in providing young children with opportunities to express their feelings verbally as well as practising and reinforcing social skills. Pretend play introduces rules and opportunities to explore feelings and to learn about the social norms expected of people, for example the 'baby' has to act the part and behave like a baby (Keenan, 2002). Pretend play can encourage children to play at a level beyond their stage in life, for example being a parent, a fire fighter or a doctor.

While nurseries and many reception classes offer a wide range of play activities for pupils, the choice often narrows as children move through the infant school and into Year 3, frequently becoming restricted to occasional work with construction kits or computer simulations. In addition an increasingly large distinction is sometimes drawn between playing and working as children get older (Bennett et al., 1997). Not only does the range of play activities become narrower, but also some teachers seem much less willing to allocate time to play. Rather than being seen as an approach to learning, play sometimes appears to be regarded as a luxury that actually takes time away from that pursuit. Although this is not surprising given the emphasis on literacy and numeracy, meeting government-set targets for SATs results and ever-increasing levels of teacher accountability at Key Stages 1 and 2, it is still a great shame as play offers a wide range of potential learning opportunities.

Along with play, talk forms a vital part in young children's learning; they use it to build relationships and improve their knowledge and understanding. In spite of this, however, communication with teachers can sometimes become restricted to question and answer formats with children engaging in little extended speech. This is in stark contrast to dialogue with their peers, which is often much more free flowing and wide ranging. Consequently teachers need to add to the question and answer format and provide children with opportunities to express themselves at greater length, to share thoughts and ideas, and to discuss and evaluate different options and alternatives. Small-group and paired work are useful situations in which to foster this kind of talk among children. With older children teacher directed *snowball* and *jigsaw* groupings can also be effective techniques to promote children's talk. In snowball groups, children talk in pairs, then different pairs get together to talk; in jigsaw groups, children move individually from home groups to different expert groups, then back to home groups for discussion.

Supporting play and talk in 3–8 settings

- Take play and talk seriously as vehicles for learning. Plan for them, set out clear educational objectives and make time for them to happen.
- Utilize outdoor as well as indoor spaces, with younger children where possible, offering *open and continuous* rather than *restricted and timetabled* access.
- Enhance the quality of play and talk by ensuring that the role-play area contains plenty of interesting and exciting equipment and materials. Introduce plenty of action rhymes, songs or examples of alliteration to foster a sense of fun.
- Use trips and visits to real locations such as shops or cafés to introduce children to new language and to provide them with ideas about ways of behaving and likely events in a given context. Where appropriate, real-life artefacts may be better than pretend ones for promoting responsible behaviour, for example tables, chairs, beds, a range of clothing (male, female, multicultural), accessories (purses/wallets, jewellery, hats) and kitchen artefacts (cooker, sink, washing machine).
- Build learning opportunities from across the curriculum into the play activities taking place. For example, water play can provide an excellent context within which to extend children's mathematical development, or their Knowledge and Understanding of the World.
- Be ready to become active participants in children's play and talk from time-to-time to support or scaffold their learning. While it is important not to let involvement become interference, teachers may well have to get drawn in if they wish their learning objectives to be realized. For example, providing access to adults can present children with insights into social protocols, how to listen, how to respond as well as models of how to use language appropriately.
- Offer opportunities for children to extend and improve their oral language skills through working in pairs and groups and by providing a wide range of shared experiences.
- Think aloud with pupils, providing opportunities for questioning, reasoning, investigating and solving simple problems verbally, and to share ideas.
- Use bilingual teachers and learning support staff to facilitate the play and talk of pupils with English as an additional language (EAL) or with special educational needs (SEN).

Planning

Much of children's learning takes place in relatively unstructured contexts outside of the nursery/school, for example at home or through the media. Teachers, however, are engaged in building on children's previous learning in a more organized fashion, based on the Foundation Stage early learning goals or National Curriculum Programmes of Study.

✔ Audit

By the end of this section you should:

- know about the planning of lessons and sequences of lessons;
- know how to develop clear learning purposes/objectives.

Why plan?

Planning is an essential skill which all teachers must master. There are many distractions in 3–8 settings which may deflect teachers from their planning but without a clear plan to begin with these distractions will come to rule; it is harder as a teacher to think on your feet if you are already thinking on your feet. An absence of effective planning can have serious consequences for teaching and learning. It can lead both to teacher inefficiency and ineffectiveness in the classroom and to learning that is, at best, patchy and uncoordinated. Effective planning provides a clear focus and purpose for lessons and schemes of work. It assists teachers in focusing on their own practice, making it easier to reflect on events, to modify future teaching, to anticipate children's needs and to have responses ready. Good planning helps teachers to avoid wasting time and missing learning opportunities. Lessons and activities that are planned are more likely to be satisfying and successful than those that are not.

This is not to say that planning should act as a straightjacket on teachers. Good teachers are able to spot opportunities for unplanned learning when they occur and good planning does not preclude this. Paradoxically, good planning can make it easier for teachers to be more responsive and flexible and to take calculated detours by enabling them to adjust their timing and modify their intentions much more easily.

Planning for the Early Years Foundation Stage

For those working with FS1 and FS2 pupils planning ought to be informed by an understanding of the fact that young children learn well in situations and circumstances that are real and relevant to their lives and through activities that are varied and interesting. While children will follow recognized patterns of development during this period, individuals vary considerably. Development may not necessarily be a smooth and continuous process; it may even be susceptible to regression. Children arrive in nursery and reception classes from a wide variety of backgrounds, with a broad range of experiences, and at different stages of development. Their experiences in 3–5 settings constitute a key stage in their learning and development. As a result planning in nursery and reception settings seeks to build upon the children's previous (home) experiences and learning and recognizes that young children's needs and interests will grow and develop over time. Children are offered opportunities to explore significant events in their lives and are encouraged to engage in self-expression and discovery. Early years practitioners also capitalize on the valuable lessons to be learned through the wider curriculum such as conventions relating to health and safety, playing sensibly in the playground, behaviour in and out of school, and involvement in events and productions such as festivals, concerts and celebrations.

Nursery and reception provision is less compartmentalized and more holistic in comparison to primary settings. The under-fives' curriculum provides a coherent framework for addressing the various discrete areas of learning and development while at the same time offering teachers and children opportunities to make links between these various areas of learning. For example, visiting the local shops with the children can offer starting points and opportunities for learning in Personal, Social and Emotional Development; Communication, Language and Literacy; and Problem Solving, Reasoning and Numeracy (DfES, 2007d). Practitioners recognize the potential for learning across a number of areas of learning and development within any one session and therefore there is likely to be a distinction between curriculum conception (i.e. the planning), in which the different areas of learning are clearly mapped out, and curriculum delivery (i.e. learning and teaching), whereby young children do not necessarily see themselves as *doing creative work* or doing *mathematics work* (Alexander *et al.*, 1992).

Young children are inquisitive; many everyday occurrences capture their imagination and provoke demands for explanations. Nursery/reception programmes attempt to make this desire to find out and the children's natural ability to soak up information work for them by providing a curriculum with opportunities for enquiry and first-hand experience. Planning includes opportunities for children to handle a range of tools and materials, to observe, listen, investigate, question, experiment and draw conclusions. This enquiry element is supported by teachers who help the children to make links between previous experiences and current discoveries and who establish an environment in which the children feel safe, secure and confident. In addition, practitioners need to ensure a balance between teacher-initiated tasks (i.e. where the teacher is guiding the children's learning) and child-initiated activities (i.e. those activities selected by a child on the basis of their personal interests and abilities).

Medium-term planning: Reception

Theme: Plants/growth   Spring term – 2nd half

	What do we want the children to learn?		How will we enable this learning to take place?	How will we know who has learned what?	What next?
	Learning intentions (based on stepping stones/ELGs)	Vocabulary	Activities/routines	Assessment	Notes on how assessments will inform future plans
Personal, Social and Emotional Development	• Take turns • Show caring for living things • Select and use resources independently	'Please can I have a turn?'	Garden centre role-play: customer/assistant Plant seeds Care for seedlings	Note which children take on roles	
Communication, Language and Literacy **Objectives from the literacy framework**	• Listen and respond to stories • Take part in role-play • Write for different purposes • Use sequence words • Hear/say phoneme 'g', 's', 't' • Recognize letters 'g', 's', 't'	 First, then, after that	Jasper's Beanstalk – Titch: Pat Hutchins Songs: Oats, Peas, Beans and Barley grow Action rhyme: Growing flowers Customers/assistants in garden centre Make labels and notices for garden centre Show others how to prepare cress for planting Find objects beginning with sounds Sort letters and objects Group objects	Note use of language in role Collect example of labels created	
Mathematical development **Objectives from the numeracy framework**	• Use number names • Count objects • Recognize numerals • Use vocabulary to compare size	Numbers 1–10 More than Less than Bigger, smaller, more	Count plant pots, bulbs and seeds Organize different sizes of plant pots	List children who know and can use numbers to 5 List children who know 5–10 and above	
Knowledge and Understanding of the World	• Identify features of plants • Show awareness of change • Recognize everyday use of ICT	Stem, leaf, leaves, root Grow/n Longer, taller More, fewer Scan, till	Sketches/paintings of plants Plant seeds in garden and inside Sow cress Use till, computer and price scanner in role-play area	Can describe plant or painting using appropriate vocabulary	
Physical Development	• Explore malleable materials • Handle tools with care	Spade, fork, trowel, dig, plant	Outside area – earth/water Planting seeds and seedlings	Record children who dig/can hold spade and control	
Creative Development	• Explore colour and texture	Rough, smooth	Collect and compare leaves Collage	Use of different textures	

(Burnett and Myers, 2004)

Short-term planning/Weekly: Nursery

Planning sheet, week beginning:

Personal, Social and Emotional Development	Communication, Language and Literacy	Mathematics
1. Work as part of a group or class, taking turns and sharing fairly, understanding that there needs to be agreed behaviour.	1. Listen with enjoyment and respond to stories, songs, rhymes and poems. 2. Sustain attentive listening, responding to what they have heard.	1. Use developing mathematical ideas and methods to solve practical problems. 2. Begin to use vocabulary involved with addition and subtraction.

Vehicles for learning:	Activity with parents	Carpet time	Mark-making	Mathematics	ICT
Mon	Name cards	Read *Oh Dear!* Introduce some farm animals	Labels for the tea room	Money game	KidPix
Tues	Can you share a book with your child?	In my shopping bag . . .	List of things you can buy at a shop	Money game Shopping game	KidPix
Weds	Number cards	Read *Don't Forget the Bacon* Play shopping game in a circle	Letter formation cards	Money game Shopping game	Leaps and Bounds
Thurs	Name cards Older children to write the alphabet	Number recognition game with This Old Man	Mark-making numbers and sequences	This Old Man Money game 1p, 2p, 5p	Leaps and Bounds This Old Man song tape
Fri	Can you share a book with your child?	Read *Noisy Farm* Money recognition	Salt in spot tray	This Old Man Number books, jigsaws and tape	Leaps and Bounds This Old Man song tape

Knowledge and Understanding of the World		Creative Development		Physical Development	
1. Select tools and techniques they need to shape, and assemble and join materials. 2. Use ICT to support their learning.		1. Use their imagination in art and design, music, dance, imaginative and role play activities.		1. Handle tools, objects, construction and materials safely and with increasing control.	

Construction	Small-world play	Role-play	Creative	Sand/Water	Games/Dance
Make different sized animal homes using stickle bricks	Farm animals on spot tray	The Three Little Pigs' house	Farm jigsaws	Threading beads	Wet sand with small moulds
Make different sized animal homes using Duplo bricks	Farm animals on spot tray	The Three Little Pigs' house	Painting pigs	Wet sand with small moulds **Outdoor area**	Hall time – responding to instructions
Duplo bricks	Farm animals on spot tray **Outdoor area**	The Three Little Pigs' house	Painting mixing different colours **Outdoor area**	Wet sand and sieves	Circle games
	Farm animals on spot tray	The Three Little Pigs' house	Painting mixing different colours Jigsaws	Dry sand and sieves	Bats, balls, hoops and ropes **Outdoor area**
Box modelling	Space Station	The Three Little Pigs' house	Jigsaws Free drawings	Dry sand and sieves **Outdoor area**	

Short-term planning/Session/Lesson: Nursery

Date:	Learning Objective(s)/Early Learning Goal: K&U p. 92 – Use ICT to support their learning.

Assessment Can the children • draw using the mouse? • use menu/icons to select colours, shapes and effects?	Activity To use a simple computer program (KidPix) with a range of tools to enable the children to draw pictures of favourite farm animals

Context (group size, in/outdoor, role-play area, etc.) Pairs/individuals in the computer area	Resources Both nursery computers, KidPix program, farm visit photographs, farm animal pictures and small-world play figures

Language mouse, double click, drag, click, animal names, shape names	Differentiation By outcome

Introduction
Model how to use the KidPix tools to draw a recognizable pig. Encourage the children to think about what shapes the pig is made up of and what colour to fill the pig in with.

Development of activity (what the children will be doing) Using the mouse and a selection of tools to draw their favourite farm animal	Teaching points (what you will do and say to support learning) Model the activity. Talk about how to control the mouse and how to change colour, etc.

Opportunities to recap/share/reinforce children's learning Children to print off their work to share with the other children and their parents	Involvement of parents/carers Mrs . . . . (parent) to work with pairs on the computers	Links to other areas of learning Creative Development

Planning to address the different areas of learning and development in the EYFS

Personal, Social and Emotional Development

Your planning should include opportunities for children to:

- become more self-confident; to express themselves and articulate their interests, preferences, thoughts and ideas;
- share their experiences with their peers and adults, identifying and recognizing their achievements and strengths, including perseverance and self-control;
- demonstrate concern for others (e.g. helping to clean up, or looking after someone in the playground);
- share resources with others;
- become more self-reliant (e.g. by encouraging them to learn their address and telephone number, to become increasingly proficient in dressing themselves after PE, and to make decisions about their work, such as when and where to seek help and support);
- become more responsible (e.g. by observing conventions and routines in the nursery/classroom such as following basic safety rules).

⇨

Communication, Language and Literacy

Your planning should include opportunities for children to develop their speaking and listening skills through:

- listening and responding to stories and rhymes;
- showing their understanding of stories by predicting outcomes;
- responding appropriately to questions;
- repeating words;
- naming letter characters and sounds;
- following simple directions;
- describing personal experiences and retelling familiar stories.

Your planning should include opportunities for children to develop their reading and writing skills through:

- identifying signs and labels;
- learning names;
- imitating writing;
- using gestures and tone of voice to communicate meaning more effectively;
- showing awareness of the conventions of written material (e.g. left to right, spaces between words, upper and lower case letters);
- identifying key features of books (e.g. title, pictures);
- using key features to understand and tell stories;
- contributing words and sentences to a narrative scribed by the teacher;
- writing simple messages (e.g. printing letters in the alphabet, writing their own name and familiar names, and simple words such as 'dog' and 'cat').

Problem Solving, Reasoning and Numeracy

Your planning should include opportunities for children to increase their understanding through:

- demonstrating their understanding of whole numbers;
- measuring (e.g. comparing length, weight, mass, capacity and awareness of time);
- identifying characteristics of simple two- and three-dimensional shapes;
- recognizing and using patterns;
- collecting, showing and understanding simple data.

Knowledge and Understanding of the World

Your planning should include opportunities for children to:

- show curiosity and enthusiasm for investigating and exploring;
- develop their concepts of place and time;
- demonstrate awareness and concern for living things and the environment;
- learn about the properties of familiar materials;
- take some responsibility for planning and organizing their work with support;
- become familiar with technology (including ICT).

Physical Development

Your planning should include opportunities for children to:

- practise personal hygiene;
- show awareness of safe and unsafe situations and resources (e.g. sharp scissors, large apparatus);
- participate in regular physical activity including dance and movement;
- use a wide range of large and small apparatus to develop gross and fine motor control (e.g. bicycles, climbing frames, barrels, balls, crayons, paint brushes, scissors);
- improve their balance, agility and spatial awareness (e.g. running and jumping, using scooters and other riding toys, using climbing frames).

Creative Development

Your planning should include opportunities for children to:

- express their thoughts and feelings using a wide range of media;
- experiment with and investigate tools, techniques and materials;
- perform (e.g. using puppet theatres, making music, dancing);
- learn songs and rhymes;
- enact and re-enact stories in the structured play area;
- respond appropriately to the tempo and mood of music (e.g. fast, slow, scary, happy);
- learn about the visual arts (e.g. colour, shape and size).

Planning to teach the National Curriculum

The following section gives a brief outline of the progression through long-, medium- and short-term planning using National Curriculum Programmes of Study, National Literacy and Numeracy Strategies and includes examples from primary settings.

Long-term planning: schemes of work

Long-term planning provides broad frameworks outlining the curriculum to be taught during a child's time in the school. Long-term planning of this sort ought to reflect the school policies and the whole staff should be involved in developing and approving the final versions. Schools draw up schemes of work to cover the full range of National Curriculum subject areas, to address coherence, continuity and progression across the various subjects and between year groups and Key Stages. Schemes of work contain:

- the content that needs to be covered within the different year groups (based on National Curriculum Programmes of Study or National Literacy/National Numeracy Strategy statements);
- the organization of that content into manageable and coherent sections;
- identification of any real links between the various aspects of the curriculum; and
- the balance between, and time available for, the various subjects and areas of learning.

Long-term planning may also be used by schools in areas such as transition between nursery and school, induction arrangements for new children, and themes, festivals and visits to be incorporated into the curriculum at various times during the year (see Chapter 1 concerning policies and guidelines).

Long term planning

Year 1

Year 2

Year 3

Breadth of study
The Victorians
Local study

Historical knowledge, skills and understanding
- Characteristic features of Victorian period (ideas, beliefs, attitudes and experiences) (2a)
- Identifying and describing reasons for and results of industrial developments in Victorian period (2c)
- Investigating how an aspect of the local area has changed over a long period of time (7)
- Learning to use a range of sources for historical enquiry (4a)
- Selecting, recording and organizing historical information (5a)
- Communicating historical knowledge and understanding in a variety of ways (5c).

Medium-term planning

Medium-term planning covers the details of the programme to be taught to a particular year group (normally) over a term or half-term period. Such planning is based on the school's long-term plans. It should involve the whole year group team within a school. Medium-term plans show where work is continuing, blocked or linked in nature (SCAA, 1995).

Continuing, blocked and linked work

- **Continuing work**: work drawn from single subject area and on going across the year.
- **Blocked work**: work drawn from a single subject, taught within a set period of time, characterized by a tight subject focus with a discrete body of knowledge, skills and understanding.
- **Linked work**: work drawn from 2 or 3 subject areas, intended to increase the coherence of the curriculum by building on common or complementary knowledge, skills and understanding across the subjects involved.

(SCAA, 1995)

Medium-term plan: Geography

Learning objectives (inc. NC PoS)	Assessment of outcomes	Activity and organization
Where do I live? How do I get to school? NC Geog 1d, 4a, 7a,	**Criteria**: Do children know and understand their own address? Draw conclusions from a graph? **Mode**: Work produced and observations	Children to write their own addresses and display these on a large map of the area. Discuss with the children who live the furthest/nearest to school. With the children carry out survey and complete a graph of how children travel to school.
How do I get to school? NC Geog 1d, 2e, 3b	**Criteria**: Can children draw a simple map? **Mode**: Children's work	Children to draw a map of their route from home to school and then describe to a partner, following the map.
What can we see in the local area around school? NC Geog 3a, 3b, 3c	**Criteria**: Can children recall physical and human features in their locality? **Mode**: Observation/Questioning	Children to look at pictures of the locality and describe the features. Children to group them in sets, near and far, buildings and features, and place them in the sequence they are seen on the route to school.
What was my school like long ago? NC Geog 1a, 5a,	**Criteria**: Can children ask geographical questions? **Mode**: Observation	Children to prepare questions to ask the visitor about the school and the local area. Listen to speaker and look at a range of artefacts, photographs and pictures.
What are our immediate surroundings like? NC Geog 1c, 2b, 5b	**Criteria**: Can the children: Describe features of the local environment? Express their opinions on the features? Identify changes in the locality? **Mode**: Questioning	Walk around the local area and school using a map (take digital photographs) to identify main features and changes. Discuss: the quality of the features and the environment; what the children like or dislike about the local area.
What are the changes taking place in our area? NC Geog 3c, 4b, 5a	**Criteria**: Can children identify how things change for better or worse over time? **Mode**: Observation/ Questioning/Work	Discuss the changes taking place using the photographs. With help of the children mark these on the large map. Discuss whether the children think these changes are good or bad. Draw a plan how they would like the school and local area to look in the future.

Medium-term plans:

- state the learning objectives drawn from the long-term plans indicating progression through the programme;
- indicate the resources needed where some form of advance action will be required, such as booking loan materials from libraries and museums;
- suggest teaching methods and ways of organizing the children;
- include opportunities for assessment.

Pupil outputs	Special resources needed	Links
• Write address • Represent various types of travel on a graph	Large map of area Computers	Maths ICT
• Draw a map showing the route • Recognize where places are	Large map of area	Literacy
• Identify sequence of features seen on their route to school • Describe the features	Pictures of locality	
• Prepared geographical questions • Used secondary sources of information	Visitor to bring artefacts, pictures and photographs	History
• Use a range of words and photographs to show their view on the environment • Know about the changes • Use digital camera	Additional adult support Digital cameras	ICT
• Realize that the process of change is continual • Develop understanding of chronology • Draw a plan	Photographs/pictures	History

Short-term planning

This focuses upon daily and/or weekly teaching and assessment. Short-term planning is derived from medium-term planning but is more specific and detailed, showing:

- clear learning purposes;
- key skills, concepts and vocabulary to be introduced or reinforced;

Short-term plan

Literacy Weekly Planner

Class: 3   **Year**: 1   **Term**: Autumn 2nd half   **Week Beginning**:   **Teacher**:

Phonic, spelling and vocabulary	Grammar and punctuation	Comprehension and composition
4. To discriminate and segment all three phonemes in CVC words.	6. To begin using the term sentence to identify sentences in text.	7. To re-enact stories in a variety of ways, e.g. through role-play and puppets.
9. To read on sight other familiar words; (house, little, then, three, once, so).		5. To describe story settings and incidents and relate them to own experience and that of others.

	Whole-class- shared reading and writing	Whole-class phonics, spelling, vocabulary and grammar	Guided group tasks	Guided group tasks
Mon	Introduce text: *Three Little Pigs*. Cover, title, familiar words.	Using large letters, show an object and children to make the word.	Guided reading White group	Familiar reading Yellow group
Tues	*Three Little Pigs*. Talk about story setting and incidents. Children to give input.	Read familiar words (house, little, then, three, once, so).	Guided reading Blue group	Familiar reading Green group
Weds	*Three Little Pigs*. Children to sequence the events in the story and me to write it on the whiteboard.	Use whiteboards to get children to write CVC words and practise letter formation.	Children to write and sequence the important events that happened in the story.	
Thurs	*Three Little Pigs*. Show a section of text without full stop and capital letters. Identify sentences.	Read familiar words; (house, little, three, then once, so).	Children to identify sentences. Put in full stops and capital letters.	
Fri	Handwriting in writing books.	CVC words (house, little, then, three, once, so).	Handwriting in books.	

- the nature of any adult intervention;
- how activities are to be differentiated;
- clear progression through the lesson from introduction to conclusion;
- the resources that will be needed;
- how and what is to be assessed;
- where feedback to children will be given.

Tasks

	Guided	Familiar	Phonics	ICT	Role-play	
Mon 11.30	White	Yellow	Blue	Green	Red	Phonic work – children to complete CVC Worksheet on 'e, o, u'
Tues 9.50	Blue	Green	White	Red	Yellow	ICT – children to write familiar captions from the *Three Little Pigs*. Using familiar words (house, little, three, then, once, so)
Weds 9.50	Red	White	Yellow	Blue	Green	Role-Play – children to re-enact the story of the *Three Little Pigs* using masks and puppets
Thurs 1.15	Green	Blue	Red	Yellow	White	
Fri 1.15	Yellow	Red	Green	White	Blue	

Group tasks			Plenary
Phonics work Blue group	ICT Green group	Role-play Red group	Look at ICT and phonic work
Phonics work White group	ICT Red group	Role-play Yellow group	Look at ICT and phonic work
		→	Read a selection of the children's writing
		→	Check sentences for full stops and capital letters
		→	Re-read the story of the *Three Little Pigs*

Lessons need clear objectives or learning purposes which indicate what the children are going to learn or practise. Trainee and newly qualified teachers need to be clear about the distinction between the purposes of a lesson and the activity that the children will do, and sharing these learning purposes with the children can help them to achieve the intended outcomes. There may be many possible activities that would allow children to achieve a particular learning objective. Learning purposes, moreover, should not be too numerous. It is both inappropriate and unreasonable to expect children in this age group to meet large numbers of learning objectives in any one lesson or session.

Literacy session plan

Day: Wednesday	**Subject:** English – literacy hour	**Class:** 3 Yr 1
Date:	**Theme:** Three Little Pigs	**Set/Group:** Whole class

Lesson objective/s:	NC/NLS/NNS ref:
• Discriminate and segment all three phonemes in CVC words • Identify and describe characters, events and settings in fiction • Use their knowledge of sequence and story language when they are retelling stories and predicting events • Sequence events and recount them in appropriate detail • Encourage children to use the text they read as models for their own writing • Write familiar words and attempt unfamiliar ones	NC KS1 En En2– 3a, 3b En3 – 1b, 1f, 2a NLS – word level objective 4

Time	Teaching strategies	Pupil tasks and learning outcomes	Support adult/s
Start:	Settle the children on the carpet in their literacy places.	Children to sit on the carpet in their literacy places.	
10.50 am	**Whole class – word work** • Explain task – children to listen carefully to words so that they can identify the phonemes (letters) and then write the word accurately on their whiteboard. Look at the word they have written and check letter formation. (Stress the importance of letter formation.) • Hand out whiteboards, pens and cloths to the children. • Read list of words, stressing phonemes. Each time wait for all children to finish then get the children to hold up their board and show the word. Check letter formation. • Collect whiteboards, pens and cloths.	• Children to pass along the whiteboards, etc. • Children to listen carefully and then write the word concentrating on the formation of their letters. • Children to hand in equipment.	NTA to assist with distribution and collection of equipment.
11.05 am	**Whole class – text work** • Ask the children to identify week's story. • Ask the children to recount events in the story. • Introduce the idea of putting the events in order of occurrence. Check children's understanding of ordering/sequencing events. Discuss. • Introduce the pictures from the story and explain that we need to put them in the correct order. Ask individual children for contributions. • Introduce group/independent work.	• Children to think about what the answer might be before putting up their hand with a suggestion. • Children to make suggestions about the meaning of 'ordering'.	

Time	Teaching strategies	Pupil tasks and learning outcomes	Support adult/s
11.20 am	**Group or independent work** Children to sit in their literacy groups. Children to think about the order of the important events within the story. Children to: • choose four key events in the story; • draw a picture of the event; • write a sentence to explain what is happening. White group – independent work Blue group – independent work Green group – teacher supervised work. Yellow group – teacher supervised work. Red group – series of pictures from the story, to be ordered. The children to talk through the story with NTA before choosing four key events and completing worksheet with support.	Children to think about the story and the important events, reflecting on what was done as a class. Children to choose four of the main events and record them in the correct order, drawing a picture and then writing an accompanying sentence.	 NTA to work with Red group.
	Extension More able children to write their own ending for the story.		
Session ends:	**Plenary** Individual children to show their work to the rest of the class, reading what they have written.		

Assessment
Criteria: Can the children:
• discriminate and segment all three phonemes in CVC words;
• sequence events and recount them in appropriate detail;
• write familiar words and attempt unfamiliar ones.

Mode:
Outcome and observations of individual children

Resources
• Whiteboards, pens and cloths
• Large pictures from the story
• Five sets of small pictures from the story
• Pencil/pencil crayons

Vocabulary
• Order or sequence
• Familiar words, house, little, three, then, once, so

Monitoring, assessing, recording and reporting

All teachers need to be proficient at monitoring and assessing children's learning, as well as recording and reporting on their progress. Teachers have always made judgements about their pupils and have used those judgements in structuring their future teaching. The results of assessment are an integral and indispensable part of the teaching and learning process. However, the introduction of the National Curriculum and the Early Years Foundation Stage, coupled with the increasing pressures associated with monitoring and public accountability, have greatly increased the amount of time and rigour being applied to this aspect of the teacher's role.

✔ **Audit**

By the end of this section you should:

- know about using different kinds of assessment for different purposes;
- know about alternative forms and methods of assessing children;
- know about different ways of recording children's progress systematically;
- know about marking and monitoring children's work; providing constructive oral and written feedback; and about some of the more common misconceptions and errors that children can hold and make;
- know about the statutory assessment and reporting requirements and know how to prepare and present informative reports to parents;
- know about Standard Assessment Tasks and tests (SATs) and the Foundation Stage Profile.

Why monitoring and assessing matter

The primary purposes of assessment are first, to improve the quality of teaching and learning; and second, to enable schools and nurseries to report on children's progress and provide summative information on their achievements. Assessment benefits all those involved in the education of young children, including the teachers and other professionals, the children themselves, and their parents.

For teachers, assessment provides a better understanding of children's learning. It offers a way to ensure progression and greater continuity for pupils as the results of assessment provide more reliable information upon which to plan the next step of a teaching programme. Assessment produces information on individual pupil experience, achievement and progress across the curriculum, identifying what children know, understand and can do. The results of assessment also provide teachers with a more valid base for evaluating the curriculum, helping them to monitor and raise standards (Hunter-Carsch, 2002). Assessment is helpful to children by enhancing their motivation and confidence through the promotion of accurate and constructive feedback from the teacher in the form of short-term learning targets and the identification of future learning needs. Assessment is also helpful for parents and others, including future teachers and the wider community, who wish to evaluate the effectiveness of a nursery/school through teachers' reports (both verbal and written) or test results. Assessment, for example, can provide information on pupil attainment to date that can be used to make the transition within and between schools more streamlined.

Purposes of assessment

Assessing children involves more than simply looking at the work they produce. Teachers also need to employ their observation and questioning skills in order to ascertain what children know, what they can do and where they need to go next. Assessment serves a variety of purposes and it is important to realize that the boundaries between the different forms are permeable; considerable overlap is possible. It can be difficult, for example, to determine whether assessment is summative or formative in nature as different teachers may wish to use the same information for different purposes.

Some assessments will be **summative** in nature and result in statements about what a child has achieved at a particular point in time, for example, on transition from the nursery to the reception class, or at the end of Key Stage 1. These assessments are sometimes referred to as assessment *of* learning (AoL). A summative assessment constitutes a record of the overall achievement of a pupil in a systematic way and can be used to answer the following questions:

- How well do children understand certain ideas or concepts?
- What level of attainment have the children reached?
- Are the children ready to move on to the next level?

Summative assessment sheet

Name:
Date of birth:
Admission date:

English

AT1: Speaking and listening comments	Rec.	Y1
Y2		
Level 1		
Talks about matters of immediate interest		
Listens to others		
Responds appropriately		

$\Rightarrow$

		Rec.	Y1
Conveys simple meaning to range of listeners			
Speaks audibly			
Extends ideas and accounts by providing some detail			
Conveys/remembers a simple message			

Level 2   Rec.   Y1
Y2

		Rec.	Y1
Shows confidence when talking and listening			
Listens carefully			
Responds with increasing appropriateness to what others say			
Develops and explains ideas			
Speaks clearly and uses a growing vocabulary			
Includes relevant detail for needs of listener			
Conveys/remembers a more complex message			
Is aware of a more formal vocabulary and tone of voice			

Level 3   Rec.   Y1
Y2

		Rec.	Y1
Talks and listens confidently in different contexts			
Shows careful listening through relevant comment and questions			
Communicates and explores ideas in discussions, shows understanding of main points			
Adapts what they say to needs of listener varying use of vocabulary and level of detail			
Is aware of standard English and when it is used			

Summative assessments have an importance that extends beyond the nursery/classroom in which they were made by providing information that is of use and interest to the whole school, the child's next school, parents and others. One example of summative assessment is the use of Standard Assessment Tasks and tests (SATs) that children take at the end of Key Stage 1. Schools can combine information from local and national SATs results with details of their own results to identify future targets for pupil achievement in the school. Although its primary purpose is not to inform the next step, the knowledge gained from summative assessment can be used in this way by subsequent teachers. An example of summative assessment being used formatively would be the use of reception teacher assessments (Foundation Stage Profile) by subsequent Year 1 teachers to inform their planning and preparation at the beginning of the year.

Summative assessment

Pupil name: Shaida

Year group: Reception

Language and literacy

Shaida always listens attentively and makes good contributions in class discussions. She loves reading and can read a range of texts independently. She is beginning to use a variety of strategies to tackle unfamiliar words and shows understanding of the main points of the book. Shaida is being encouraged to write at greater length and to extend her ideas. She can structure a simple story or account, and spell simple words correctly. Her handwriting is legible and she is working towards the more consistent use of upper and lower case letters.

Mathematics

Shaida has a good grasp of early number concepts in addition and subtraction to 20, and is developing mental recall of these facts. She has completed measurement activities involving length, weight and capacity and can use non-standard units. She can sort and classify objects and name and describe the properties of simple two-dimensional shapes. She can continue and make repeating patterns involving shape and colour with two changes.

Other areas of experience

In classroom tasks, Shaida has made observations, talked about her findings and made recordings of these in words and pictures. She can recognize similarities and differences in living things and objects, and demonstrates a good general knowledge. She draws, paints, cuts and makes with care and has plenty of ideas for her work. She shows good coordination when moving on the floor and apparatus during PE lessons. She likes to sing and can play percussion instruments.

Personal, Social and Emotional Development

Shaida has made excellent progress in all curriculum areas, most notably in English and mathematics. She settles quickly to tasks, works hard and takes part in all areas of school life with growing confidence and a happy disposition. She is helpful and reliable and an asset to the class. I am sure that Shaida will continue to build on this super start. She is a pleasure to teach.

Number of attendances out of total number possible 312: 300

Number of unauthorized absences: 0

This report may be discussed with . . . . on . . . .

at . . . .

Summative assessments have their uses as measures of performance. However, there can be limitations to some of these measurements. In the case of SATs, for example, they cannot hope to measure more than a small part of a child's overall capability. A further limitation of summative assessment is its limited use in assisting teachers who are seeking to identify and respond to the learning needs of their pupils during the course of the year; to do this teachers need to engage in ongoing formative and diagnostic assessment.

Assessment ought to take place on a regular basis; it should be ongoing throughout the school year not just intermittently at the end of term, year or Key Stage. It is a continual process, sometimes referred to as assessment *for* learning (AfL). **Formative assessment** is used to inform the next stage in a child's learning. Its purpose is to recognize the achievements of a pupil so that these might be discussed and the appropriate next steps taken. **Diagnostic assessment** occurs when teachers seek to scrutinize and classify learning difficulties so that appropriate guidance can be given and intervention can take place. Formative assessment therefore is about where the child has progressed to; diagnostic assessment looks at why a child is not progressing. Both inform the next step in terms of what the children should be learning and how to teach it. Formative/diagnostic assessment can be used to answer the following questions:

- What do the children know/not know about a topic/subject?
- What do they know/not know about specific ideas/skills/procedures?
- Are any aspects of the topic causing problems for children?
- Can the children apply learning in new situations?
- Do the children hold any misconceptions?
- Is the pace and level of teaching set at appropriate levels?

Assessing a little bit at a time on a regular basis using systematic observation (watching, listening and talking to the children) is one method of assessing formatively/diagnostically. Teachers and schools also retain samples of pupils' work and/or photographs as a source of concrete evidence to support formative/diagnostic judgements based on these observations. It is, however, easy to allow the focus of assessment to be on the outcomes of a lesson rather than the process. It may seem easier to make judgements about the accuracy of a piece of writing than to assess how it was produced, but for useful diagnosis it is helpful for teachers to have some idea of both. Failure to diagnose difficulties accurately means that the identification of suitable future tasks and differentiation are harder to do. Teachers therefore review work with children to gain insight into processes as well as the products and use neutral or open-ended questions to get quality responses when making formative/diagnostic assessments of children. Children can be asked to report on their progress and what they have done so far. Similarly they can be questioned about how they completed an activity or accomplished a task.

Assessment can also be used to evaluate and influence policy and practice in a school or nursery on a wider scale than merely the planning of follow-up lessons or topics by individual teachers. This type of **evaluative assessment** is used to determine the extent to which the goals of the wider teaching programme are appropriate for the pupils and how effective the teaching programme is in achieving these goals. Evaluation involves making a judgement of some kind based on the information obtained through assessment which provides a more valid base for these judgements than the use of impression alone. The results of assessment therefore can be helpful in keeping track of the breadth and balance of the curriculum and in ensuring progression and continuity in children's learning as they move through the school from nursery and reception, to Key Stage 1 and on to Year 3.

An evaluative assessment of reading materials

Mrs Wilson was appointed to the post of English Coordinator in a primary school. Part of her responsibilities included monitoring and overseeing the loan of reading books to pupils for homework tasks. Parents were asked to help their children and the school by indicating in a report book what the children had read, how they had coped and what they thought of the stories. When Mrs Wilson reviewed the comments from parents she realized that they were strongly negative concerning the age, quality and content of the reading material. When Mrs Wilson spoke to children about the books available she discovered a reluctance to get involved in reading at home because the books were old, tatty and 'boring'. Mrs Wilson presented her assessment of the situation to her colleagues and the headteacher, who in turn discussed the matter with the governing body. The governors decided to make funds available for the school to buy new books for homework tasks and to release Mrs Wilson for two afternoons to organize the resources and loans system.

Irrespective of whether teachers are concerned with the assessment of or for learning, assessing children in the nursery/classroom requires them to adopt a mixture of formal (i.e. planned) and informal (i.e. unplanned) approaches. **Informal assessment** is an activity in which teachers are constantly involved, providing a very wide-ranging evidence base, considered over an extended period of time. Children's work, comments and behaviour may reveal unplanned for and unanticipated evidence. It makes an invaluable contribution to formative assessment for learning and acts as the basis for a considerable amount of good quality and immediate feedback to pupils in the form of a smile, a frown, spoken comments on the amount of effort being made, or written comments on pieces of work. Informal assessment can occur as a result of looking at the concrete outcomes of activities and often occurs as a result of routine discussions and observations; indeed, it is such a normal part of classroom life that it can be overlooked and is sometimes undervalued.

Formal assessment meanwhile takes place when teachers have planned for it, at times that have been identified and where the results will be formally recorded. While informal assessment constitutes an integral part of work with young children, a natural part of the minute-by-minute interactions in the nursery or classroom, these unplanned assessments tend to centre on those things which *draw themselves to the practitioner's attention*. While important, they do not necessarily offer a more rounded picture; they may, for example, fail to pick up the events that take place quietly. While it is not possible to assess everything that goes on in the nursery/classroom, making use of more planned, targeted and focused assessments may well serve to complement the informal, unplanned and ongoing kind as well as sharpening a practitioner's skills in this area generally. Formal assessments may, for example, challenge adult assumptions about children and their capabilities because they offer information that might otherwise be missed (Edgington, 1998, pp. 127–8).

Informal and formal assessment

Informal assessment: Unplanned observation

John and Ruth had been paired to work on a design and technology activity. It became clear to the teacher from their expressions that John was feeling self-conscious about working with a girl and that Ruth was well aware of his attitude. Although the learning objectives were centred on the subject of design and technology, the teacher had an ongoing commitment to encourage children to work constructively together. She responded immediately to her informal assessment of the situation by intervening quickly to offer encouragement and support to both children and to help them to organize themselves to tackle the activity in such a way that both children had real roles in the task.

Informal assessment: Examining work produced

Miss Lee was moving around her class of Y1/2s, who were engaged in number work activities as part of their regular numeracy hour. She noticed that two or three children were making the same mistake. She intervened to help the children to tackle the problem individually and made a note to pursue the matter with this group in a subsequent lesson.

Formal assessment: Planned observation

Mrs Jones had been conducting formal assessments of her children's scientific skills, knowledge and understanding during the week. The focus was on forces and, in particular, floating and sinking. She had arranged for non-teaching support and/or parents to be in the classroom while she assessed the children in groups. The children were testing objects in the water tank and discussing their observations and ideas with Mrs Jones, who was noting down any evidence of attainment against a checklist. She asked the children to predict which objects would float and which ones would sink. Wayne suggested that the apple would float. Mrs Jones asked him to explain why he thought this was the case. 'Because it was floating this morning, Miss.'

In addition to the mixture of formal and informal approaches, teachers also need to be able to employ both criterion- and norm-referenced systems when assessing children's learning. Assessment that is **criterion-referenced** seeks to assess pupils' achievement against a set of standards or competences, normally utilizing increasingly more demanding descriptions to judge and report on attainment. Such criteria can be helpful for teachers in sharing the purpose of the activity with the children. The National Curriculum level descriptions and Foundation Stage statements are examples of criterion-referencing; the Professional Standards for the Award of Qualified Teacher Status are another. **Norm-referenced** assessment involves making comparisons between the achievements of different children, for example *Child A finds letter formation harder than his classmates*, or *Child B is a better painter than Child C.*

It may seem that criterion-referenced assessment offers teachers a fairer, less subjective approach to assessment as it utilizes universally applied measures of attainment. Unfortunately, producing criteria or descriptions that are universally understood and unambiguous is not as easy as it might sound (Knight, 2001). Furthermore, large numbers of criteria can result in an atomized view of the curriculum making it hard on occasion to see the bigger picture. Most teachers therefore draw on both criterion-referenced and norm-referenced techniques when making assessments of young children.

Methods of assessment

When planning to assess children, teachers need to consider what they want to assess; how they will know if the children have achieved the learning objectives; and how they will collect evidence to support their judgements. The assessment methods/modes available to teachers include:

- classroom observations (watching children's actions, listening to their discussions, asking questions to check on comprehension and understanding);
- making judgements based on outcomes (models, pieces of writing, drawings, paintings, number work);
- making judgements against previous outcomes (benchmarking).

Observing children

While there will be times when children produce concrete evidence of their awareness and understanding, many of the judgements made by practitioners about young children's learning and development will be based on *classroom observations*. Such observation is integral to work with young children and is essential for their continual assessment (Hobart and Frankel, 1999). Observations can be both informal, such as watching children interacting with one another, and formal, such as structured observation to ascertain learning against a particular element of the National Curriculum Programmes of Study. Observations may involve the whole class, small groups, or individuals. These observations, such as an overheard conversation between children, or being presented with a striking piece of artwork, provide a means by which children's knowledge, skills and dispositions can be checked and explored and can help to define more clearly any individual contributions to a group task.

Although the term observation suggests passivity on the part of the teacher, the reality is usually far more active and involves more than just sitting and watching. Practitioners often have to check their observations through careful questioning, discussion and further observations. Discussing activities with children as part of classroom observation is a very useful device for locating evidence of a child's success, diagnosing learning difficulties, monitoring progress over a period of time, and developing some insight into the ways in which a particular child learns and works. An observation is akin to a *camera shot*; while it does not lie, it can distort. A child's initial response to questioning is not necessarily an accurate or reliable guide to knowledge and competence; similarly, actions and behaviour can be misinterpreted (SCAA, 1997). Consequently practitioners need to base their judgements and assessments about children's capabilities on more than one such snapshot (Sharman *et al.*, 2007).

Assessing children through observation requires good classroom organization and management, particularly where teachers wish to assess a small group of individuals in situations where non-teaching support is limited or non-existent. Assessing through observation requires attention and concentration and teachers therefore need to consider not only the child or children being assessed, but also the rest of the children in the class.

The *assessed* and the *rest*

- How involved will you become in the activity itself? Too much involvement could make collecting the evidence difficult. Sitting too close to the children can make disengagement and note-taking almost impossible. Simultaneously teaching, listening and making notes is not easy.
- How many children will you assess at any one time, and against how many learning objectives? It can be difficult to collect evidence for large numbers of children through observation and discussion. Likewise, trying to assess children against large numbers of learning objectives can become unmanageable. It is important to have a clear and uncomplicated set of objectives.
- Are the children aware of the purposes for both the task and the assessment? Explaining what you are going to be observing gives the children the chance to show if they know or can do it.
- Frequent interruptions will play havoc with your attempts to conduct assessments in the nursery/classroom. Yet young children are much more dependent upon their teachers than their older counterparts. It is important therefore to make maximum use of any learning support staff in the classroom and to plan low-intervention tasks for children where such support is limited or unavailable.
- Assessment through observation or discussion does not necessarily mean that the teacher has to be with the children being assessed at all times. Planning which considers the balance between independent activity and teacher participation or group discussion may be a useful approach to take. For example, when assessing a group of children teachers could visit the group at regular intervals of time throughout an activity, they could visit the group at fixed points in the programme of activities, or they could work down a list of the children. Whichever option is chosen, it is important to ensure that there will be sufficient time to gather the necessary information without ignoring the needs of the rest of the class.

Observations should also be made on a broad front reflecting the breadth of the 3–8 curricula. Below are some examples of indicators of progress and learning that teachers might look for; the list should in no way be seen as comprehensive. Trainee and newly qualified teachers should refer to the further sources of information at the end of this chapter to extend their knowledge and understanding.

Indicators to watch for

Possible indicators of achievement in PSED/PSHE and citizenship

The child can:

- express feelings;
- communicate appropriately in social situations;
- initiate conversations with peers and adults;
- work cooperatively with peers;
- persevere when faced with a challenge;
- cope effectively with changes in routines or staffing.

Possible indicators of achievement in Communication, Language and Literacy/English

The child can:

- ask and answer questions;
- seek information;
- participate in discussions and imaginary play;
- respond appropriately to a speaker;
- demonstrate listening behaviour;
- recall experiences/retell stories;
- model (pretend) reading; select books;
- understand that text has meaning;
- recognize familiar signs, letters, words;
- engage in reading and writing.

Possible indicators of achievement in Problem Solving, Reasoning and Numeracy/mathematics

The child can:

- form recognizable numbers and shapes;
- understand that mathematical symbols represent number and shape;
- understand and apply concepts such as behind, above, below, large, small;
- use number in everyday contexts;
- count and order;
- estimate and approximate;
- measure and make judgements.

Possible indicators of achievement in Knowledge and Understanding of the World/science, design and technology, geography, history, ICT and RE

The child can:

- use five senses and ask questions about the world;
- suggest solutions to problems;
- demonstrate an awareness of cause and effect;
- predict consequences;

- make comparisons and identify similarities and differences;
- distinguish between living and non-living things;
- identify significant places in the locality (e.g. shops, mosque, post office) and beyond;
- demonstrate an understanding of past, present and future involving people, places and events;
- make things using a range tools and materials safely and effectively; and
- incorporate ICT into play situations and use ICT to support their learning across the curriculum.

Possible indicators of achievement in Physical Development/physical education (PE)

The child can:

- move safely about the learning environment;
- participate in physical activities;
- use equipment safely and in a variety of ways;
- initiate own challenges;
- demonstrate hand–eye coordination and gross motor skills;
- demonstrate fine motor skills (e.g. manipulating scissors, pencils, construction materials);
- describe ways of keeping healthy;
- describe ways of keeping safe.

Possible indicators of achievement in Creative Development/Art and Music

The child can:

- use a range of responses in imaginary play;
- select materials for creative activities;
- participate in movement activities involving music;
- respond appropriately to different music (e.g. fast, slow, cheerful, sad);
- experiment with different art media;
- demonstrate awareness and appreciation of aesthetics, colour, shape and pattern.

Looking at children's work

The **concrete outcomes** of an activity can also be a useful guide to learning, and small collections of children's work can illustrate their attainment very effectively. Such portfolios can provide a way of displaying a range of work, not simply written or number work but also project, ICT, two- and three-dimensional creative work. Concrete outcomes assessed in conjunction with teacher–pupil discussions can be very helpful in enabling children to become more involved and take an active part in the process of assessment. This approach can help children to gain some insight into their own progress, strengths and weaknesses. It can also provide a useful starting point for setting targets for future learning.

When considering methods of assessing attainment through outcomes, teachers can also consider **benchmarking**. Benchmarking requires the teacher or the school to collect exemplar material (i.e. samples of children's work) as a way of indicating the quality of work that should be expected at different levels from particular groups of children. Benchmarking not only acts as an aid to teachers in trying to determine the level of a particular piece of work but can also provide pupils with insights into standards and expectations and can act as a spur to greater effort and higher achievement.

Many activities in 3–8 settings, however, will not result in concrete outcomes, for example much of the work that takes place in nurseries or PE. In addition, concrete products alone may prove insufficient and inconclusive as evidence of attainment. Many factors could influence the final outcome and lead teachers to misjudge children's learning. For example, where the collaborative setting actually belies the individual nature of the assessments being made, teachers will need to devise strategies for discerning individual contributions and comprehension. It can also be difficult to identify the features of a piece of work which indicate achievement and it may be necessary to support judgements made on the basis of outcomes with reference to either observations of the process or discussions of the work with the child. Look at the two examples of concrete products produced by nursery pupils. Using the Early Years Foundation Stage what assessment would you make of these children's abilities based solely on this work?

Example A: computer printout

```
DFGHJKLL;POYREW2W21ZRYUJK,MNBVC14789 632ACDKG
```

Example B: nursery drawing

Now read the commentary on the two pieces of work below. How does this information alter your assessments of the children concerned?

Assessments of concrete products

Commentary on Example A

Helen types at random using the computer keyboard and prints out her writing. She points at the screen and says to a nearby adult: 'That's my name!'
    Adult: 'Oh, have you written your name? Can you read it to me?'
    Helen: 'Helen!'

Commentary on Example B

The nursery teacher asked Ellen to tell her about the drawing. In the subsequent discussion Ellen explained that the picture represented her daily journey from home to school (a *map*, perhaps) and gave details on who she travelled with, which route she took and what things she passed on the way, for example cars. Ellen was also able to talk to the teacher about her previous experience of other modes of transport, including the aircraft.

The contribution of parents and other adults to assessment

Attempts to gain information on children's needs and abilities upon entry to nursery or school settings can be enhanced by the involvement of parents and other adults in the process of assessment. In reception classes, where staffing levels are often lower than those in nursery, good organization and planning are essential if a parental contribution is to be obtained in a timescale of use to the practitioner. Initial assessments involving parents in the nursery/classroom may necessitate provision for the care of younger siblings while discussions take place. Parents need to be reassured that the information they are supplying is for positive reasons and will not be used to discriminate against their child. Parents also need to know that in instances where special educational needs are identified some of the information they give may also be passed on to other professionals involved in the education and welfare of young children.

An early assessment sheet completed jointly by parents and the nursery teacher

Name:

Date of birth:

Admission date:

Asks questions e.g. Why? Who? When? Where? What? ☐

Independence/decision-making skills ☐

Expresses needs and wants, using speech and gestures ☐

Comments and directs, e.g. 'Come on', 'I like' ☐

Uses language in play ☐

Joins in conversations/interchanges with three or more turns ☐

Listens to and enjoys books, songs and poems ☐

Book skills ☐

Understands that print carries meaning ☐

Reads own 'writing' ☐

Can recognize own name ☐

Knows letter sounds ☐

Scribbling ☐   Writing ☐
Letter shapes ☐   Key words ☐

Colour identification
red ☐   blue ☐   yellow ☐
green ☐   orange ☐   purple ☐
black ☐   brown ☐   pink ☐
white ☐

Shape identification
square ☐ circle ☐   triangle ☐
rectangle ☐   oval ☐
star ☐

Matching
by colour ☐   by shape ☐
   by type ☐   by more than
          one attribute ☐

Sorting
by colour ☐   by shape ☐
by type ☐   by more than
         one attribute ☐

Counting 1–5 ☐   5–10 ☐
       more than 10 ☐

Number symbol/quantity ☐

Conservation of number ☐

Ordering ☐

Follows pattern and sequence ☐

Time ☐

Can order
by size ☐   big/little ☐
short/tall ☐   heavy/light ☐
full/empty ☐

Reports previous experiences ☐

Identifies and describes similarities and differences ☐

Reasoning skills ☐

Ability to predict ☐

Play
Solitary ☐ Parallel ☐ Cooperative ☐
Exploratory ☐   Self-pretend ☐
     Sequence pretend ☐

Fine motor skills e.g. threading, small construction, pencil, brush, glue spreader, scissors ☐

Gross motor skills
coordination ☐   balancing ☐
climbing ☐   riding ☐
catching ☐   kicking ☐
throwing ☐

The parental contribution to assessment can also continue after transition has taken place and parents can keep teachers informed of their children's achievements through ongoing contacts such as parent meetings, curriculum events and working alongside practitioners in the classroom.

In addition to the contribution that parents and carers can make to assessment, learning support staff (e.g. nursery nurses, learning mentors, TAs and HLTAs) can play an invaluable role in monitoring and reporting on young children's achievements and progress with the help of clipboards, post-it notes and observation notebooks. The teacher cannot be everywhere at once and the involvement of the whole team under the guidance of the teacher makes the task of focusing on groups and individuals much more manageable in terms of creating time and opportunities to observe and talk with the children. Furthermore, given the importance of establishing a team approach to the teaching of young children, assessment that excludes all but the teacher from making judgements about children's learning is likely to undermine the team.

Some principles of assessment

- Make assessment an integral part of the learning and teaching in your nursery/classroom.
- Be clear about why you are assessing children. Enabling them to progress should have a high priority in these deliberations.
- Make sure the assessment allows pupils to demonstrate the appropriate skills, knowledge and/or attitudes.
- Assessment should not be limited to academic attainment alone. It should also provide information on progress in a child's development as an effective learner, including physical, social and emotional development.
- Share the results of assessment with pupils and parents in order to improve confidence and motivation.
- Remember that parents, carers and non-teaching colleagues can make a valuable contribution to assessment.
- Assess using a variety of methods and in a variety of contexts depending on the needs and capabilities of the children and the nature of what is being assessed. This diversity will:
  - help to minimize possible bias in assessment;
  - provide a more balanced picture of children's capabilities;
  - help to allow for the age and level of pupils;
  - take into account children whose first language is not English;
  - be more sensitive to the sometimes different interests of boys and girls; and
  - acknowledge the fact that the context in which assessment takes place can have a significant impact upon children's performance.

Recording and reporting on the results of assessment

Recording young children's learning and experiences is an inevitable concomitant of assessment and evaluation. All schools and nurseries have to keep up-to-date records of children's progress and achievements. Since the introduction of the National Curriculum and the Foundation Stage Profile the scale of recording and reporting has greatly increased, sometimes in response to the demand for accountability rather than in recognition of the role it plays in the teaching and learning process.

Recording

There is a great deal of guidance available to 3–8 teachers on recording systems but no universally imposed one. Although this approach has been beneficial in allowing for flexibility, it has also led some nurseries and schools to overestimate what is needed. Some 3–8 teachers spend considerable amounts of time trying to meet the requirements of unnecessarily complicated systems whose creation owes more to worries over increasing teacher accountability rather than to the need to inform teachers, pupils and others about children's progress.

Purposes of record-keeping

- To inform future teaching, enabling teachers to develop and evaluate their teaching programmes.
- To ensure that the school or nursery has an accurate and up-to-date profile of individual children's learning.
- To provide the basis for reporting to parents and carers about the children's achievements and development.
- To inform future teachers about a child's progress, needs, interests and capabilities, facilitating transition within and between schools.
- To help teachers in monitoring pupil progress over time, revealing patterns or problems and underpinning summative statements.
- To inform discussions with children on target-setting.
- To provide evidence for a review of nursery/school policies and practices.

Recording children's progress often involves collating notes from observations and the collection of samples of children's work as evidence to support statements about attainment. The latter can be problematic at times for teachers working with the youngest children where much of their learning and development does not always result in a concrete product and could well be demonstrated outside the confines of the nursery/classroom, for example during a break time, while on a visit or in an assembly. Fortunately new technologies such as digital cameras offer ways round some of these difficulties. Primary pupils, however, are more likely to produce a wide range of concrete evidence on which teachers can base their judgements, including drawings or sketches, computer printouts, digital photographs, written work, graphs and charts, junk models, clay work, diagrams, paintings, diaries, plans and posters.

The evidence collected ought to arise from a broad range of activities. This increases the chances of making accurate judgements concerning the whole child and not simply about a narrow range of subject specific skills and knowledge. A narrow range of learning approaches therefore will lead to a more impoverished evidence base. That said, teachers recording and collecting everything the children say or do is simply not practicable; excessive amounts of evidence are unwieldy and teaching would grind to a halt. Good records are a compromise between what is informative and what is manageable. Teachers should therefore provide sufficient evidence to back their judgements. A minimum amount of useful evidence should be the aim and 3–8 teachers will need to decide what to collect and how long to retain it. Evidence collected over an extended period of time is in some cases likely to be superseded by subsequent examples, and so the evidence base needs to be reviewed from time to time.

Not only are practitioners involved in the completion of records but they also need to make use of the information being provided. This may seem an obvious, not to say trite, statement; however, it is the case that some teachers like to form their own impressions of pupils and feel that others' records and evidence of past performance will colour their judgement. Yet subjective judgement is not eliminated by not looking at records and first impressions are no more reliable than any other impression. In addition, past performance ought to be the starting point for future teaching and learning. If teachers are not going to use the previous teacher's records it undermines the whole basis for keeping them.

In part, some of the records kept by schools and nurseries will be formed by planning documents; these will provide information on the timing and content of topics that the children have experienced. Schemes of work and lesson/session plans are a form of record, albeit of future intentions. Such whole-school/nursery planning greatly reduces the need for individual teachers to spend time recording coverage of the curriculum. A session/lesson plan that has been modified or adjusted in the light of experience in order to better address the learning needs of the children also forms a concrete record of how assessment has been used to inform future teaching.

A very common approach to recording children's learning and the activities and elements of the curriculum that they have experienced or completed is to make use of *tick lists/tick charts*. However, although they are relatively quick to use, a tick means only that a child has done something; it does not necessarily indicate the level of performance or achievement. Tick lists/tick charts also have an additional problem in that they can become very long and unwieldy. They can be made more informative and have the capacity to record not just what has been covered but also the degree of success or achievement by using more than one symbol or by including a comments box.

All teachers keep *written records* of some kind and often use notebooks, clipboards or post-it notes to jot down incidents and observations. Given the hectic and dynamic nature of 3–8 settings it is often impossible to remember the details of observations for any length of time; indeed, it is possible to forget the detail of a child's remark by the end of a busy day, let alone a term. However, it is neither necessary nor desirable to note down everything as it happens and teachers need to exercise their professional judgement as to what is useful to record and what is needless paperwork. Some written comments may be placed directly onto children's work and thus form part of teachers' constructive feedback to pupils on their progress and attainment (see pp. 201–2).

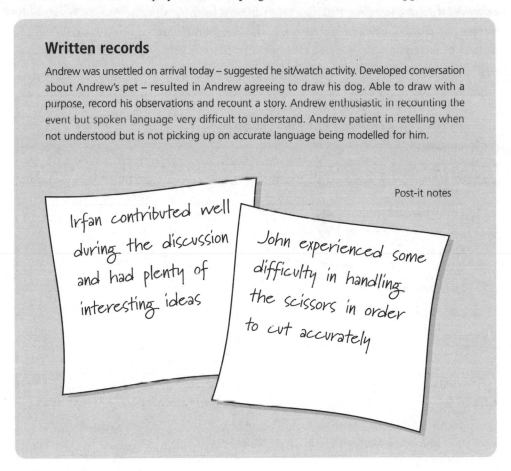

Written records

Andrew was unsettled on arrival today – suggested he sit/watch activity. Developed conversation about Andrew's pet – resulted in Andrew agreeing to draw his dog. Able to draw with a purpose, record his observations and recount a story. Andrew enthusiastic in recounting the event but spoken language very difficult to understand. Andrew patient in retelling when not understood but is not picking up on accurate language being modelled for him.

Post-it notes

Irfan contributed well during the discussion and had plenty of interesting ideas

John experienced some difficulty in handling the scissors in order to cut accurately

Many schools and nurseries compile **portfolios** or **Records of Achievement and Experience (RAE)**. Portfolios of pupils' work, selected by the teacher, show children's achievements to date and can include information across the curriculum, not just on core subjects. Compiling portfolios of work can be time-consuming for teachers and there is a danger of duplication, especially where the children's workbooks contain much of this evidence already. However, collections of work of this sort provide concrete evidence in support of the judgements and assessments that teachers are making. Just as importantly they enable teachers to go back in time. Reviewing children's previous work contained in a portfolio can be an illuminating activity for teachers and can provide graphic evidence of both progress and regression.

Records of Achievement and Experience (RAE) offer a more child-centred approach to the use of portfolios for monitoring achievement insofar as the child selects the examples/ evidence for inclusion in the portfolio, in discussion with the teacher. This approach is useful as a way of encouraging children to take greater responsibility for their own learning and to get involved in self-assessment. Furthermore, such records will not be restricted to achievement in school, but can also include successes beyond this context. However, as with other portfolios, compiling RAE can be a time-consuming process not least because the samples need to be reviewed and updated with the children each term. It is a good idea to dispose of or send home outdated examples of children's achievements in the interests of accuracy and manageability.

Record of Achievement and Experience

Reception

I like to . . .

I don't like to . . .

I know these colours

red

blue

yellow

purple

green

orange

I can draw this picture

I can . . .

build with bricks

go to the toilet on my own

ride a bike

do a jigsaw

say a nursery rhyme

play with my friend

sing songs

put on my own coat and shoes

count to 5

My favourite story is

My favourite song is

I can write my own name

Some principles of recording

Records should:

- show individual progress and achievements, and indicate areas for improvement;
- be accessible for all those using them, including colleagues, parents and other adults with a right to the information and, in the case of Records of Achievement and Experience (RAE), the pupils themselves;
- be ongoing and cumulative in nature, based on regular assessment in the form of systematic observations, discussions, directed tasks and tests;
- be linked to evidence which supports the judgements recorded;
- be kept up-to-date and be manageable for teachers, allowing information to be included and retrieved quickly and easily;
- be used by future teachers.

Reporting to children: marking, giving constructive feedback and responding to misconceptions and errors

Discussions between teachers and pupils on their progress take place every minute of every day in most nurseries and schools. By utilizing their communication skills effectively teachers can do much to provide accurate, helpful and motivating feedback for children. It is not just a matter of what is communicated but also how. Using positive phrases and statements in relation to difficult tasks can help to reduce children's fear of failure and let them see that challenges are actually good, interesting, exciting and, once overcome, represent progress (DfES, 2004b). Teachers also need to be aware of the non-verbal messages they give to children as well as the oral and written feedback that they provide. Their body language, facial expression and gestures can all be used to reinforce and emphasize the messages they give to children about their achievements and what they need to focus on in the future. While much of this feedback is informal and constitutes part of the normal, everyday exchanges in the classroom, it is possible to institute more formal approaches by dedicating time to joint target-setting and self-appraisal/assessment with children; even quite young children can get involved less formally in this type of self-assessment and reporting.

Marking is an important, although time-consuming, aspect of providing constructive feedback to children and it sends an important message to the children about the importance of what they are doing. Marking also enables teachers to monitor what the children have done and to assess where they need to go next. Marking as children are working helps teachers to notice learning needs and to set learning targets in an ongoing and formative fashion. However, in a classroom where there may be as many as 30 pupils it is unreasonable to expect the teacher to be marking everywhere at once. If teachers attempt to do all their marking in this way they may not leave themselves with any time to discuss pupils' attainment. Furthermore, as children get older and are able to cover increasing quantities of work, the task of marking as the lesson proceeds becomes increasingly challenging.

> It was Jaspers birthday aN he
> went to the shopAe Lookdt at
> the toys. He got a Little
> cat Just like him.
>
> 13.7.99

> could read his own writing, and spell cvc words.

> Well done
> You can work
> more quickly

In some instances (where there are clear right and wrong answers) children can be encouraged to do some of their own marking. While there is always a danger that some children may adjust their answers to obtain perfect scores, their peers will normally alert the teacher to what is going on. In situations where judgements are more subjective, teachers will need to adopt an approach that is manageable by marking sufficient work during the lesson to ensure that encouragement and direction are possible, without trying to do everything and be everywhere at once. In these circumstances teachers need to make sure that they vary their focus to ensure that all the children experience this ongoing feedback on a regular basis even though they may not all receive it at the same time.

Reporting to pupils: marking and offering constructive feedback

- Find something positive to say or write (see p. 199 for suggestions).
- Share and set targets with the children at the start of an activity, for example 'Today I want you to remember to use capital letters at the start of a sentence'. Identify future targets/goals for children to work towards at the end of the session/lesson.
- Try to use your feedback to help the children improve and develop; make sure your comments include references to any learning objectives.
- Where children are self-marking, conduct spot checks from time to time to inhibit cheating and to ensure opportunities for feedback to children on their performance. Offer praise and recognition for honesty and keep reinforcing the message that only honest self-marking is of any value.
- Praise effort and achievement at the end of the lesson or day by telling the rest of the class when a child has tried especially hard or been particularly successful.

Misconceptions

Trainee and newly qualified 3–8 teachers need to appreciate that children's mistakes or misconception may actually constitute partial understanding that can, and will, become more complete as they mature and gain in experience. It is not possible in the space available to deal with this area over the whole curriculum; this section will therefore restrict itself to some general remarks on the subjects of English, mathematics and science.

In English, mistakes often arise from an incomplete understanding of grammatical rules, for example 'I weren't!' or 'Miss, we done it'. Children may also experience problems over letter formation and spelling, make errors in reading and have difficulties with punctuation. In mathematics, children may experience difficulties associated with counting on, have misunderstandings over place value, or be unclear over the order of subtraction. The use of the phrase *take away* when referring to subtraction is acceptable when young children can physically take away items such as sweets, bricks or marbles; however, they will also need a more extensive repertoire of terms including *from* and *subtract*. Some difficulties in mathematics can also arise from the fact that there may be numerous ways of asking children to do the same thing, for example 'find the sum of 1 and 5'; 'add 5 to 1'; 'add 1 and 5'; 'what number is 5 more than 1'?

In science, some pupil ideas and misconceptions can arise from the fact that, although the children are familiar with a particular word, they have only ever heard its everyday usage. They may be unaware that it also has a much more precise scientific meaning; the concept of energy is one example. Children also experience difficulties as a result of the counter-intuitive nature of some scientific ideas, for example explaining the forces acting on a ball after it has been thrown. The number of variables coupled with limited life experiences can also lead to misconceptions and incomplete understanding, for example *plants aren't living things*, how can they be, they do not move, breathe or eat, after all?

Scientific ideas encountered by 3–8 student teachers during an infant teaching practice

- Strawberries classified as animals.
- Big things sink, little things float.
- Big things are heavy, little things are light.
- We see things because light shines out of our eyes.
- Plants need to be put in a greenhouse, in the sun, in order to germinate and grow.
- Heavy objects fall faster than light objects because they are heavier.
- Seeds contain miniature plants.
- *Material* and *fabric* mean the same thing.

Having identified pupil ideas, errors and misconceptions, and having made some judgements concerning possible causes, teachers are then faced with the question of what to do about them. Young children can develop certain ideas, make errors and hold misconceptions for a variety of reasons. Language use can be at the root of some problems; teachers may be using vocabulary that is inappropriately advanced or strange to the children, or children may confuse similar-sounding words. Problems can also occur when children draw incomplete conclusions from their first-hand experiences and observations.

The teacher is more than just a provider of first-hand experiences

A group of reception children had been exploring whether a range of objects would float or sink when immersed in the water tray. Their teacher joined them and asked them to suggest how they could tell whether an object would be a floater or a sinker. The children replied that *red things sink and the other colours float*. When the teacher looked at the objects tested she realized that in this particular instance that was indeed the case.

Reporting to pupils: responding to misconceptions

- Allow for the age and maturity of the child. What might constitute an error for an 8 year old might be a reasonable level of understanding for a reception child.
- Respond in supportive and helpful ways that promote progress and do not belittle and demotivate pupils. Children can learn a lot from mistakes if they are handled in a sensitive way and are accompanied by regular experiences of success.
- Some sensitive correction can be instructive for children and may even be motivating as they feel more skilled and knowledgeable as a result. Picking up on every little error and correcting incessantly, however, is likely to make children less confident and less willing to take risks and *have a go*.
- Introduce activities and experiences that result in challenges to children's current understanding (causing disequilibrium) to encourage them to modify their ideas.
- Do not make the intellectual jump required of pupils so large that they are unable to link contrary experiences with their existing ideas.
- Remember that experience alone guarantees nothing. Be aware that some children may incorporate contrary experience into their existing schemas rather than alter the schema. Teachers need to intervene to help children develop their skills, knowledge and understanding (scaffolding). Using focused questions and making time to discuss children's experiences and ideas are useful ways of doing this.

Reporting to parents

In nurseries and infant schools where there is a high level of day-to-day contact between teachers and parents a great deal of informal and ongoing reporting is already taking place. In addition, every parent whose child is of statutory school age is entitled to an annual written report on their child's performance and achievement during the year.

Following a consultation exercise in 2001 concerning baseline assessment for reception pupils, a national system of assessment within the Foundation Stage was developed and introduced in 2002–3 (QCA, 2002). The new scheme is referred to as the Foundation Stage Profile (FSP). Practitioners contribute to the ongoing maintenance of the profile throughout a child's time in the Foundation Stage. Final completion of the profile takes place at the end of the Foundation Stage (usually during the second half of the summer term in reception) and is followed by reporting to parents before the end of the school year. Foundation Stage Profile assessments seek to identify the strengths and learning needs of individual children. This information enables future teachers to plan appropriate teaching and learning activities to meet these needs and to inform discussions with parents and staff on progress and performance. The Foundation Stage Profile aims to provide:

- a summative record of pupil attainment for parents and teachers and a formative and diagnostic tool for future Year 1 teachers;
- information that is useful to a school as a whole in helping it to plan and manage its provision in terms of curriculum and resources; and
- a benchmark against which a school and inspection teams can make judgements on the extent of pupils' progress by the end of Key Stage 1.

The FSP applies throughout the maintained sector and includes statements covering all six areas of learning contained in the Early Years Foundation Stage in an effort to properly reflect the breadth of learning in which children have been engaged. This does, however, have implications in terms of manageability as the FSP is largely based on teachers' observations of children's performance in everyday classroom activities. Manageability is a key issue as many reception classes lack the staff–pupil ratios to be found in nursery/FS1 settings, often have more than one intake during a year and include rising-5 pupils (children who will reach the age of 5 in the coming term). Recording and conducting FSP assessments in such a changing environment therefore is heavily influenced by:

- the perceived benefit to the teacher;
- the extent of the paperwork involved;
- the numbers, ages and full-time/part-time status of the children;
- the amount and quality of learning support available.

The introduction of the FSP caused concern among some practitioners who feared downward pressure and the establishment of a culture of over-assessment characterized by excessive use of tick boxes. These concerns and others were exacerbated by the manner in which the FSP was introduced whereby reception practitioners had little time to familiarize themselves with the documentation and intended procedures before having to complete the profile at the end of the year. However, the FSP does not involve testing and should be based on ongoing observations throughout the Foundation Stage, in a wide range of contexts, not simply at the end of the reception year. The FSP also gives parity of esteem to all areas of the Foundation Stage curriculum and provides for input from parents and carers and other early years practitioners (e.g. non-teaching colleagues). At the time of writing it remains to be seen whether the FSP proves to be a boon or a burden to children and their teachers. Trainee and newly qualified teachers wishing to look at the documentation that teachers have to complete, plus the guidance notes to support this process, can locate the information on the Qualification and Curriculum Authority website (www.qca.org.uk/ca/foundation/profiles).

In primary schools meanwhile annual reports have to contain brief particulars on the child's achievements in the form of a series of short statements outlining successes and areas of weakness. The report should also contain information on a pupil's general educational progress which might include remarks on behaviour and attitude as well as academic attainment.

Annual report to parents

Pupil name: Stephen

School Year:

English

Stephen always listens attentively in class discussions, and he confidently makes thoughtful and interesting contributions. He continues to enjoy reading and can read a wide range of simple texts independently. He is developing the ability to use a range of strategies to read new words, and shows that he understands what he has read through oral questioning and comprehension exercises. He is always keen to write and puts real effort into his work. Stephen can develop his ideas for stories and accounts, and is working hard to use capital letters and full stops consistently, and to use descriptive language. He spells many words with regular spelling patterns correctly and is learning irregular words.

Mathematics

Stephen can use addition and subtraction when solving problems involving up to 20 plus objects. He has begun to understand the place value of each digit in a number and can use this to order numbers to 100. He has mental recall of number bonds to 20, and is developing this with higher numbers. He is working on early multiplication through continuous addition and counting-on activities. He can use non-standard and some standard units to measure and order objects. Stephen has made data collections and recorded these in simple charts.

Science

He has completed science tasks about sound and light, forces, and plants. He can describe and name the simple features of objects, living things and events, and recognize similarities and differences. He can offer suggestions about how to find things out, has made predictions and tested his ideas. He asks and answers questions related to a task with interest. Stephen has made individual and group recordings of his work in a variety of ways including simple tables. He has an excellent general knowledge and is always eager to find out more.

Design and technology

When designing and making Stephen can select from a range of materials and techniques and explain his choices. He has developed his skills in cutting, joining and assembling. He has made pictures and models to show his designs and can discuss his ideas and suggest improvements.

Information technology

Stephen can recognize a range of IT equipment and has learned to control and operate different devices. He has used the computer to communicate in pictures and text and learned more about using the keyboard and the mouse.

History

Stephen can recognize changes in his own and others' lives and use related vocabulary to describe the passing of time. He has used objects, books and photographs to find out more about the past, and can sequence objects and events into simple chronological order.

Geography

He has made observations and recordings about the features of the local environment – the types and uses of buildings and land, and the people and their roles. He has talked about attractive and unattractive features and made simple plans and routes.

Art

Stephen has worked practically and imaginatively with materials, tools and techniques to create pieces of artwork. He is developing his use of colour, pattern and texture, and takes care in observational work.

Music

He has learned songs and rhymes, and is an excellent singer who confidently performs on his own. He has learned to name and play simple percussion instruments, and to explore and select sounds to express ideas.

Physical education

Stephen is well coordinated and moves confidently on the floor and apparatus during PE lessons. He has developed and refined his skills in using small apparatus, and works enthusiastically in games.

Religious education

Stephen has listened to Bible stories and learned about the life of Jesus and the work of the church. He always shows care and concern for others, and has a responsible and reliable attitude.

General comments

Stephen approaches all his work with enthusiasm and a desire to do well. He has made very good progress in his work across all areas of the curriculum. He is a happy, friendly member of the class who has been a pleasure to teach. Thank you for your home support which, coupled with Stephen's hard work, will ensure his continuing success.

Number of attendances out of total number possible 312: 302

Number of unauthorized absences: 0

This report may be discussed with . . . . on . . . .

at . . . .

In addition to annual reports Year 2 teachers are also involved in reporting on the Standard Assessment Tasks and tests (SATs) that all Y2 pupils undertake during their final term of Key Stage 1. The final overall results of these tasks on a school level will be made public, but only teachers, parents and pupils see the detailed results for individual children. Schools are expected to report annually to parents on the SATs results, and teacher assessments (also based on the National Curriculum level descriptions) are reported alongside the test results. For many people formal assessments, particularly public examinations or tasks such as SATs, are seen as being more objective than the judgements and critical appraisal made by individual teachers. Yet the concept of objectivity may be something of an illusion as the fact that an assessment is universal does not automatically mean that it is fair and unbiased. The manageability of assessment is crucial, and the need for it often results in compromises over validity, reliability and objectivity. SATs may be valid in that they assess what they say they are assessing, and they may be reliable in that they offer consistency of results over different activities and times, but that is not the same as saying that they are objective and hence should be given primacy over teacher assessments.

In many ways SATs are a product of the tensions inherent in a system which is seeking to measure children's performance as a means of supporting the teaching and learning process while at the same time measuring that performance as a way of ensuring teacher accountability. In a climate characterized by high levels of this type of accountability, assessments such as the SATs can skew the curriculum away from a broad and balanced education and towards passing the test, sometimes undermining the professionals' capacity to determine children's wider achievement and potential in the process. SATs are inherently reductionist; they can offer useful comparisons, but they are across a relatively narrow front.

Some principles of reporting and accountability

When reporting on pupil attainment:

- begin your comments by referring to positive factors and ensure any subsequent criticism is constructive in nature;
- make reference to children's achievements in relation to the Early Learning Goals or National Curriculum level descriptions;
- include some description of children's achievements in relation to the wider curriculum;
- suggest areas and ways in which children can improve on their attainment to date;
- maintain a professional commitment to confidentiality;
- value the contribution made by pupils, parents and learning support staff in assessment and recording;
- use methods that are manageable and understandable for all involved.

Catering for individual pupil needs and abilities

Children vary: from each other, from day to day, from year to year, in their abilities, in their behaviour, and in their attitudes. Young children can learn in different ways, at different speeds, can experience a variety of different learning difficulties, and can reach very different levels of attainment. The concept of **personalized learning** contained in current legislation and guidance for teachers is a recognition of this fact (DfES, 2004a; 2004c). Most teachers would acknowledge that diversity exists in their classes and they respond by employing organizational strategies such as ability grouping, by adjusting the curriculum for different children, and by tailoring expectations according to individual pupils' needs and abilities.

✔ Audit

By the end of this section you should:

- understand how to match learning objectives and content to the needs and abilities of pupils;
- be aware of the importance of challenging children and having appropriate expectations for children's learning;
- understand the need to build on prior attainment, and to share the content and purposes of lessons and activities with the children;
- be familiar with ways in which teaching and learning can be adapted and modified in response to some of the special educational needs (SEN) that might be encountered in mainstream settings.

Differentiation

Differentiation is an important element in effective teaching and learning as a means of maximizing *the motivation, progress and achievement of each student* (Stradling and Saunders, 1993). When planning and teaching practitioners think about the children's abilities, their previous experiences, their interests, their knowledge and skills, as well as paying attention to the subject matter and the range of teaching styles and methods. Differentiating in this way is intended to result in the provision of tasks which will enable all the children to:

- consolidate their existing understanding;
- practise their existing skills;
- build on such understanding and skills;
- encounter and master new ideas and enlarge their knowledge of a subject;
- engage in creative and imaginative thinking and action.

(Alexander *et al.*, 1992)

A key factor to consider when differentiating is that ability is not necessarily fixed. The notion that children have habitual levels of achievement is supported by common sense and anecdotal evidence rather than by hard facts. It is entirely possible that achievement is domain specific rather than universal, and is unstable rather than fixed (SCAA, 1994, p. 26). A pupil's ability may well alter over time as a result of maturation and could depend on the context or the subject matter. In addition, the domains in question may not be different subjects, such as English and art, but could quite easily be between different aspects of the same subject such as writing and reading (e.g. children who can read words that they cannot yet spell).

Models of ability

- **Universal ability**: a child's ability is the same across the whole curriculum.
- **Fixed ability**: a child's ability relative to his/her peers will not alter over time.
- **Domain specific ability**: a child performs better in some areas of the curriculum than in others.
- **Unstable ability**: a child's ability can improve and regress over time and in different contexts.

Given that ability may be domain specific and unstable, those working in 3–8 settings need to start from the premise that every child is good at something, and success in one area can breed success and increased confidence in other areas. In conjunction with this article of faith, teachers need to retain a degree of flexibility and deploy a range of different strategies, including differentiation by outcome, differentiation by support and differentiation by task.

Differentiation by outcome involves a group or class of pupils undertaking the same task while working at their own level. While this will always be a useful option, differentiation by outcome should not be used as an excuse for not considering differentiation at all, or in other words, differentiation *by accident*. When teachers differentiate by outcome they recognize the implications. First, activities and materials must be equally accessible to all children and ought not to be dependent upon knowledge and skills which only some of the children have. Second, there should be a range of possible answers and outcomes. Ultimately, if a task is to be truly defined as differentiated by outcome it needs to offer all the children involved the chance to make progress.

Differentiation by support refers to a variation in the level of teacher intervention provided and in the level of autonomy offered to children during activities. Although the difficulties involved in differentiating should not be underestimated, much of what is already common practice in nurseries and classrooms could be classed as differentiation by support. Most teachers already adapt, alter and adjust the demands placed on children during teaching and learning in order to support or extend particular individuals or groups. This can have implications for the organization and management of lessons and activities, as it is sometimes the case that the dialogue and interaction between teachers and individual children is less than it might be, for example when it is primarily concentrated at the start and conclusion of sessions.

Differentiation by task may take a number of forms, including:

- children covering the same content but at different levels;
- children covering the same content but with different activities;
- children covering the same content, activity and level, but being taught using different approaches.

When differentiating by task teachers need to remember that children have an entitlement to certain skills and knowledge within the National Curriculum and Foundation Stage. In order to ensure that differentiation by task and the entitlement curriculum are compatible, a distinction needs to be drawn between the purpose of an activity and the way in which that purpose is addressed. For example, if teachers wish children to learn to *count reliably up to 20 objects* then there are many ways in which they can set about achieving this (QCA, 1999, p. 62).

It is sometimes hard to say with any certainty where one form of differentiation ends and another begins, particularly as different approaches could be employed at different points within the same lesson or activity. A task might be identified as differentiated by outcome on the surface, yet within that the teacher may use a range of different techniques (including challenges, questions and procedures) for different individuals and groups.

The example below outlines a design and technology activity for a class of Year 2 infants following a visit to the local playground. The teacher's primary purpose was to teach the pupils to *measure, mark out, cut and shape a range of materials* (QCA, 1999, p. 92). The columns show how the same task could be differentiated either by outcome or by task/support.

A design and technology class activity

Differentiation by outcome	Differentiation by task and/or support
When *clarifying the task* the children talked about their visit to the site and were then told that they would be designing a piece of apparatus. The teacher discussed the features of playground apparatus with the children and they decided that all the products should be fun to use and safe.	When *clarifying the task*, following the visit, some children were asked to respond to the broad question 'What would make an exciting piece of playground equipment?' Others were asked to respond to much more specific queries such as 'What should our climbing frame be like?' The teacher assisted and guided one group of children closely as they began to identify criteria and specifications arising from the answers to the second question. The first group was expected to operate more independently and to make a written list in pairs.
The children were then asked to *design* their apparatus in pairs using pencil and paper.	Some of the children *designed* their models verbally and by handling the materials at their disposal to show their intentions. Most of the class drew their designs. Three very able children were asked to review different designs in catalogues and to produce two alternative designs of their own and then to select the best.
When *making* their playground models the teacher put out a limited selection of tools and materials (including hacksaws, bench hooks, square section softwood, cardboard, PVA adhesive, string and scissors) to which all the children had access.	When *making*, different children were provided with different materials and equipment. For the majority of the class this meant scissors, paper, card, softwood and hacksaws. One pair, which was proceeding rapidly and effectively, was offered additional tools and materials with which to produce their final model. One pair was asked to construct their climbing frame using a commercially produced construction kit.
When *evaluating* their models the children all used the original criteria of fun and safety.	When engaged in critical reflection and *evaluation* of their work some children used a worksheet, while a small group who had difficulty with writing discussed their views with the teacher acting as scribe. The teacher employed different types of questions with different children including procedural questions such as 'How are you going to do that?'; questions about outcomes such as 'Have you done what you set out to do?'; and questions about understanding such as 'How does it work?' and 'How could you make it work better?'

The ability to differentiate tasks based on judgements about children's needs and abilities plays an important role in helping pupils to achieve their full potential. However, differentiation is a demanding task for teachers, one that is made even more difficult in situations where teachers experience a lack of access to support from other adults (e.g. curriculum coordinators, TAs, HLTAs, learning mentors and parents); where resources are insufficient or not available; and where class sizes are large and the available space is limited. The realities of nursery and primary classrooms can sometimes make these things *aspirations rather than absolutes* (Alexander *et al.*, 1992, p. 28). Eliciting children's ideas and using knowledge of their strengths, weaknesses and previous experiences to inform planning and teaching cannot be expected to result in 30 or more separate lesson plans. Not only would such an approach be unmanageable but it would also ignore the fact that while there are many individual differences between children, there are also similarities and common needs. Fortunately these similarities can make differentiation more manageable, as matching tasks to pupils may involve consideration of groups and classes as well as individuals.

Differentiation checklist

- Monitor your teaching materials to ensure that they support, extend and allow for achievement by all the children.
- Alter the amount, range and complexity of information given.
- Adjust the degree of independence and responsibility for organizing and running tasks and activities. Structure a task tightly for some children while allowing others more room to plan, organize and manage themselves.
- Identify those children likely to struggle and plan ways of assisting them to cope with the demands of the lesson or session.
- Identify those children likely to find the task easy and plan ways of making the task more demanding to ensure they are suitably challenged.
- Use a wide range of recording methods.
- Recognize the successes of all pupils and challenge them to extend their knowledge and skills.
- Organize the nursery/classroom to support group work and collaborative learning as well as class and individual teaching.
- Monitor children's experiences, target your time and attention towards certain children at certain points, and alter the intensity of teacher intervention between levels that could be described as high, medium, or low.
- Undertake formative assessment and enter into dialogue with pupils as a way of setting new targets and identifying learning difficulties.
- Make effective use of other adults and learning support staff in the classroom, including parents, TAs and visitors.

Meeting the needs of children with SEN

It has been estimated that as many as one in five children will have some form of special educational need at some point during their school lives (Dearing, 1993). Teachers of young children play an important part in identifying and providing appropriate educational experiences for them. The reader is advised to refer to sections in the other chapters on the range of SEN that might be encountered in nurseries and schools, the Code of Practice and the underlying rationale behind the policy of inclusion and attempts to remove potential barriers to achievement (DfES, 2001b, 2004d).

Developing inclusive provision may involve consultation and collaboration with external agencies and others to discuss and plan learning programmes aimed at meeting children's specific needs. Where a teacher has suspicions or knows that a child has a special educational need advice and guidance ought to be sought from those with relevant expertise and experience such as parents, the school's SENCO and/or local support services as any strategies employed will need to fit with the school's SEN policy and procedures. The teacher's role in responding to SEN includes:

- providing support for learning in the classroom;
- establishing a learning environment that enables children to have equal access to the curriculum;
- providing appropriate learning experiences, including social ones.

Efforts to support children with SEN can be greatly aided by positive relationships with parents and carers. Parental involvement can be highly effective in assisting children to overcome cognitive, linguistic, behavioural or emotional difficulties. Parents and carers should be included and involved in the decision-making concerning their child and be encouraged to contribute and support their child's development in partnership with the nursery or school (Paige-Smith, 2002). Where such involvement is encouraged, parents are more likely to have a positive attitude towards the process and their child. Where such involvement is not encouraged, parents may feel threatened or criticized and may be reluctant either to accept that a need exists or to support the efforts of professionals to help their child achieve their full potential.

Involving parents and carers

- Listen to what parents have to say.
- Include parents and carers at an early stage.
- Demonstrate an understanding of, and respect for, the feelings of parents and carers.
- Make every effort to maintain good channels of communication so that children's progress can be reported.

The remainder of this section briefly considers some of the strategies that student and newly qualified teachers may wish to employ to help children with SEN to achieve; the reader is urged to seek more detailed information in the further sources of information section (p. 243).

In some cases children will be forced to interrupt their schooling as a result of **medical needs**. Such needs could be short term and temporary or long term and even permanent (Dewis, 2007). Breaks of any kind are likely to disrupt a child's educational progress to some extent. If the breaks in question happen over an extended period of time, if they involve painful treatment regimes or cause higher than normal levels of stress and anxiety as a result of the medical prognoses then the educational disruption could be considerable. Schools and teachers are expected to play their part in supporting a Local Authority's attempts to ensure coherent and continuous educational provision for children with medical needs. As a result teachers may be asked to liaise with home and hospital tutors, they may work closely with the school's SENCO to develop plans to properly reintegrate a child with medical needs back into school following an absence and they will also have to consult and communicate closely with parents.

Other children that do not experience any significant interruptions to their nursery/school attendance can still experience barriers to the curriculum as a result of **physical disabilities**. Some children with physical disabilities may need additional time or alternative ways to complete activities. For example, teachers need to anticipate likely triggers for asthma attacks, or the need for diabetic pupils to keep their blood sugar levels stable. Places where children can sit, rest or be quiet are a good idea. Similarly, under certain circumstances, completing written and other work could be made easier by making the most of educational technology (e.g. video/DVDs, audio recorders, word processors, concept keyboards). Teaching Assistants and other learning support staff need to be properly briefed about supporting the health and education of these children; for example, an adult working with an epileptic pupil who experiences an absence attack may need to repeat or check on information and instructions given.

Resources too may need to be carefully chosen to ensure participation by all including those pupils who, for example, may experience visual impairments or have difficulties with gross or fine motor skills; handling objects and accessing out-of-nursery/school sites are two areas that may present difficulties. The stability of equipment can be improved (e.g. using Velcro), as can ease of handling/control (e.g. attaching handles, or increasing the size of resources) and the accessibility of resources (e.g. attaching strings/cords for movement or retrieval; providing multisensory experiences to maximize participation levels). Where necessary, practitioners may need to provide some physical assistance for children. In some cases teachers may need to look for alternative learning objectives even though all the children are engaged in the same activity. Providing entirely different activities altogether ought to be a last resort when it is the only way to meet a child's needs.

Adapting/altering learning objectives to support inclusion

Class objective: matching shapes and recognizing similarities (QCA, 2000, p. 80).

Objective for pupil with mobility difficulties: reaching, grasping, releasing.

Supporting the learning of a visually impaired child

- Make sure that the child is close enough to see *or* allow the child to use other senses (e.g. touch, smell, hearing) to investigate the world around him/her.
- Allow additional time for the completion of certain tasks.
- Use alternative recording methods.
- Make sure that the lighting where the child is working is not too dim.
- Make sure the child can use aids such as glasses or magnifiers.

Supporting the learning of a hearing impaired child

- Provide visual clues to support oral work.
- Rephrase/emphasize spoken language (e.g. key words or phrases).
- Reduce background noise levels.
- Face the child when talking and articulate words clearly.
- Check that instructions/information are understood.
- Use assistive technologies (e.g. induction coils and microphones).

Pupils with **learning difficulties** are more likely to work best and stay on task longer in situations where routines are clearly understood, where they are able to exercise some control over their work with support, and where work is set at an appropriate level. Teachers may have to build a series of shorter activities into lessons/sessions. Similarly, taking care to avoid overly long strings of instructions is useful. Autistic pupils, for example, may respond better to statements, instructions and directions rather than asking questions and seeking choices. Teacher-centred or high pupil autonomy approaches (e.g. *chalk and talk*, dictation, note-taking from books, or unstructured/free writing) are the least effective teaching methods to employ. Children with learning difficulties will need plenty of opportunity for reinforcement and repetition, as well as using and applying similar vocabulary and ideas in different contexts. Teachers may need to keep referring to previous work and experience to help children make sense of what is going on.

Supporting the work of pupils with learning difficulties

- Be ready to simplify and rephrase instructions. Use shorter, less complex sentences that draw on concrete first-hand experience.
- Provide verbal and visual cues and prompts as well as written information. Use concrete materials, demonstrations and examples. Utilize a range of non-text based teaching methods (e.g. drama and socio-dramatic play, visits, guest speakers or storytelling).
- Differentiate tasks to enable children to engage in them at different levels of comprehension and/or capability.
- Provide numerous opportunities to practise skills.
- Model language and skills.
- Recognize the distinction between communication and comprehension; the latter may be sophisticated even though the former proves challenging.
- Use assistive technologies and/or augmentative communication systems including ICT to facilitate pupils' ability to communicate and demonstrate comprehension.
- Adapt written material by simplifying and translating texts into language that is easier for the children to understand. Précis longer texts into single paragraphs or short sentences.
- Read with or for a child and/or act as a scribe.
- Mark pages in reference books to enable children to find the information they want more easily.
- Use key words, worksheets or writing frames to help children structure their written work, to organize information and to express themselves, rather than asking them simply to *write about it*.
- Work around, rather than shoot down, incorrect or partial answers. Foster discussion among children to develop partial into more complete answers.

Children with **emotional and behavioural difficulties (EBD)** may struggle to concentrate and focus on a task for the same length of time as their peers. It is often assumed, mistakenly, that children with EBD are seeking attention and that they obtain satisfaction from that attention. Unwanted behaviour, such as aggression, may result from frustration and alienation or may be because the child has never learned or been taught strategies for resolving conflict and confrontation. Some of the difficulties may therefore be susceptible to some modification and improvement over time by examining and altering the setting. Looking at when and where disruption occurs is the first step in this process, for example the sorts of lessons, the times of day, classroom organization, or teacher or pupil activity. Difficult situations may be exacerbated by teacher reactions or pupil actions.

Trying to keep the child productively engaged and on task is the aim. Liaison with learning support staff on the best ways of providing extra support in group settings can be helpful and appropriate pacing of lessons too can make a big difference to children with emotional and behavioural difficulties.

Supporting the work of pupils with emotional and behavioural difficulties

- Structure lessons to avoid *dead time* and a lack of supervision.
- Establish expectations, conventions and routines that reduce the need for constant teacher instruction at key points during the day such as transition times.
- Develop your ability to anticipate events. Classroom layouts that create blind spots are likely to exacerbate disruption and task avoidance.
- There may be ways in which the child can be assisted in modifying his/her behaviour and to develop new strategies for coping with school. Teach children to verbalize anger, for example by asking for equipment/resources to be returned or expressing their feelings, and praise them for doing it.
- Monitor progress, provide positive feedback and include children with EBD in setting simple goals and targets that can be achieved within a short period of time.
- Offer an easy task to do, stay with the pupil while the task is completed and make sure positive feedback is given. Success in one area can *breed* a more positive attitude in other areas.
- Find out what children with EBD see as a reward, and ensure that they are rewarded when they show determination, perseverance or consideration for others.
- Be prepared to step in quickly if you spot the build up of disruptive behaviour. It is sometimes possible to head off, divert or defuse an imminent outburst using questions, offering a change of task, a change of location or simple housekeeping chores that children enjoy and which confers responsibility on them for which they can receive praise and recognition.

Children who are considered **gifted and talented** are likely to be capable of pursuing their learning in greater depth and at a faster pace than their peers. There has been considerable debate over the concept of giftedness and singling out children as gifted and/or talented has been seen by some as potentially damaging (i.e. raising of expectations that put undue pressure on a child). The arguments can be further complicated by the suggestion that singling out pupils as gifted or talented is an elitist approach to education. However, if there are children in mainstream education who are very able or more than very able then ensuring that their needs are met ought to be seen as an equal opportunities issue rather than elitism (Ofsted/DFE, 1994). Children who are thought to be gifted and talented may:

- display a good memory for facts, people or events;
- possess good powers of observation;
- like to know how things work or happen;
- be able to follow relatively complex instructions;
- have a wide vocabulary which they use accurately;
- possess good physical coordination and control;
- have a high level of visual and spatial awareness;

- display a high degree of independence, self-sufficiency and initiative;
- be ambitious, setting themselves high goals;
- display good social skills with older children and adults, and have a well-developed sense of humour, yet they may experience difficulties with their peers.

(DfES, 2006a)

It is essential to maintain the interest and motivation of gifted and talented pupils by presenting curriculum content in clear and exciting ways. Gifted and talented pupils can easily become bored and disruptive, can dominate their more average peers and can be intolerant. They may be sensitive to criticism and rejection, troubled by their difference and may even be tempted to underachieve to conform. Gifted and talented children may also frighten or annoy their teachers. The speed and pace at which these children often work, as well as the high levels of thought, autonomy and independence of which they are capable, can make great demands on already overloaded professionals.

Although able to complete teacher-set tasks quickly these pupils may benefit from opportunities to have additional time and from being asked to study in much greater depth than their peers. Teachers should not hesitate to use more challenging vocabulary and language with them, as well as offering them greater variety and autonomy in tasks. Research skills can be a particularly productive area in which gifted children can be challenged, and it is one that fits well with their characteristic thirst for knowledge and experience. Providing gifted and talented children with opportunities to use and apply ideas and skills in a range of different contexts puts them in the position of having to make deductions, develop and test hypotheses, and take their research into new areas. Gifted and talented children can also be encouraged to share their learning and skills with their peers as a way of raising the knowledge and understanding of the whole class.

Supporting the work of gifted and talented pupils

- Provide extension work and enrichment activities with greater depth and variety (some of which may be extra-curricular).
- Challenge pupils to think at a higher level (e.g. querying assumptions).
- Give them the chance to solve demanding problems.
- Provide opportunities for autonomous and independent learning such as project work.
- Find a way to enable them to work at their own pace to cover the normal curriculum more quickly, combined with opportunities to engage in more sustained work without timetable interruptions.
- Make sure that *giftedness* or *talentedness* do not become exclusiveness; gifted and talented children need experience of working with non-gifted/talented peers.
- Do not make the assumption that because a child is exceptionally able teacher intervention is unnecessary. Thoughtful teacher intervention, inspiration, challenge and constructive criticism are vital in avoiding underachievement.

Enabling environments: organizing and managing learning and teaching

This section is based in part on the premise that a great deal of learning takes place outside of the classroom. It also takes the view the strategies such as class teaching and group work are not inherently good or bad but are simply options open to teachers, who have to make choices about the best way to organize and manage a particular lesson or session. Teachers should group children on the basis of fitness for purpose rather than on the basis of dogmatic adherence to established practices.

✔ Audit

By the end of this section you should:

- understand how to make effective use of teaching time in whole-class and group situations;
- know about ways of creating safe and stimulating environments (indoors and outdoors) to support teaching and learning;
- know how to plan for learning beyond the nursery/school through extended schooling, homework tasks and educational visits;
- know about a range of teaching methods which will help to support children's learning by sustaining the momentum of pupils' work and keeping pupils engaged.

Organizing the children

Young children have always experienced some form of *class teaching* whether at morning registration, at story time, in PE or in dance and movement. As a method of organizing the children for learning, it has become increasingly common in infant schools, particularly with the advent of literacy and numeracy hours. Class teaching is an essential part of a teacher's repertoire, placing the onus on her/him to be an organizer, a giver of information, a leader and the focus of attention (Alexander *et al.*, 1992).

Potential benefits and disadvantages associated with class teaching

Benefits

- Useful for introducing new topics as well as summarizing learning
- Higher order questioning
- More detailed explanations
- Higher levels of pupil performance.

Disadvantages

- Too much teacher talk
- An absence of active learning by children
- Individual differences ignored.

(Alexander *et al.*, 1992)

When working with a large number of young children, trainee and newly qualified teachers need to bear in mind the age and maturity of these learners. Teachers who keep young pupils sitting passively for too long are asking for trouble. So too are teachers who do not check that their instructions have been understood before setting the children to work. The following suggestions are intended to assist trainee and newly qualified teachers in organizing the children and teaching effectively in whole-class situations.

Teaching a whole class

- Ensure that the necessary resources are set out or readily available.
- Think about the language and vocabulary that you will use.
- Obtain and maintain the children's attention. Waiting for silence can be done actively through effective use of your voice and non-verbal communication. Having something interesting to show can be very effective as a technique for getting little eyes, ears and minds all pointed in the right direction. A teacher whose whole body says, *Look at me! This is going to be really interesting* is more likely to gain the children's attention, and gaining this attention is crucial if you are to create a window of opportunity.
- Do not squander your chance to start a lesson well. A prompt start, followed by an appropriate, yet business-like pace will help to set the tone for the lesson and avoid the creation of dead time.
- Share the purpose of the session with the class. Some practitioners use the WALT (*we are learning to*) and WILF (*what I'm looking for*) systems.
- Pacing and timing are crucial. Some children may be left floundering if the pace is too rapid. Others may lose their concentration and enthusiasm if the pace is too languid; they may start fiddling or interrupting. You can lose the initiative and spend unnecessary amounts of time trying to regain their attention.
- Make the session as engaging and interactive as possible for the children by:
  - getting children to discuss ideas in pairs for a couple of minutes;
  - asking for their contributions, thoughts, predictions or demonstrations;
  - exploring any interesting responses in more depth;
  - referring to and making links with prior learning;
  - introducing eye-catching props, artefacts and visual aids, including ICT resources.

- Give some thought to transition times within a lesson, for example moving from a whole-class situation into groups or back again. Use strategies such as checking on instructions and staggered movement times to reduce disruption. For example, 'Let's see who's sitting up nicely and is ready to start'.
- Finishing class lessons in an organized fashion is every bit as important as starting them well. It is part of the learning process, providing opportunities for review and reflection and giving you a chance to ascertain the extent of the children's experiences and learning.
- Being overtaken by time is often a problem for trainee and newly qualified teachers when teaching the whole class. When planning, allow time for plenary sessions and putting things away. Learning to put things away properly is a long-term process with young children, and will require determination and consistency on your part. Encourage children to take some responsibility for tidying up and looking after their learning environment; a shared classroom ethos in which the children have had an opportunity to decide that 'In our class we always . . .' will help.

A significant amount of teaching with the 3–8 age range takes place using *group work*. Grouping for learning (on the basis of ability or needs) can be a very effective and efficient way of teaching. However, if the groups are permanent two problems can arise. First, children pick up unspoken messages about their ranking and status in the classroom; they soon know that the Red group is the *top group*, for example. For those children who see themselves as less able this can have an adverse effect on their self-esteem and motivation. Second, teachers themselves can be affected in that their expectations can be coloured by their own groupings, leading to under- and overestimating ability.

Some teachers will seek to group children by age/maturity. This is frequently the case in vertically grouped classes (e.g. Y1 and Y2 together) that often appear where school numbers dictate. Grouping by interest or enthusiasm is another option. Although not really practical as a permanent arrangement it can be very powerful for short-term projects. Grouping by friendship meanwhile can also be a powerful motivator for children but there are dangers here too:

- single sex groups may appear where you would prefer mixed sex groups;
- there can be children that no one wants to work with (i.e. *the last child on the bench* in PE);
- *like with like* can fail to challenge and stimulate, it risks stifling the introduction of new ideas, and can even become exclusive or elitist.

In some cases an apparently collaborative and group work setting belies the fact that children are actually engaged in a task as individuals. In other instances group work involves true collaboration with small numbers of children working collectively on the same task (Alexander *et al.*, 1992). It is also worth noting that in some Foundation Stage settings the membership of groups can be unstable and short-lived as young children are able to opt into and out of group tasks, albeit usually with adult support and direction.

Potential benefits and disadvantages of group work

Benefits

- Encourages pupil–pupil interaction and learning from one another
- Promotes more in-depth discussion
- Fosters cooperation, negotiation, sharing and problem-solving skills
- Encourages children to take more responsibility for their own learning, setting the pace, asking questions and developing answers
- Promotes participation, high involvement and commitment

Disadvantages

- Can be quite slow
- The positive social dynamics of group work are not automatic and can require input from the teacher
- Can be difficult to manage several groups simultaneously

Children need to be in a position to work effectively as a group. The self-discipline and social skills required for greater concentration, perseverance and effective group work take time to develop. Encouraging children to articulate their feelings about themselves can be a good starting point when trying to promote these skills. Readiness for group work can also be underpinned by providing common experiences for all the pupils involved, such as a class visit.

Group work indicators

Children:

- can play cooperatively, work collaboratively, share and take turns;
- have developed positive relationships with others in the classroom, demonstrated by a willingness and an ability to initiate verbal and non-verbal interactions with adults and peers;
- are able and willing to participate in discussions;
- can identify the effects of their behaviour on others with help;
- are able to observe and adhere to rules and conventions such as accepting and respecting differences;
- are developing an ability to cope with change;
- are developing strategies for coping with frustration, for example having another go or trying different approaches;
- are displaying an increasing confidence to try things out independently.

Supporting young children's learning in groups

- Ensure that everyone in the group knows the purpose of the task.
- Think about roles in groups. Who is going to do what? Are there real roles for all?
- Offer the group guidance on procedures at the start, and remind them about class conventions and timescales.
- Do not play a numbers game. A group is not defined by the number 4 or 6. The larger the group, the easier it is for some young children to find themselves on the margins of an activity. The size of the group also interferes with procedure. It can take pupils all their time just to decide what they want to do and then there is no time left to do it.
- Allow for variety and flexibility when grouping children; this is determined to some extent by the purposes or objectives of the activity and the fact that relationships change over time.
- Remember that younger children's need for security can be undermined by constantly chopping and changing groups.
- Capitalize on the similarities between pupils in order to make children feel more secure in groups.
- Capitalize on the differences between pupils in order to encourage creativity and excitement. Groups based on diversity can benefit from the challenges and tensions created by differences, but you must ensure that these challenges are tackled in a positive and supportive fashion.
- Provide opportunities for reflection about group work. For children to become better at group work they need to be given the chance to think about how they worked together. Praise and recognition reinforce desirable behaviour.
- Where will you be and what will you be doing while group work is taking place? When will adult interventions be needed? Have you made effective use of other adult support?
- Do not attempt to chair multiple groups simultaneously by yourself. Use a classroom map to predict potential clashes, avoid trying to be everywhere at once and make effective use of learning support colleagues in the classroom.
- Make sure that there are some sessions when groups engaged in structured play and practical and creative activities also receive higher levels of teacher attention.

Using a classroom map to plan for group work

Red: High intervention. Needs you most/all of the time.

Orange/amber: Medium intervention. Needs you some of the time, for example, starting the group off and monitoring from a distance.

Green: Low intervention. Needs occasional visits and checks.

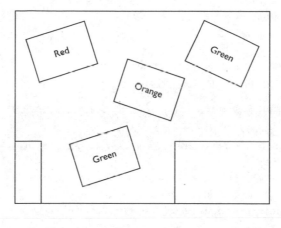

Organizing the learning environment: indoors

The physical environment of the nursery or classroom can say a lot to children, parents and others about teachers, their standards and their expectations. Physical celebrations of individual success such as displays can enhance pupil motivation (DfES, 2004a). The physical environment can also have a much more direct impact on learning. Surroundings that are language and number rich with alphabets, books, number lines, labels, puzzles, questions, learning objectives and planning on view can all help to support learning.

Within classrooms, many teachers operate a mixed economy with their equipment and resources. Some resources will be assigned to individual classes or teachers, some will be available to teams of staff (e.g. the nursery team or the Y2 classes), others may be held centrally for use by the whole school; some are teacher-controlled, others are open-access. The issue of access will often be shaped by concerns about health and safety and classroom management. At the same time the physical environment should be welcoming and designed with younger children in mind. Safety gates and doors in nursery settings and scaled-down furniture in Key Stage 1 classes are two examples.

Creating a safe learning environment: a checklist

Does the nursery/school have:

- safety glass or plastic covering for low windows and doors?
- well-lit stairways?
- slow closing internal doors?
- safety gates?
- safe floor coverings?
- fire-retardant curtains and soft furnishings?
- guards on fires or radiators?
- protected power sockets?
- closely supervised use of heavy or sharp equipment?
- fire exits clearly marked and accessible?
- non-lockable toilets?
- hygienic toilet facilities?
- rubbish points that are inaccessible to children?
- systems for recording and reporting accidents, especially head injuries?
- safe car parking?
- effective supervision of children before and after nursery/school?
- effective supervision of children in the playground?
- high standards of organization and management during off-site visits?

(Leeds City Council, 1996)

In addition to thinking about the resources, fixtures, fittings and furniture, the use of display helps to create an attractive learning environment and can be instrumental in motivating children, setting standards and communicating information to parents and other visitors about the children's experiences and work. A good display can start children talking, thinking, asking questions and working, as well as offering a means of praising, recognizing and encouraging achievement. Putting children's work on display shows publicly the value that the teacher places on their efforts, and children's involvement in some of the decision-making about what to display, and where and how to display it can help to ensure that a display is used and referred to.

An unusual display

A class of Y2/3 children made a model of a Pteranadon out of bin liners (for wings) and large cardboard boxes. They painted it bright blue with red eyes the size of plates. One of the children had learned that no one could be sure what colour dinosaurs were but since it flew in the sky the pupils thought it should be blue. Their teacher decided to surprise the children by arriving especially early the next day and suspending the model from the ceiling. It took the children more than 30 minutes to notice the model hanging six feet above their heads. If young children can miss a prehistoric monster with a 10-metre wingspan, how much easier is it for them to miss a drawing or a piece of writing?

Displays should be professionally presented; a sloppy display can make good work look poor and does not do justice to the efforts of the children. Not all 3–8 teachers have artistic talents, nor is this necessary in order to produce a professional display.

Display checklist

- Whose work is displayed and why? If the aim is to motivate pupils, then it ought to be the children's work not the teacher's that is displayed.
- Include *effort* alongside *outcome* as a criterion for judging which pieces of work are put on show. If effort is not used as a criterion for selection, then some children may be consistently overlooked while others may receive disproportionate recognition.
- Make sure that displays reflect the variety and breadth of the 3–8 curricula, showing practical activities as well as written work, celebrating personal and social development as well as academic achievement, and showing the development of skills as well as the acquisition of knowledge.
- Utilize a range of techniques which include two-dimensional as well as three-dimensional ones, and hands-on interactive displays as well as static ones.
- Use and refer to displays around the classroom in your teaching.
- Change displays on a regular basis.
- Ensure that displays are professionally presented by:
  - making certain that the display conforms to school/nursery conventions (e.g. single/double-mounted, approved colour schemes);
  - cutting mounts using a guillotine to ensure they are straight and even, with square corners;
  - making the margins on mounts of equal width or if they are unequal, then this should be based on the aesthetics of the display and not the result of carelessness;
  - providing labels with correct spellings and the children's names;
  - making sure handwriting on display conforms to nursery/school guidelines;
  - avoiding overcrowding; remember that the spaces between work are as important as those occupied by the work;
  - thinking about the height and level at which work is displayed; pieces of writing six feet up a wall will be unreadable by the children;
  - making sure the overall impression is one of neatness and tidiness, with evidence of the pride taken in the children's work on display.

Organizing the learning environment: outdoors

An important resource and additional learning environment is the space outside the nursery/classroom. For many children today there is less access to outdoor spaces than in the past as a result of increased traffic or parental fears about child abduction, and when children do get access it is often adult organized (e.g. attendance at sports clubs) rather than roaming freely (Edgington, 2002). Lack of outdoor experiences of this sort could inhibit children's risk assessment abilities making them overly nervous or reckless as they get older. At the same time the rise of TV, video and computer technologies may also lead some children to get less experience of outdoor play and raises the spectre of health problems arising from a lack of exercise (BBC, 2004).

Many teachers of nursery/reception children make extensive use of outdoor areas as a way of broadening their pupils' experience. These areas offer opportunities for a wide range of activities including imaginative play, construction play, traditional games (e.g. hide and seek) and physical play (e.g. running, throwing, climbing) (Garrick, 2004). Many primary teachers too take advantage of opportunities to use outdoor areas, for example collecting minibeasts in the school garden or teaching PE on the school field. While much of this work can be done inside the nursery/school, the outdoor area provides an alternative arena for learning, one that may suit some children better and one that may also compensate for changes in lifestyles. Well-resourced outdoor areas consist of spaces on a number of levels, containing a variety of soft and hard surfaces. In addition, there will be a mixture of open and secluded areas to allow for both boisterous play and more reflective activities.

Resources for the outdoor area

- Climbing area – stepping stones/tyres, climbing frame, planks, tunnels/barrels, A-frames
- Open space for running and riding – use parking spaces, road markings and signs to reduce collisions
- Playground markings – snakes, hopscotch, *follow the footsteps*, wall targets/goal mouths
- Small equipment – balls, bats, bean bags, hoops, coits, skipping ropes, bins, buckets and nets
- Quiet area – blankets/mats, chairs and tables, umbrellas/parasols, writing/drawing materials, books, easels, paints, tape recorder, radio
- Hiding places – natural (i.e. dens under bushes) and manufactured (i.e. tents blankets over 'A' frames, play house or large cardboard boxes)
- Role-play materials – dressing up clothes, props
- Wild/garden area – logs, mulched surface, soil, sand, flower pots, plants, magnifiers, binoculars, cameras, streamers, wind socks/chimes, mirrors
- Large-scale construction kits
- Sand, water and small world play area – sand pit, water trough, buckets and spades, containers, pipes, tubes, funnels, dolls, figures, cars, programmable vehicles
- Wet weather clothing – hats, Wellington boots, waterproof jackets.

(Edgington, 2002)

Not only must nurseries and schools provide appropriate outdoor spaces, but also teachers need to make effective use of them. Just because children are working in the outdoor area does not mean that planning, teaching and assessment cease to be necessary. This means treating the outdoor area as if it were an extension of the classroom. While the opportunities for using the outdoor area to support children's Physical Development are obvious, this space should also contribute to learning across the curriculum. Teachers therefore may wish to complement the balls, bikes and climbing frame with seating areas and benches or tables to facilitate play and work in other areas of learning.

Opportunities for learning across the curriculum in the outdoor area

• Personal, Social and Emotional Development • PSHE and citizenship	• Developing positive relations with others (e.g. suggesting ideas, sharing, taking turns, negotiation) • Developing self-confidence, independence, responsibility, and risk assessment skills • Experiencing a sense of achievement
• Communication, Language and Literacy • English	• Developing speaking and listening skills • Reading and writing/mark-making in quiet areas
• Problem Solving, Reasoning and Numeracy • Mathematics	• Counting activities • Number recognition (e.g. number the tricycles and bicycles) • Measuring distance, time and volume
• Knowledge and Understanding of the World • Science • Design and technology • ICT • Geography • History • RE	• Investigating plants, animals and the natural environment – introduce bird tables and feeders into the garden area, plant and grow seeds, carry out weather work (i.e. experiencing the wind, rain, sun or snow) • Explore the properties of materials (e.g. wet and dry) and forces (e.g. floating and sinking, building structures) • Exploring the built environment • Taking digital photographs
• Physical Development • PE	• Developing physical strength and skills including coordination and control through the use of a wide range of equipment and resources
• Creative Development • Art • Music	• Listening to sounds in the environment (natural and man-made) • Playing musical instruments • Observational drawings and paintings

Managing the learning environment in 3–8 settings

- Managing the space and resources involves outdoor as well as indoor provision.
- Remember the learning environment needs to facilitate an inclusive approach to teaching and learning. Factors to consider might include lighting, noise levels, visual/auditory input, layout, accessibility and adapting equipment.
- In the case of shared resources and loans, advance action may well be needed in order to ensure access to them at the right moment, for example booking library loans.
- Label storage areas and containers with words and pictures. Encourage children to refer to the labels.
- When arranging and organizing resources used on a daily basis consider ease of access and rules.
- Encourage pupils to make choices, to select equipment and materials, to take responsibility for keeping things tidy, and to develop their own resource management skills. Teachers and children can help caretakers and cleaners by ensuring that the nursery/classroom is properly tidied up at the end of the day.
- Do not put potentially hazardous tools and materials (such as hot glue guns) on open access. Ensure that children understand the importance of safety and restrict usage of some resources to adults only, or situations where strict supervision is available. Make sure that any chemicals (such as cleaning fluids) and medicines are securely locked away, and find out who the trained first aider on the staff team is.
- Remember that teachers and other responsible adults are the most valuable resource available. High adult–child ratios help to make the most effective use of materials and equipment; they help to foster a sense of security, and are important in reinforcing learning in young children. Adults are also very important as role models for children.
- Use furniture to mark out and define areas, including quiet areas, but bear in mind the need to be able to observe and monitor children.
- Plan and establish a mixture of clearly defined areas and general purpose spaces. There should be sufficient and varied space for a range of activities. Include a wide range of interesting objects, materials and equipment to create a stimulating environment. Use bright, colourful, interesting and interactive displays in the nursery/classroom.
- Some activities will be noisy and messy, others quiet and orderly. Different activities can be separated by time as well as by space. Try to keep messy indoor activities near the sink.

After-school learning: extended schooling and wrap around care

Many schools and teachers have offered after-school learning opportunities for children for a very long time, often involving a variety of clubs or societies. However, one outcome from the Every Child Matters agenda in recent years has been the drive to expand greatly the range and scope of these after-school activities and childcare. The stated purposes are to improve pupil engagement, participation and achievement, to support learning and teaching and to improve access for children and their families to wider services related to areas such as health, parenting or family support (DfES, 2007b). **Extended schools** (often working in partnership with other local agencies and groups) seek to provide a range of additional services before, during and after the school day. Although teachers may have direct involvement in some of these activities it is not a requirement and other professional groups and volunteers are also likely to be heavily involved in any extended provision. Examples of extended school activities include:

- breakfast clubs;
- after-school clubs and activities (e.g. art, music or sport);
- enhanced use of learning mentors to support individual pupils;
- setting up advice and guidance services on health and social care for parents;
- programmes of activities and events designed to increase levels of parental involvement in their children's education;
- additional support for children and parents with English as an additional language (EAL).

Out-of-school learning environments: home and homework

Homework refers to any work which children are asked to do outside lesson time, either on their own or with parents and carers. Children do not normally encounter formal homework tasks prior to Key Stage 1. Homework tasks can offer schools a way of developing further their partnership arrangements with parents and carers by involving them actively in their children's learning. Tasks can provide opportunities for children to talk about what they are learning to an interested adult and to practise key skills in a supportive environment. They can, for example, be helpful in supporting individual children's consolidation, reinforcement and understanding of literacy and numeracy skills. This said, if children have been working hard all day homework tasks need to be set carefully so as not to overburden them. The overall burden of homework also needs to take into account the impact on others involved in the activity; excessive and unreasonable homework is not fair on parents either. Children with special educational needs (SEN) meanwhile should not automatically be excluded from homework. They may benefit from special tasks separate from those given to their peers; however, it is also important that they do as much in common with other children as possible. Homework for pupils with SEN will need to have a very clear focus, be varied (not just written assignments) and where appropriate will need to be linked to their Individual Education Plan (IEP) targets.

Examples of homework tasks at Key Stage 1

- Playing simple word/number games
- Learning spellings (once a week)
- Learning number facts (once a week)
- Reading together (daily). All children should either read to their parents/carers or be read to. Fluent readers need to read on their own for at least ten minutes each day.

Both parents and teachers have a part to play in making homework policies an effective device for raising standards of achievement. Teachers need to ensure that they monitor or follow up on any homework, which they and the school set. Where homework remains unmarked or where children's efforts remain unacknowledged then the status of any future home tasks will be undermined both for the children and for those who have worked with them. The role of parents and carers meanwhile is equally crucial. Homework can provide a means of contact and communication between the school and parents, for example through reading record diaries. For parents who may find it harder to visit the classroom (e.g. some fathers) homework may provide a valuable opportunity to get involved in their child's education; the tasks set may also provide an insight for parents into the nature of the curriculum and their children's abilities and achievements (DfES, 2007a). Teachers can also use any comments made by parents as a means of informing their own assessments. Although some parents may worry about their ability to help their children with homework teachers can reassure them that they do not need to be *experts*. Parental encouragement, parental interest and parental willingness to engage in the process of learning alongside the child are easily the greatest assets that they can bring to the activity. Schools need to liaise with parents to ensure that they realize just what a pivotal role they play in:

- ensuring that the child has a reasonably peaceful place in which to work;
- making it clear to the child that time spent completing homework is valuable and worthwhile time spent together;
- encouraging and giving lots of praise to the child when they are completing their homework.

Out-of-school learning environments: educational visits

Trips and visits can be a wonderful stimulus for teaching and learning across the curriculum. Using the local environment makes a contribution to the intellectual and practical development of pupils as individuals and as informed members of society. Educationally, outside visits offer real opportunities for community interaction and for linking nursery and school experiences with the wider world, enabling young children to become more aware of the diversity of people, places and objects. There are, however, major implications in terms of health and safety for the teacher. Educational visits will test a teacher's relationships, control and organization. Teachers who fail to encourage their children to exhibit responsible behaviour in the nursery or classroom can hardly expect them to suddenly exhibit it on the local bus. Outside the school gates, the children are beyond their normal closed environment and consequently they are not so easily observed, not as easily held accountable and are subjected to wider influences. In this looser context it is not as easy for teachers to exercise control and lack of control carries with it potential risks to the health and safety of the children.

Know your pupils

Philip, a final year student teacher, arranged a visit to the local canal, situated approximately three-quarters of a mile from the school. There were 30 Y1/2 pupils in the class, one of whom suffered from arthritis. Philip knew about the arthritis but had not appreciated the implications and had not considered it in his planning. Halfway to the canal it became clear that the child was experiencing some discomfort and that if the walk continued this discomfort would become more serious. Philip gave the child a piggyback ride all the way there and all the way back rather than abort the visit for the whole class. Not surprisingly this was not an ideal solution. Other children wondered why they could not have a ride too and, by the time they returned to the school, Philip was also aching all over.

Preparation can greatly increase the chances of a safe and successful visit. Local walks can give young children useful training in crossing roads, public behaviour, and staying with designated adults. Such walks provide teachers with good opportunities for making it clear to the children that in the outside world the standards of behaviour expected are even more rigorous than those in school or nursery. Ensuring good behaviour is not just a method of preserving the teacher's sanity; it is a prerequisite for safety and learning. Teachers of young children should always conduct a risk assessment prior to a class visit. It is important to bear in mind the need to give consideration to likelihood as well as severity, and to be prepared to deal with any accidents should they occur.

Reception/Y1 visit to the local park: risk assessment

Risk	Small brook running through the park, danger of pupils falling in	Dogs off the lead
Severity	Water very shallow – low	Potentially high
Likelihood	Medium to high	Medium to high
Action	Pack spare clothes, allocate specific children to specific adults for better supervision and brief adult helpers about the risk	Talk to children prior to the visit about not approaching strange dogs, suggest strategies such as ignoring animals and staying with adults. Alert adult helpers

A well-organized and executed visit can inspire and enthuse young children and the momentum can last for quite some time. A poorly organized and riotous visit endangers the children and could rebound on the nursery/school, and hence on the teacher in charge. Trainee and newly qualified teachers are advised to consult the DfES good practice guide on Health and Safety of Pupils on Educational Visits for further information on the responsibilities, planning, supervision, preparation, liaison and emergency procedures involved in taking children beyond the nursery/school gates (DfES, 2001a).

Suggestions of things to consider before taking young children on walks and visits

The children

- Do any of the children have a medical condition such as epilepsy or asthma which needs to be taken into account?
- Do any of them suffer from travel sickness and if so, do their parents give them medication prior to journeys?
- Have the children been told where they are going, with whom, why and what's expected?
- How will they remember and/or record their experiences?

The parents/adult helpers

- No child can be taken out of nursery/school without the parents' permission. Letters therefore need to be sent to parents informing them of the details of the visit such as appropriate clothing, date, time and cost.
- Accompanying parents should be briefed as to what is being asked of them. Which children are they to accompany? What should they wear? Why are the children going, and what are the (learning) purposes of the visit?
- Make sure that there are enough adults to supervise the children adequately (3 to 1 in nursery and 6 to 1 with infants are considered optimum ratios although clearly some children may need individual support).

The route

- On local visits it is advisable to check the route. What are the safest crossing points? Are there any toilets en route just in case?
- Are you familiar with details such as bus times, stopping places and alternative buses in the event of a bus not arriving? In some areas it is necessary to ring the bus company beforehand to inform them of the trip; failure to do so could mean drivers refusing to take the party on board.

The occasional emergency

- Careful and responsible supervision, combined with good preparation, will do much to reduce the risk of emergencies. However, some cotton wool and a flask of clean water for cuts and grazes can be very useful.
- Sick bags are essential if using road transport.
- Spare clothes are a good idea if travelling anywhere near water.

The site

- Where will the children eat, sit, keep dry, go to the toilet?
- Are there any particular hazards to avoid?
- What are the procedures in the event of an emergency, for example a fire alarm?
- Wherever possible teachers should check the site before setting out with the children. This may be done in person or, in the case of more distant locations, by telephone. Even if the teacher has been to the site in previous years, things change.

Check the details

Hannah arranged a whole-day visit to a zoo in the next county for two reception classes while on teaching practice. The school hired two coaches, parents were recruited and the headteacher decided to accompany the party. The children were prepared for the visit and, in particular, for the reptile house, which was the main focus of the trip. When the coaches arrived at the zoo they were informed that the reptile house was closed that day and that, had Hannah contacted the zoo beforehand about the visit, they could have informed her of this fact.

Effective teaching methods

As a trainee teacher or newly qualified teacher, it is important to learn about and acquire a range of effective teaching strategies as soon as possible. Without the ability to do this, the learning opportunities planned for the children may never be realized. This section concentrates on some of the key skills 3–8 teachers need to acquire in order to support children's learning by sustaining the momentum of pupils' work and keeping pupils engaged. It will touch upon one important aspect which is often at the forefront of trainees' and NQTs' minds – discipline and control, and the reader is advised to refer back to Chapter 1 for further information on this topic. However, although good discipline is a prerequisite for successful teaching, it is not a sufficient condition on its own and it must be underpinned by positive, professional teaching methods.

Awareness and mobility

Teachers of young children need to maintain a high degree of vigilance at all times. This awareness, sometimes referred to as *withitness*, is a crucial skill for anyone attempting to ensure high quality teaching and effective class management with 3–8 pupils. It takes time to develop a fully fledged appreciation of young children; however, it is possible to acquire and master the skills associated with awareness by making a conscious effort in the early stages of training and teaching. Retaining a degree of mobility in the classroom greatly increases a teacher's awareness. The mere presence or proximity of an adult can have a calming and controlling effect; simply being there can do much to help young children stay on task. At the same time, moving around can also help to avoid long queues of children requesting the teacher's attention. Finally, awareness and mobility are prerequisite skills for identifying and consolidating children's learning.

Expect the unexpected

Joanne, a newly qualified teacher, had just finished a very well-organized and structured PE lesson with a Y1/Y2 class. The children were getting changed at one end of the hall and Joanne moved away from them for a short time to return some balls to a box. On her return, Suzanne approached her to say that she could not find her leotard. Everyone helped to look for it, corners were explored, kit bags were emptied, apparatus boxes were opened. Every possible place where a leotard might have been mislaid was investigated. There appeared to be no sign of it. Meanwhile the class was becoming unsettled and disruptive. The next class was queuing to come into the hall, and their well-established teacher was looking disapprovingly through the glass. A horrible suspicion began to dawn on Joanne. 'Suzanne, just lift your T-shirt up one moment will you, please?' She did, and the mystery was solved: Suzanne was still wearing the leotard!

Maintaining your awareness

- Make a point of scanning the immediate teaching area at intervals.
- Remember to check to the sides and rear.
- Demonstrate a degree of prescience by trying to anticipate events.
- Make a conscious effort to listen to the noise in the classroom; there is a qualitative difference between a busy hum and the sound of children who are off-task.

Communication

The ability to communicate effectively and appropriately with young children is another essential teaching skill. Clear and concise instructions play a valuable part in effective classroom organization and management, while exposition (discussing, explaining and outlining things verbally) and questioning offer ways in which a teacher can inspire, motivate and guide children (DfES, 2004a).

Preparing the ground

Mrs Clark asked all her Y1s to stop what they were doing and look at her. After a minute or so, during which time she asked one or two individuals by name to look her way, she then informed the children that in five minutes they would have to start clearing away ready to go to assembly. She asked the children to start to finish off the piece of work that they were doing, and checked with one or two 'key' individuals that they had understood what they had to do. When Mrs Clark stopped the children again five minutes later and asked them to start clearing up, the transition went very smoothly – the children were prepared for the task.

Teachers of young children use their communication skills in the nursery/classroom to:

- generate interest and curiosity;
- review and consolidate previous learning;
- share the programme and purposes of a session/lesson;
- offer encouragement and support;
- organize the children and maintain good order.

Questioning in particular can be a powerful means of sparking children's interest, getting them to focus, helping them to draw on and apply previous learning and illuminating what they know or are struggling with. However, questions can take a number of forms and serve different purposes.

Question categories

- **Managerial questions**: these focus on behaviour and tasks, they are concerned with the day-to-day running of the class, e.g. *Have you got a pencil?*
- **Information/Closed questions**: these test knowledge recall, e.g. *How many sides does a rectangle have?*
- **Higher order/Open questions**: these are designed to make children think critically and creatively about ideas, concepts and problems, e.g. *How do you know?*; *What if?*

(DfES, 2004a)

The key to effective questioning is to do it sensitively by asking *fewer, better and more demanding* questions and by using alternatives to questioning to keep children interested and stimulated (DfES, 2004a, p. 64). Open questions require children to think more deeply about things. This is not to say that managerial and closed questions are somehow *bad*, they are not; they serve useful purposes in reminding children of previous learning as well as providing a degree of cognitive challenge, for example what is the answer to 7 multiplied by 9? Questions are central to teaching but they are not the only basis for dialogue between teachers and children; indeed, over-questioning could have the effect of stifling children's learning rather than enhancing it.

Improve your questioning technique

- Use a mix of closed and open questions.
- Tailor your questions for different children.
- Avoid always asking the same child/children.
- Encourage fuller answers and give children the confidence to answer by offering the occasional clue, giving them the space and time to answer, and listening positively and actively, prompting, probing and praising.
- Challenge answers that are correct but that could be expanded upon as well as those that are incorrect.

Exposition is a second key communication skill for teachers. Not only does the teacher's ability to articulate clearly and concisely contribute to the efficient management of the learning environment, but also it is a powerful means of aiding children's understanding and enthusing them for a topic. Thinking beforehand about an explanation gives a teacher the chance to make sure that she/he has the necessary subject knowledge as well as the time to work out the best order and sequence to follow, the right level for the age and ability of the children and the most appropriate examples to use. Planning an explanation in advance also gives practitioners the opportunity to organize any supporting resources such as artefacts or visual aids that may help children's comprehension (DfES, 2004a). That said, by their very nature, discussions of this sort can often be spontaneous and even those that can be predicted are likely to involve a few *detours*. Teachers need to be ready to deal sensitively but efficiently with unexpected contributions, taking on board children's comments while avoiding being sidetracked.

Gentle steering of a discussion

A class of Y1 children were listening and responding to questions about a story that their teacher was reading. The teacher asked the children what they thought was about to happen. Ellen put up her hand and the teacher said, 'Yes, Ellen. What do you think will happen?' Ellen responded, 'I went to my gran's on Saturday.' The teacher replied, 'Did you? That's very interesting, do you think you could tell us a bit more about it when we've finished our story? Thank you. Now then, can anyone tell us what they think is going to happen next?'

Improving your communication skills with children

- Exposition, questioning and discussion ought to be thought about beforehand. A list of key questions, useful vocabulary and explanations can be helpful.
- Use a wide range of questioning techniques including:
  - higher order, e.g. What makes you think that?
  - information, e.g. What are you trying to do?
  - managerial, e.g. How are you going to do that?
- Use question and answer times to make judgements about children's understanding and learning needs, and to pick up on any pupil misconceptions.
- When discussing things with young children or asking questions, be prepared to show a little patience while they marshal their thoughts.
- Use praise and recognition to foster participation.
- Be inclusive. Avoid addressing the front and centre of the group or class while ignoring pupils at the back and sides.
- Promote respect for others. Follow rules, such as 'hands up and await your turn'.
- Make sure that instructions are clear and concise and that you have the children's attention before giving them.
- Do not string multiple instructions together. Young children may not be able to remember them all.
- Check that your instructions have been understood.

Monitoring the controlling the learning process

While planning and preparation are prerequisites for effective 3–8 education, teachers still have to make their plans work. They have to control the learning process, ensuring that the timing and pacing of activities is appropriate, that transitions between tasks are managed smoothly and that children's progress is monitored and consolidated in an ongoing fashion. Teachers slow activities down, they provide an accompanying commentary for the children to make the purpose explicit, and they give children opportunities to try things for themselves (DfES, 2004a).

Teachers need to be able to scaffold and guide the learning process in part by demonstrating, modelling and explaining skills which children can subsequently practise independently, as well as introducing knowledge and ideas to extend children's understanding. With younger children this means actively participating in children's work and play as a co-player/co-learner, offering ideas and knowledge to help children sustain the learning. Teachers have to be able to mediate between the children themselves and to mediate between the physical environment and the children (Jones and Reynolds 1992 in DECS, 1996). In these mediated learning experiences (MLEs) the adult adapts the activity to a child's needs, arousing care, curiosity and alertness and helping him/her to understand and succeed in the activity (Sayeed and Guerin, 2000).

Mediated learning experiences

In an MLE the child:

Selects an activity

Focuses on relevant aspects

Perceives and understands similarities
and differences

Transfers learning to a new situation

In an MLE the adult:

Helps the child to select an activity and
reduce its complexity

Exposes the child to the activity repeatedly

Reinforces learning

'Bridges' by connecting the child's past,
present and future experiences

(Sayeed and Guerin, 2000)

Monitoring and consolidating learning

- Have a clear focus for the activity or lesson and share this with the children.
- Think about any checking and monitoring that needs to take place during a lesson/session; retaining a degree of mobility will help. Ongoing monitoring has two advantages. First, it enables you to consolidate learning and assist children at a point of need while simultaneously reducing your work at break time and at the end of the day. Second, it shows pupils that you are interested in and value their work; this can be a powerful source of motivation for children.
- Have a clearly identified location where work is to be placed, such as a finished work box. This makes it easier to locate material for checking or marking later on and stops a lot of time-consuming queries from children.
- Base your standards and expectations on your knowledge of the children's abilities and include attention to the process of learning as well as to the outcomes of that process. The finished product is important but the commitment shown by the children, their willingness to concentrate and persevere, and their ability to cooperate and work constructively and positively with their peers ought to be equally worthy of comment and feedback.
- If engaged on a teaching practice with unfamiliar pupils or working with your first class, look back at previous work from time to time. It can be a useful way of identifying pupils whose work seems to be deteriorating rather than progressing.
- When errors or misconceptions arise, deal with them in a sensitive and humane fashion.

Establishing conventions and routines

Establishing and maintaining simple conventions and routines within the nursery/ classroom underpins a teacher's efforts to achieve good class management. Not only are ground rules important from the point of view of health and safety, but also young children feel much more secure in an environment where certain boundaries are clearly understood (Cowley, 2006). Establishing such conventions can require a major effort at the beginning of a year or term. However, it is an investment that will more than repay the teacher as the year progresses. Classroom conventions need to be appropriate for the age and maturity of the children and it is a good idea to keep these conventions simple and few in number so that they are manageable and understandable for the children.

Instances where conventions might apply

- Lunchtimes
- Putting things away
- Not taking things that do not belong to you
- Not running across roads, hitting or biting
- Movement as a class (e.g. to PE, assembly, or out to play)
- Movement by individuals within the class (e.g. Does it have a purpose? Does it limit the freedom of others?)
- Noise levels (e.g. not shouting out but raising hands, listening while others speak, using normal voices when speaking individually to one another)
- Handling equipment and materials sensibly (e.g. lifting, not dragging, chairs).

Promoting good behaviour and independence through classroom conventions

- 'In our class we share things and look after things.'
- 'In our class we look after one another.'
- 'In our class we are kind to one another.'
- 'In our class we put things back where they came from.'
- 'In our class we don't shout.'
- 'In our class we don't run.'

Using praise and recognition for displays of honesty, fairness and respect can help to positively reinforce desired behaviours. Teachers need to be consistent about classroom conventions through firm, though gentle, insistence and where minor infractions do occur, to handle the situation in a calm, firm and fair manner. It is important to remember that obedience is a means to an end, not an end in itself. Although rules and conventions underpin good behaviour in the nursery/classroom, so too does experience of freedom, exercising responsibility and making choices. It is through being able to exercise their decision-making skills that children can begin to grow up into responsible, independent and self-disciplined adults. Such abilities cannot be acquired simply through being told, they need to be fostered by first-hand experience. Children can therefore be included in the decisions on what form classroom conventions will take as a way of encouraging them to take ownership of, and responsibility for, the rules and routines that are eventually agreed upon. Discussing conventions in terms of personal responsibility, consequences and feelings can help children to appreciate their importance and to understand *right* and *wrong* behaviours. Like learning purposes, such expectations need to be communicated to the children and reinforced at every opportunity.

Instances where free choice and decision-making might be promoted

- Choosing games and toys;
- Choosing which friends to work with;
- Choosing which activity to go to;
- Developing role-play scenarios;
- Selecting equipment.

Further sources of information

Promoting positive relationships and active learning

- Bilton H. (2002, 2nd Edition) *Outdoor Play in the Early Years: Management and Innovation*. London: David Fulton.
- Bilton H., James K., Wilson A. and Woonton M. (2005) *Learning Outdoors: Improving the Quality of Young Children's Play Outdoors*. London: David Fulton.
- Bliss, T. and Tetley J. (2006, 2nd edition) *Circle Time*. London: Paul Chapman Publishing.
- DfES (2004a) *Excellence and Enjoyment. Creating a Learning Culture: Conditions for Learning*. London: DfES.
- DfES (2007d) *The Early Years Foundation Stage. Setting the Standards for Learning, Development and Care for Children from Birth to Five*. Nottingham: DfES.
- Mosley J. (2005) *Circle Time for Young Children*. London: Routledge.
- Rogers S. and Evans J. (2007) *Young Children's Role-playing in School*. London: Routledge.

Planning

- DfES planning templates for literacy and mathematics: www.standards.dfes.gov.uk/primaryframeworks/planningtool
- DfES (2007d) *The Early Years Foundation Stage. Setting the Standards for Learning, Development and Care for Children from Birth to Five*. Nottingham: DfES.
- Drake J. (2001) *Planning Children's Play and Learning in the Foundation Stage*. London: David Fulton.
- Moyles J. (2002, 2nd Edition) 'What shall we do today? Planning for learning: children and teachers!', in Moyles J. and Robinson G. (Eds) *Beginning Teaching: Beginning Learning in Primary Education*. Buckingham: Open University Press.

- Qualifications and Curriculum Authority (1999) *The National Curriculum: Handbook for Primary Teachers in England Key Stages 1 and 2*. London: QCA.
- Qualifications and Curriculum Authority (2000) *Curriculum Guidance for the Foundation Stage*. London: QCA.
- Smidt S. (2002, 2nd Edition) *A Guide to Early Years Practice*. London: RoutledgeFalmer.

Monitoring, assessing, recording and reporting

- DfES (2004) *Excellence and Enjoyment. Assessment for learning*. London: DfES.
- Hobart C. and Frankel J. (1999, 2nd Edition) *A Practical Guide to Child Observation and Assessment*. London: Stanley Thornes.
- Hunter-Carsch M. (2002) 'Keeping track: assessing, monitoring and recording children's progress and achievement', in Moyles J. and Robinson G. (Eds) *Beginning Teaching: Beginning Learning in Primary Education*. Buckingham: Open University Press.
- Sharman C., Cross W. and Vennis D. (2007, 4th Edition) *Observing Children and Young People*. London: Continuum.

Catering for individual pupil needs and abilities

- DfES (2001) *Special Educational Needs Code of Practice*. London: DfES.
- DfES (2007) 'Personalised learning': www.standards.dfes.gov.uk/personalisedlearning/
- DfES (2007) *The Early Years Foundation Stage. Setting the Standards for Learning, Development and Care for Children from Birth to Five*. Nottingham: DfES.
- Paige-Smith A. (2002) 'Parent partnership and inclusion in the early years', in Miller L., Drury R. and Campbell R. (Eds) *Exploring Early Years Education and Care*. London: David Fulton.
- Porter L. (2005, 2nd Edition) *Gifted Young Children: A Guide for Teachers and Parents*. Maidenhead: Open University Press.
- Roffey S. (2001, 2nd Edition) *Special Needs in the Early Years: Collaboration, Communication and Coordination*. London: David Fulton.
- Wall K. (2006, 2nd Edition) *Special Needs and Early Years: A Practitioner's Guide*. London: Paul Chapman.

Enabling environments: organizing and managing learning and teaching

- Casey T. (2007) *Environments for Outdoor Play: A Practical Guide to Making Space for Children*. London: Paul Chapman.
- Cowley S. (2006, 3rd Edition) *Getting the Buggers to Behave*. London: Continuum.
- DfES (2001) *Health and Safety of Pupils on Educational Visits*. London: DfES.
- DfES (2004) *Every Child Matters: Change for Children*: http://www.everychildmatters.gov.uk/ete/extendedschools/
- Miller L., Cable C. and Devereux J. (2005) *Developing Early Years Practice*. London: David Fulton.
- Olpin J. (2005) *Displays and Interest Tables*. London: David Fulton.
- Pollard A. (2005, 2nd Edition) *Reflective Teaching*. London: Continuum.

The First Year of Teaching and Beyond

Introduction

Successfully completing your initial teacher training is just the beginning of an exciting and stimulating career. Having found the right job, your professional development will continue once in post in your NQT year and beyond. Teachers need to be ready, able and willing to continue to learn from experience, guidance and training in order to adapt and improve their practice throughout their careers.

✔ Audit

By the end of this chapter you should:

- know a number of useful strategies to use in locating, applying and being interviewed for teaching posts in 3–8 settings;
- be aware of the Career Entry and Development Profile (CEDP) and the arrangements for the induction of newly qualified teachers;
- understand the need to take responsibility for your own professional development in the longer term and to keep up to date with research and inspection evidence as well as pedagogical developments in the subjects/age phases that you teach.

Getting your first teaching post

Applying for a first teaching post is likely to be a time consuming and sometimes nerve wracking process at a time when many applicants are already preoccupied with other time consuming and nerve wracking activities such as final teaching practices and dissertations. Given the intellectual and emotional capital invested in the process of applying for jobs, being systematic in your approach is one way of reducing stress levels and improving your chances of success.

✔ Audit

By the end of this section you should:

- know how to locate information on vacancies in good time;
- know how to complete an application that will meet the selection criteria and get you to interview;
- know how to be successful at interview.

Finding vacancies

Information on teaching vacancies can be found in many places. Many local CYPS produce vacancy brochures or bulletins and the information should also be available online by going to their websites. Individual nurseries and schools may also choose to advertise teaching vacancies in the local and national media, through websites or through agencies and organizations with an interest in teacher recruitment. Some areas organize *pool* applications for NQTs; being accepted into the pool, however, is not a guarantee of a job; a school may decide not to appoint a pool interviewee and the interviewee also has the right to decline a job offer made through the pool system.

Useful websites for teaching vacancies

- Times Educational Supplement: www.tes.co.uk
- Guardian: www.guardian.co.uk
- Telegraph: www.telegraph.co.uk
- Independent: www.independent.co.uk
- Catholic Teachers Gazette: www.e-ctg.co.uk
- Church Times: www.churchtimes.co.uk
- The Voice: www.voice-online.co.uk
- Select Education: www.selecteducation.co.uk
- E-teach: www.eteach.com
- Local Government Jobs: www.lgjobs.com
- Public Jobs and Careers: www.jobsgopublic.com
- Fish4 jobs: www.fish4.co.uk/iad

It is important to act in good time when searching for vacancies. Leaving it until the last minute is likely to result in missed opportunities and hurried applications. Some CYPS pools, for example, advertise as early as December/January for the following September. Teachers meanwhile are usually expected to give a minimum of three months' notice of their intention to leave their current post; this means that most individual teaching jobs that start in September will be advertised between Easter and the summer holiday. It is a good idea to get into a routine of regularly checking the press and electronic media from early spring onwards.

Completing your application form and writing your supporting statement

Completing the application form is undoubtedly a hurdle but it is also an opportunity for you to research the job and the setting and to decide whether this is the job for you. There could be many, many applicants but selection panels will probably shortlist no more than four candidates to interview for a single post. Your application form therefore has to be good enough to persuade the panel that you should be one of the four. Read everything that you are sent about the job, especially the job description and/or person specification and fill out the application form with great care. You cannot afford spelling mistakes, grammatical errors, crossings out or even the use of blue ink if the form asks you to use black, so check everything. You may even wish to photocopy the blank form and have a trial run before filling in the form proper. The information you receive should set out what the job will entail and may also include a list of essential and desirable selection criteria. If your application form does not or cannot show that you have met all the essential criteria then you will not be called for interview.

Sample selection criteria

Area	Criteria	Demonstrated through application (App)/ interview (Int)	Essential (E)/ Desirable (D)
Experience	Experience with FS and KS1 pupils	App	E
	Experience of children with SEN and EAL	App/Int	E
	Experience of KS1 literacy and numeracy	App/Int	E
Knowledge/ training	QTS	App	E
	3–8 training course	App	E
	Knowledge of SEN policies and practices	App/Int	E
	Knowledge of planning processes	Int	E

⟹

Skills	Good classroom organization skills	App/Int	E
	Other	App/Int	E
	Good ICT skills	Int	D
	Ability to work effectively as part of a team	App/Int	E
Other	Positive approach to learning and teaching	App/Int	E
	Commitment to inclusive education	App/Int	E
	Willingness to take part in after/out-of-school activities	Int	D

If the school is reasonably close you may be able to visit it prior to applying. Some schools have set times when prospective applicants can visit and ask questions. In other cases schools build the tour into the interview process itself. Being able to listen to the headteacher talk about the job and being able to see the facilities and sometimes the staff first-hand can help you to decide whether or not you wish to continue with your application for the post and may also give you some valuable insights into any issues that are particularly important to the school.

At some point on the application form, having provided lots of factual details about your circumstances, experiences and qualifications, you will then be asked to provide any further information in support of your application. This is your supporting statement and it is a difficult piece of writing. The space provided is unlikely to be sufficient so if the form permits it you may wish to submit the information on a separate sheet or sheets. This has an added advantage of allowing you to word process and edit the supporting statement as it will need drafting and redrafting just like an essay. The style and tone of this statement are important; you need to present yourself as enthusiastic without gushing, take care not to be too chatty, avoid exclamation marks (!) and *steer clear* of slang and colloquial language such as *kids*. At the same time you need to let the selection panel see that you are energetic and professional in your approach, a human being, not a robot. Make sure you use what are sometimes referred to as action words in your statement and that you illustrate some of your claims with reference to your teaching practice experiences.

Action words

- Started
- Supervised
- Organized
- Managed
- Planned

- Prepared
- Devised
- Initiated
- Set up
- Achieved

There is no rule that says how long a supporting statement has to be, however, between one-and-a-half and two sides of A4 should allow enough space to cover the necessary ground. Anything over that length is likely to overwhelm the selection panel.

Opening and concluding statements are always tricky to compose but two options are:

- **Opening**: 'Please find below further information in support of my application for the post of . . .'
- **Conclusion**: 'I hope that the information I have provided above demonstrates that I could be a useful addition to your nursery/school and I would welcome the opportunity to discuss these and other matters further at interview.'

While every job is different, selection panels will want to know that applicants have the relevant skills, knowledge and experience to be effective as a teacher and so the following aspects of the role will probably need to feature somewhere in your supporting statement (although not necessarily in this particular order):

- the kind of teacher that you are (i.e. your beliefs, values or philosophy);
- the classroom ethos/atmosphere that you try to establish, how and why;
- your approaches to and experience of planning;
- your approaches to and experience of assessment, recording and reporting and the ways in which your assessments inform any future planning and teaching;
- the sort of learning environment you like to create;
- how you differentiate learning and teaching to meet the needs of individuals and groups;
- how you motivate, encourage and provide positive feedback for children;
- how effective you are as an organizer and manager of the classroom;
- how and why you seek to involve parents in their children's education;
- your ability to work as part of a team;
- your views on and experiences of inclusion and equal opportunities;
- your commitment to and experiences of the wider life of the school (e.g. your involvement in visits, clubs or whole-school events).

Excerpts from two supporting statements

1 My teaching course has furthered my knowledge and experience of working with children with special educational needs. During my final teaching practice in a reception/Foundation 2 class I had the rewarding experience of working with a child who had autism; this gave me the opportunity to plan and differentiate lessons to meet each child's individual learning needs. My teaching is based on setting high expectations and raising attainment for all; however, I believe that these expectations need to take into account each child's capabilities.

2 I feel it is important to deliver a broad, balanced and progressive curriculum to all children taking into account the children's special educational needs and the cultural diversity of society. In all of my placements, I have had experience of working with children who have IEPs and I incorporated their needs into my planning. As part of the government's initiative of assessment for learning, I have worked in a school where individual targets were set for all the children and these were shared with the children so that the children knew what they were going to achieve. I also worked closely with the child psychologist to initiate a mini-schedule for a boy with severe behavioural, emotional and social problems while he was in the process of having a Statement of Special Educational Needs issued.

Could you improve on either of these statements?

Do you prefer one over the other? If so, why?

Being interviewed

If you have been called for interview then congratulations, you have cleared the first hurdle and the odds of your eventual success have improved considerably from as low as one in a hundred to probably one in four. Make sure you confirm your intention to attend promptly, either in writing or by phone. If for any reason you will not be attending (e.g. you have just accepted another post) then you should also inform the school of this.

You are likely to be nervous on the day and there are things that you can do beforehand to ease the pressure:

- Research the route and likely journey times to avoid being late or even feeling that you might be.
- Try to anticipate the sorts of questions you might be asked and rehearse the sorts of things you might say in response.
- Organize what you intend to wear beforehand to avoid discovering on the morning of the interview that something you need is actually in the washing basket.
- Get any sample materials together in advance. Interviewers may be interested to see examples of your planning or photographs of the learning environment or children's work.
- On the day of the interview make sure you eat something before you leave home no matter how poor your appetite; you do not want your answers drowned out by a gurgling stomach.

It is becoming increasingly common for the interview process to include a task of some kind. This might involve giving a short presentation or teaching a class or group of children. Schools should inform you of this when they invite you to the interview so that you will have time to prepare. Take spare copies of any session plans for the observers and be ready to be asked afterwards about how you thought your lesson went. Your ability to appraise your own performance and the children's learning are as important as the session itself.

In some cases applicants will spend time together in a waiting room, in others interviewees are asked to attend at a set time and so never meet the other candidates. If you do meet the other candidates you should be polite and professional. In the interview room keep your head up, avoid fidgeting and make eye contact. Remember your posture will say a great deal to the panel; do not slouch, do not fold your arms, get a grip on any tapping feet or fingers and do not cover your mouth with your hand. It is only natural to be nervous but try to avoid either gabbling or rambling. Instead engage with the interviewers, treat them to the occasional smile and if you are not sure about the meaning of an interviewer's question do not be afraid to ask for clarification. The panel know you are an NQT, they will not expect perfection; they will expect enthusiasm and a willingness to learn. Show that you can be thoughtful and reflective about your own practice. Make sure you have reviewed your classroom experiences to date and be ready to draw on your work with nursery/infant children to illustrate the points you want to make.

Sample interview questions

- 'Can you tell us a bit about yourself?'
- 'Why do you want to work at this school?'/'What do you think you can contribute to this nursery?'
- 'Talk us through and evaluate the session you taught this morning.'
- 'If I came into your classroom in September what would make me think I had appointed the right person?'/'What do you think makes a good teacher?'
- 'How would you involve parents?'/'A parent complains that the standard of her daughter's work has dipped since being in your class. What would you do?'
- 'What behaviour strategies have you found useful in your teaching and why?'/'How would you deal with a disruptive child?'
- 'What assessment for learning strategies have you used and do you know about?'/'How would you ensure your children could become independent learners?'/'How would you know your children are achieving?'
- 'Describe a lesson that went really well and explain why.'/'Tell us about an area of your teaching which was particularly successful on teaching practice, and how do you think you moved the children's learning forward?'
- 'Describe a lesson that didn't go to plan and reasons as to why this was.'/'What would you say were your weaknesses as a teacher?'

- 'What is a current educational issue that you are aware of and that has had an impact on your teaching?'/'How would you address the five strands of the Every Child Matters document in your teaching?'/'What does the Excellence and Enjoyment document mean to you and how would you address this in your classroom?'
- 'What does the term special educational needs mean to you and what would you do about it in your classroom?'/'How would you remove barriers to achievement for children with SEN in your class?'
- 'How would you utilize Teaching Assistants in your classroom?'
- 'What makes an effective display?'
- 'Besides teaching what would you bring to the school and where do you see your career in five years' time?'/'What are your strengths and how would you like your career to develop?'

At the end of the interview process the chair of the interview panel will normally ask if you have any questions for them. One or two intelligent questions on school policies and practices can be a good idea but avoid long lists of questions on relatively trivial matters. You may feel that you already have all the information you need in which case you should explain to the panel that you were going to ask about X or Y but that these questions have now been answered during the course of interview. The panel may also ask you whether you would accept the job if it was offered. If your answer would be 'No' then perhaps you should ask yourself why you are there.

Where candidates are all together the panel may make its decision while you all wait and then call the successful candidate back into the interview room to offer her/him the post while the unsuccessful candidates are then offered feedback on their performance. In other cases candidates may be sent home following their interview and the offer/feedback process is then conducted by phone or in writing. It is not pleasant to be told you have been unsuccessful in a job application and it may be tempting to want to forget about the experience as soon as possible, however, interviewees can benefit greatly from good quality feedback on how to do better next time so if it is not offered do not be afraid to ask for it.

The induction year

Once appointed as an NQT you should plan to spend some time in the school before the start of the new term. There will be a huge amount to do including planning, getting the classroom ready, getting to know some of your new colleagues and clarifying any arrangements to start your induction year.

> **✔ Audit**
>
> By the end of this section you should:
>
> - know about becoming part of a team of staff;
> - know about the arrangements for the induction of newly qualified teachers;
> - understand the need for continuing a reflective approach to your practice;
> - know about the need to keep up to date with developments in your area.

Settling in to your first post

One of the most daunting environments when you first start teaching could be the staffroom. Being part of a wider staff team can provide a considerable sense of support and reassurance for newly qualified teachers but it can also make you feel exposed, vulnerable and acutely conscious of all the things you do not know. You will know from previous teaching practices that, trivial though it is, familiarizing yourself with refreshment and seating arrangements can help to avoid some awkward and uncomfortable moments with certain colleagues in the staffroom. You may also be aware from previous school experiences that you will have to navigate your way around some complex relationships between colleagues, teaching and non-teaching. It takes time to find your way round these networks and personalities; discretion and diplomacy are essential skills for the NQT. It is also worth remembering your position as *new girl/boy* on the staff; perhaps something could be done better or differently but you need to display a degree of sensitivity about how, when, or indeed whether, you should say so. Remember to talk to your mentor or a senior member of staff about any concerns or questions that you have and avoid getting tangled up in any staffroom politics and disputes.

A key thing to bear in mind during your first year of teaching is that you have to pace yourself very differently in comparison to your final teaching practice. Constant colds and an overtaxed voice box are likely to be noticeable features of your first term and while maintaining a breakneck pace may be just about possible for 6–8 weeks, any attempt to maintain a similar pace for an entire academic year is likely to lead to a physical and/or mental collapse. As an NQT it is only natural to want to make an impression and to demonstrate to your colleagues that the interview panel made the right decision by offering you the post but it is important to adopt levels of activity that, while still busy, are ultimately sustainable over the longer term. If you have any worries then mentors, other colleagues and senior staff can all provide you with reassurance that you are putting sufficient effort in.

Induction arrangements

The introduction of teacher appraisal, performance management and arrangements for the induction of newly qualified teachers are intended to ensure that a willingness to learn from the practice of others and the ability to evaluate one's own practice effectively will continue to be important throughout a teacher's career. Trainee teachers are required to complete the first part of a Career Entry and Development Profile (CEDP), known as Transition Point 1, towards the end of their initial teacher education. A copy of the CEDP and instructions on how to complete it can be found on the Training and Development Agency for Schools' (TDA) website. At this stage trainees are asked to reflect on those aspects of their practice that they find rewarding, those that are strengths, those where they feel further development would be useful in their first year of teaching and how they would like their career to develop. The decisions about what constitute strengths and areas for further development are made in discussion between trainees and trainers. These discussions will be heavily influenced by teaching practice reports from nurseries and schools, although ITE students may also draw on a wide range of evidence to compile their response to Transition Point 1 including planning sheets, assignments and teaching practice files.

Career Entry and Development Profile

Transition Point 1 Date:

Note down your response to the questions, where you might find evidence to support your thinking, and/or the reasoning that led you to this response:

Interesting aspects of teaching

- Encouraging and motivating children to be excited about their learning (teaching practice file)
- Planning and teaching around Physical Development/Physical Education (final placement report).

Strengths

- Knowledge and understanding of how young children learn (coursework assignments)
- Good organizational and classroom management skills (final placement report)
- Good interpersonal skills (final placement report)
- Use of display (final placement report).

Further experience sought

- Experience of children with English as an additional language (EAL) (little opportunity during placements to date)
- Wider experience of children with SEN (encountered only one case of Asperger's Syndrome to date on placement)

- Appropriate uses of ICT in nursery and reception classes (computer was broken on final teaching practice).

Professional development and aspirations

- Work with a range of age groups within early years and primary (to widen future employment opportunities)
- Develop curriculum coordination skills (to gain management experience).

Check: How well have you . . .

- reflected on your broader experience and the relevant skills and expertise you have developed?
- thought about why you are motivated towards some particular aspects of teaching?
- identified why you want to explore some areas of teaching further?

Once appointed, NQTs on full-time permanent contracts will have an induction programme that will last for three terms. Newly qualified teachers on short-term or part-time contracts will spend an equivalent period being inducted; for example, an NQT on a 0.5 permanent contract will have an induction period lasting six terms. They do not have to start their induction year immediately but once commenced they are normally expected to complete it within five years (NASUWT, 2006). The final decision on whether NQTs have successfully completed the induction year is based on their ability to meet a set of Induction Standards, which follow on from and are intended to build upon the Professional Standards for the Award of Qualified Teacher Status. Newly qualified teachers are expected to continue to consistently meet the QTS standards albeit with increased professional competence in an employment context, and to meet the Induction Standards outlined below as well.

Induction Standards

Professional values and practice

- Work collaboratively with colleagues to raise standards by sharing effective practice.

Knowledge and understanding

- Show commitment to Continuing Professional Development by identifying areas for improvement and taking steps to address these needs.

Teaching

- Plan effectively to meet the needs of SEN pupils.
- Liaise effectively with parents/carers on pupils' progress and attainment.
- Engage in effective teamwork, including directing the work of other adults.
- Secure appropriate behaviour in the classroom and deal effectively with inappropriate behaviour.

(TDA, 2007b)

Headteachers have overall responsibility for ensuring that NQTs are properly inducted and will appoint a member of staff whose role it will be to act as mentor during the induction period. Headteachers may decide to take this mentoring role themselves. The Career Entry and Development Profile provides the starting point for newly qualified teachers and their mentors in planning and monitoring the induction year. Meetings at the start of the induction period between the NQT and her/his mentor form Transition Point 2 during which time the NQT has to respond to four questions:

1 What are your most important professional development priorities at this stage and why?
2 How have these priorities changed since Transition Point 1?
3 How would you prioritize your needs during the induction period?
4 What preparation, support, training and development activities will you need to help you make progress?

Newly qualified teachers are entitled to a reduced teaching load of around 90 per cent of a standard timetable; this reduction is in addition to any other entitlements as a result of agreements on allowances for planning and preparation time (PPA). The purpose of this additional reduction in contract time is to facilitate the induction process by creating space for NQTs to reflect on their progress, to take part in meetings with mentors or to observe more experienced colleagues in action either in their own school or in another school where effective practice is taking place. During induction, NQTs are monitored, supported and assessed by their induction mentor and/or headteacher. Lesson observations should be conducted on a half-termly basis and will focus upon a particular aspect of the NQTs' teaching. Such observations are accompanied by follow-up discussions during which time the NQTs and their mentors can analyse the lesson. In addition, NQTs will be expected to take part in professional reviews of progress in which future targets will be negotiated and set. Summative review meetings take place towards the end of each term.

> **Agenda for summative meetings**
> - **End of first term**: assessing the extent to which the NQT is consistently meeting the Professional Standards for the Award of QTS and is beginning to meet the Induction Standards.
> - **End of second term**: gauging the NQT's progress towards meeting the Induction Standards.
> - **End of third term**: determining whether the NQT has met all the requirements for the satisfactory completion of the induction period. Completion of Transition Point 3.

At the end of the induction year successful NQTs return once again to their CEDP in consultation with their mentor in order to prepare for the next stage of their careers. At this point NQTs are required to respond to six key questions:

1 What have been your most significant achievements during your induction year?
2 How have you built on the strengths identified at the end of your initial teacher training?
3 Which targets/objectives did you achieve during the year and why?
4 Were any targets/objectives not addressed during the year and what will you do about this in the coming year?
5 What are your professional development priorities over the next two to three years?
6 What opportunities for professional/career progression are you considering?

After your induction year: Continuing Professional Development (CPD)

Becoming increasingly effective as a teacher will depend upon the continued acquisition of skills and knowledge through personal experience; the support and training received from other, more experienced professionals; and as a result of keeping up with recent research and literature.

> **✔ Audit**
>
> By the end of this section you should:
>
> - know about sources of professional and research-based advice and guidance for teachers;
> - understand the value of remaining a reflective practitioner in your future career.

Learning from others

Newly qualified teachers can continue to inform and improve their practice by accessing sources of information on recent educational research, new guidance on practice and ideas for work with children. Professional journals, magazines, professional organizations and government agencies are all useful sources.

Useful periodicals and journals

- *Childhood Education*
- *Early Childhood Research Quarterly*
- *International Journal of Early Years Education*
- *Nursery World*
- *The Curriculum Journal*
- *Times Educational Supplement*

Many publications arising from the work of government departments and other agencies and organizations can be located on the internet. These often contain recent press releases, information on circulars and lists of publications. Ofsted inspection reports, for example, can be a useful source of information for trainee and newly qualified teachers wishing to keep up to date with what constitutes quality teaching and learning in the 3–8 age range. Such sites can be helpful for trainee and newly qualified teachers wishing to keep abreast of the latest thinking about the 3–8 curriculum and good practice generally.

More useful sources of inspection evidence, current research and publications on 3–8 education

- British Educational Communications and Technology Agency (BECTA): www.becta.org.uk
- Department for Children, Schools and Families (DfES): www.dfes.gov.uk
- Economic and Social Research Council (ESRC): www.esrc.ac.uk
- Early Education: www.early-education.org.uk
- Standards Site: www.standards.dfes.gov.uk
- National Grid for Learning (NGFL): www.ngfl.gov.uk
- Office for Standards in Education (Ofsted): www.ofsted.gov.uk
- Qualifications and Curriculum Authority (QCA): www.qca.org.uk
- Teachernet: www.teachernet.gov.uk/professionaldevelopment/
- Training and Development Agency for Schools (TDA): www.canteach.gov.uk

---

Remaining a reflective practitioner

High quality teaching and learning can be supported and enhanced by many factors but newly qualified 3–8 teachers would do well to continue to conduct themselves as thoughtful and reflective professionals. Teachers who engage in self-evaluation (critically reflecting on their practice and how to improve it) are likely to master a wider range of effective teaching methods more quickly than those who do not (Pollard, 2005). Such evaluation can be used to improve performance over both the long and the short term. Without ongoing self-evaluation there can be no progress that is not accidental or very slow. Reflective teachers evaluate their performance in order to progress more rapidly and in those directions where progression is most needed, whether this is to do with knowledge or skills. Reflective practitioners acknowledge that they do not know all the answers and recognize the steep learning curve that confronts them but they accept that to manage learning in the classroom in increasingly effective ways they must recognize their achievements and build on them, while simultaneously identifying any gaps and plugging them (Moyles and Robinson, 2002).

Self-evaluation is not simply a summative task to complete at the end of a lesson or term (reflection *on* action). Good teachers are constantly evaluating their practice including during teaching (reflection *in* action). It is this ongoing evaluation that generates a decision to rephrase something differently in order to communicate an idea more effectively, or encourages a teacher to pick up the pace of a lesson in response to the early signs of fidgeting. Good teachers automatically reflect on their practice as they teach but they also need to reflect on it afterwards in order to draw useful lessons for the medium and long term. It is a continual process throughout a teacher's career as achievements and gaps change over time. Clearly this longer-term evaluation will be based at least in part on everyday observations and evaluations. However, it is also necessary to move beyond the specific to consider the larger picture. Newly qualified teachers may wish to use similar headings to structure their longer-term evaluation but ought to avoid wasting time by regurgitating chunks of lesson evaluations. They should concentrate instead on the wider picture and make an accurate appraisal of their performance and issues relating to their future practice.

Reflecting on your performance over the longer term

- Start with what is going well. Why is it going well? How do you know? What is your evidence?
- Is there an aspect of your current practice that is not going so well? Why is this? How do you know? What is your evidence? What could you do about it?
- To what extent are your teaching objectives (knowledge, skills, attitudes, new vocabulary) achieved? How do you know? What is your evidence?
- How effective are you at differentiation and meeting the needs of individual children? How do you know? What is your evidence?
- How effective is your organization and management (timing, pacing, resources, transitions)? How do you know? What is your evidence?
- To what extent are good order and a positive learning atmosphere maintained? How do you know? What is your evidence?
- What would you like to do differently/better in the future? Why? What are you going to do to achieve these goals?

Further sources of information

- Bubb S. (2006, Reprinted) *The Insider's Guide for New Teachers: Succeed in Training and Induction*. London. RoutledgeFalmer.
- Cowley S. (2003) *How to Survive Your First Year in Teaching*. London: Continuum.
- Cowley S. (2004) *Sue Cowley's A–Z of Teaching*. London: Continuum.
- Moyles J., Adams S. and Musgrove A. (2002) 'SPEEL: study of pedagogical effectiveness in early learning'. DfES Research Brief No. RB363. www.dfes.gov.uk/research/
- National Association of Schoolmasters Union of Women Teachers (2006) 'Finding your first teaching post'. www.nasuwt.org.uk
- Pollard A. (2005, 2nd Edition) *Reflective Teaching*. London: Continuum.
- Siraj-Blatchford I., Sylva K., Muttock S., Gilden R. and Bell D. (2002) 'Researching effective pedagogy in the early years'. DfES Research Brief No. 356. www.dfes.gov.uk/research/
- The Training and Development Agency for Schools offers information and advice on induction for newly qualified teachers on their website: www.tda.gov.uk/teachers.aspx
- The following union sites also offer useful guidance and advice on what to expect during your induction year as well as information on when, where and how NQTs can undertake their induction:
  - National Union of Schoolmasters Union of Women Teachers: www.nasuwt.org.uk
  - National Union of Teachers: www.teachers.org.uk

References

Abbott L. and Rodger R. (Eds) (1994) *Quality Education in the Early Years*. Buckingham: Open University Press.

Ager R. and Kendall M. (2003) 'Getting it right from the start: a case study of the development of a Foundation Stage learning and ICT strategy in Northamptonshire, UK'. http://crpit.com/confpapers/CRPITV34Ager.pdf

Alexander R., Rose J. and Woodhead C. (1992) 'Curriculum organisation and classroom practice in primary schools: a discussion paper'. London: Department of Education and Science.

Alliance for Childhood (2004) 'Tech tonic: towards a new literacy of technology'. www.allianceforchildhood.net/projects/computers/pdf_files/tech_tonic.pdf

Anderson G. T. (2000) 'Computers in a developmentally appropriate curriculum'. *Young Children*, March, pp. 90–3.

Anti-Bullying Alliance (Accessed 2007): http://www.anti-bullyingalliance.org.uk

Athey C. (1990) *Extending Thought in Young Children: A Parent–Teacher Partnership*. London: Chapman.

Baldock P., Fitzgerald D. and Kay J. (2005) *Understanding Early Years Policy*. London: Paul Chapman.

Barratt-Pugh C. (1994) '"We only speak English here, don't we?" Supporting language development in a multilingual context', in Abbott L. and Rodger R. (Eds) *Quality Education in the Early Years*. Buckingham: Open University Press.

BBC (2004) '"Couch potato" toddlers warning: toddlers have as inactive a lifestyle as office workers, researchers have warned'. http://news.bbc.co.uk/1/hi/health/3399811.stm

Bennett N., Wood, L. and Rogers S. (1997) *Teaching through play: Teachers' thinking and classroom practice*. Buckingham: Open University Press.

Bertram T. and Pascal C. (2002) 'Effective early learning programme: child involvement scale'. www.eddept.wa.edu.au/lc/pdfs/involvementworkshop.pdf

Bertrand L. (2006) 'Children and time: what they usually know when'. www.wondertime.go.com/learning/article/0806-children-and-time

Blenkin G. and Kelly V. (2000) 'The concept of infancy: a case for reconstruction'. *Early Years*, Vol. 20, No. 2, pp. 30–8.

Brierley J (1994, 2nd Edition) *Give Me a Child Until He Is Seven: Brain Studies and Early Childhood Education*. London: The Falmer Press.

Bruce T. (1997, 2nd Edition) *Early Childhood Education*. London: Hodder & Stoughton.

Burnett C. and Myers J. (2004) *Teaching English 3–11*. London: Continuum.

Christensen P. and James A. (2000) 'Childhood diversity and commonality: some methodological insights', in Christensen P. and James A. (Eds) *Research with Children: Perspectives and Practices*. London: RoutledgeFalmer.

Cooper B. and Brna P. (2002) 'Hidden curriculum, hidden feelings: emotions, relationships and learning with ICT and the whole child'. Conference Paper, British Educational Research Association.

Cowley S. (2006, 3rd Edition) *Getting the Buggers to Behave*. London: Continuum.

Cox S. and Watts R. (Eds) (2007) *Teaching Art and Design 3–11*. London: Continuum.

Craft A. (1999) 'Creative development in the early years: some implications of policy for practice'. *The Curriculum Journal*, Vol. 10, No. 1, 135–50.

Curry M. and Bromfield C. (1995) *Personal and Social Education for Primary Schools Through Circle Time*. Nasen Enterprises. www.nasen.org.uk

David T. (Ed) (1998) *Researching Early Childhood Education: European Perspectives*. London: Paul Chapman.

Davies D. (1997) 'The relationship between science and technology in the primary curriculum: alternative perspectives'. *The Journal of Design and Technology Education*, Vol. 2, No. 2, Summer, pp.101–11.

Davies D. and Howe A. (2003) *Teaching Science and Design and Technology in the Early Years*. London: David Fulton.

Dearing R (1993) 'The National Curriculum and its assessment: final report'. London: SCAA.

Department for Education and Children's Services South Australia (DECS) (1996) *Curriculum Framework for Early Childhood Settings: Foundation Areas of Learning* Adelaide: DECS.

Dewis P. (2007) *Medical Conditions*. London: Continuum.

DfEE (1995) *Circular 10/95. Protecting Children from Abuse: The Role of the Education Service*. London: HMSO.

DfEE (1997, Reprinted) '"Starting with Quality": the 1990 report of the committee of inquiry into the quality of the educational experience offered to 3- and 4-year-olds'. Chaired by Mrs Angela Rumbold CBE, MP.

DfEE (1998a) *Circular 10/98. The Use of Force to Control or Restrain Pupils*. London: DfEE.

DfEE (1998b) *The National Literacy Strategy*. London: DfEE.

DfEE (1999) *The National Numeracy Strategy*. London: DfEE.

DfES (2001a) 'Health and safety of pupils on educational visits'. London: DfES.

DfES (2001b) *Special Educational Needs Code of Practice*. London: DfES.

DfES (2003a) *Historic Agreement to Reform School Workforce*. www.dfes.gov.uk/pns

DfES (2003b) *Aiming High: Raising the Achievement of Ethnic Minority Pupils*. London: DfES.

DfES (2004a) *Excellence and Enjoyment. Creating a Learning Culture: Conditions for Learning*. London: DfES.

DfES (2004b) *Excellence and Enjoyment. Assessment for Learning*. London: DfES.

DfES (2004c) *Every Child Matters. Change for Children*. London: DfES.

DfES (2004d) *Removing Barriers to Achievement: The Government's Strategy for Special Educational Needs*. Nottingham: DfES.

DfES (2004e) 'Report of the National Advisory Committee on creative and cultural education'. London: DfES.

DfES (2005) 'Safeguarding children in education: dealing with allegations of abuse against teachers and other staff'. DfES/2044/2005. London: DfES.

DfES (2006a) 'What do we mean by gifted and talented'. www.standards.dfes.gov.uk/giftedandtalented/

DfES (2006b) 'Phonics and early reading: an overview for headteachers, literacy leaders and teachers in schools, and managers and practitioners in early years settings'. www.standards.dfes.gov.uk/

DfES (2007a) 'Homework'. www.standards.dfes.gov.uk/homework/

DfES (2007b) 'Extended schools'. www.teachernet.gov.uk/wholeschool/extendedschools/

DfES (2007c) 'Personalised learning'. www.standards.dfes.gov.uk/personalisedlearning/

DfES (2007d) *The Early Years Foundation Stage. Setting the Standards for Learning, Development and Care for Children from Birth to Five.* Nottingham: DfES.

DfES (2007e) *Letters and Sounds: Principles and Practice of High Quality Phonics.* London: DfES Publications.

Drake J. (2001) *Planning Children's Play and Learning in the Foundation Stage.* London: David Fulton.

Edgington M. (1998, 2nd Edition) *The Nursery Teacher in Action: Teaching 3-, 4- and 5-Year Olds.* London: Paul Chapman.

Edgington M. (2002) *The Great Outdoors: Developing Children's Learning Through Outdoor Provison.* London: The British Association for Early Childhood Education.

Edwards A. and Knight P. (1994) *Effective Early Years Education: Teaching Young Children.* Buckingham: Open University Press.

Ellis J (1986) *Equal Opportunities and Computer Education in the Primary School.* Sheffield: Equal Opportunities Commission/Microelectronics Education Support Unit.

Farmery C. (2002) *Teaching Science 3–11: The Essential Guide.* London: Continuum.

Fitzgerald D. (2004) *Parent Partnership in the Early Years.* London: Continuum.

Fitzgerald D. (2007) *Coordinating Special Educational Needs.* London: Continuum.

Fleer M. (2000) 'Working technologically: investigations into how young children design and make during technology education'. *International Journal of Technology and Design Education*, Vol. 10, pp. 43–59.

Gardner H. (2003) 'Multiple intelligences after twenty years'. Paper presented at the American Educational Research Association, Chicago, Illinois, 21 April.

Garrick R. (2004) *Playing Outdoors in the Early Years.* London: Continuum.

Geographical Association (2007) 'Primary Curriculum Review: Early Years and Primary Phase Group commentary'. www.geography.org.uk/eyprimary

Golbeck S. L. (2005) 'Building foundations for spatial literacy in early childhood'. *Young Children*, Vol. 60, No. 6, pp. 72–83.

Goleman D. (1995) *Emotional Intelligence: Why It Can Matter More than IQ.* New York: Bantam.

Hobart C. and Frankel J. (1999, 2nd Edition) *A Practical Guide to Child Observation and Assessment.* London: Stanley Thornes.

Hope G. (2004) *Teaching Design and Technology 3–11.* London: Continuum.

Hughes M. (1986) *Children and Number*. Oxford: Blackwell.

Hunter-Carsch M. (2002) 'Keeping track: assessing, monitoring and recording children's progress and achievement', in Moyles J. and Robinson G. (Eds) *Beginning Teaching: Beginning Learning in Primary Education*. Buckingham: Open University Press.

Hyson M. C. (1994) *The Emotional Development of Young Children: Building an Emotion Centered Curriculum*. New York: Teachers College Press.

Isaacs S. (1951, Abridged Edition) *Social Development in Young Children*. London: Routledge Kegan Paul.

Kay J. (2003, 2nd Edition) *Protecting Children*. London: Continuum.

Kay J. (2006) *Managing Behaviour in the Early Years*. London: Continuum.

Kay J. (2007) *Behavioural, Emotional and Social Difficulties*. London: Continuum.

Keenan T. (2002) *An Introduction to Child Development*. London: Sage.

Kerawalla L. and Crook C. (2002) 'Children's computer use at home and at school: context and continuity'. *British Educational Research Journal*, Vol. 28, No. 6, pp. 751–71.

Knight P. (2001) 'Assessment series No. 7. A briefing on key concepts: formative and summative, criterion and norm-referenced assessment'. Learning and Teaching Support Network

Leeds City Council, Under Eights Service (1996) 'Let's get it right'. Leeds City Council.

Loveless A. (2003) *The Role of ICT*. London: Continuum.

Macintyre C. (2001) *Enhancing Learning Through Play: A Developmental Perspective for Early Years Settings*. London: David Fulton.

MacNaughton G. (1997) 'Who's got the power? Rethinking gender equity strategies in early childhood'. *International Journal of Early Years Education*, Vol. 5, No. 1, pp. 57–66.

Marsh J., Brooks G., Hughes J., Ritchie L., Roberts S. and Wright K. (2005) 'Digital beginnings: young children's use of popular culture, media and new technologies'. The University of Sheffield and Esmée Fairbairn Foundation.

Miller L., Drury R. and Campbell R. (Eds) (2002) *Exploring Early Years Education and Care*. London: David Fulton.

Moyles J. and Robinson G. (2002, 2nd Edition) *Beginning Teaching: Beginning Learning in Primary Education*. Buckingham: Open University Press.

Myer C. (2002) *Not Just Pictures: Children Developing Creativity Through Art*. London: The British Association for Early Childhood Education.

National Association of Schoolmasters Union of Women Teachers (2002) 'Race Relations (Amendment) Act 2000 and the Code of Practice: implications for schools and colleges'. www.teachersunion.org.uk

National Association of Schoolmasters Union of Women Teachers (2006) 'The induction period: a guide for students and newly qualified teachers, England'. www.nasuwt.org.uk/

National Curriculum Council (1990) *The Whole Curriculum*. York: NCC.

National Union of Teachers (1998) '1265 and all that'. London: NUT.

National Union of Teachers (2002) 'Conditions of service: notes'. London: NUT.

NSPCC (Accessed 2007) 'Bullying: a selection of materials for children, parents and schools'. http://www.nspcc.org.uk/inform/onlineresources/readinglists/bullying/bullyingwebresources_ifega28 284.html

Nutbrown C. (1996) *Threads of thinking*. London: Sage.

O'Hara L. and O'Hara M. (2001) *Teaching History 3–11: The Essential Guide*. London: Continuum.

O'Hara M. (2004) *ICT in the Early Years*. London: Continuum.

Ofsted (2005) 'Framework for the inspection of schools in England from September 2005'. HMI2435. www.ofsted.gov.uk

Ofsted/DfE (1994) 'Exceptionally able children. October 1993 report of conferences'. London: Ofsted.

Owen D. and Ryan A. (2001) *Teaching Geography 3–11: The Essential Guide*. London: Continuum.

Paige-Smith A. (2002) 'Parent partnership and inclusion in the early years', in Miller L., Drury R. and Campbell R (Eds) *Exploring Early Years Education and Care*. London: David Fulton.

Passey D., Rogers C., Machell J. and McHugh G. (2004) 'The motivational effect of ICT on pupils'. University of Lancaster: DfES Research Report No. 523.

Pike G. and Selby D. (1988) 'Human rights: an activity file'. University of York: Centre for Global Education.

Pollard A. (2005, 2nd Edition) *Reflective Teaching*. London: Continuum.

Prentice R. (2000) 'Creativity: a reaffirmation of its place in early childhood education'. *The Curriculum Journal*, Vol. 11, No. 2, pp. 145–58.

QCA (1998a) *Maintaining Breadth and Balance at Key Stages 1 and 2*. London: QCA.

QCA (1998b) 'Early years conference report'. www.qca.org.uk

QCA (1999) *The National Curriculum Handbook for Primary Teachers in England Key Stages 1 and 2*. London: QCA.

QCA (2000) *Curriculum Guidance for the Foundation Stage*. London: QCA.

QCA (2002) *The Foundation Stage Profile*. www.qca.org.uk/foundation

QCA (2004) 'Religious education: the non-statutory national framework'. London: QCA.

QCA (2007) 'National Curriculum in action: how can you spot creativity?' www.ncaction.org.uk/creativity

Robertson J. (1989) *Effective Classroom Control*. London: Hodder & Stoughton.

Roffey S. (2001, 2nd Edition) *Special Needs in the Early Years: Collaboration, Communication and Coordination*. London: David Fulton.

Roffey S. and O'Reirdan T. (2001) *Young Children and Classroom Behaviour: Needs, Perspectives and Strategies*. London: David Fulton.

Rogers S. (2003) *Role Play in the Foundation Stage: Role play with early years children*. London: David Fulton.

Sarama J. (2003) *Technology in Early Childhood Mathematics: Building Blocks as an Innovative Technology Based Curriculum*. Buffalo and Wayne State, State University of New York.

Sayeed Z. and Guerin E. (2000) *Early Years Play: A Happy Medium for Assessment and Intervention*. London: David Fulton.

SCAA (1994) *Evaluation of the Implementation of Science in the National Curriculum at Key Stages 1, 2 and 3. Vol. 3: Differentiation*. London: SCAA.

SCAA (1995) *Planning the Curriculum at Key Stages 1 and 2*. London: SCAA.

SCAA (1997) *Looking at Children's Learning*. London: SCAA.

Sharman C., Cross W. and Vennis D. (2007, 4th Edition) *Observing Children and Young People*. London: Continuum.

Sharp J., Potter J., Allen J. and Loveless A. (2002) *Primary ICT: Knowledge, Understanding and Practice*. Exeter: Learning Matters.

Siraj-Blatchford J. and Siraj-Blatchford I. (2002) 'Guidance for practitioners on appropriate technology education in early childhood'. www.ioe.ac.uk/cdl/datec

Sowden S., Stea D., Blades M., Spencer C. and Blaut J. M. (1995) 'Mapping abilities of four year old children in York, England'. *Journal of Geography*. May/June, pp. 107–11.

Stradling B. and Saunders L. (1993) 'Differentiation in practice: responding to the needs of all pupils'. *Educational Research*, Vol. 35, No. 2, Summer, pp. 127–37.

Teachernet (Accessed 2007) 'The VAK model'. http://www.teachernet.gov.uk/supplyteachers/detail.cfm?&vid=4&cid=15&sid=92&ssid=4010503&opt=sectionfocus

Telegraph (13 September 2006) 'Modern life leads to more depression among children'. http://www.telegraph.co.uk/news/main.jhtml?xml=/news/2006/09/12/nosplit/njunk112.xml

Training and Development Agency for Schools (Accessed 2007a) *Standards for the Award of Qualified Teacher Status*. http://www.tda.gov.uk/teachers/professionalstandards/currentprofessionalstandards/qtsstandards.aspx

Training and Development Agency for Schools (Accessed 2007b) *Induction Standards*. http://www.tda.gov.uk/teachers/professionalstandards/currentprofessionalstandards/inductionstandards.aspx

Training and Development Agency for Schools (Accessed 2007c) *Learning Support Staff*. http://www.tda.gov.uk/support/learningsupportstaff.aspx?keywords=learning+support

Turbill J. (2001) 'A researcher goes to school: using technology in the kindergarten literacy curriculum'. *Journal of Early Childhood Literacy*, Vol. 1, No. 3, pp. 255–78.

Turner-Bisset R. (2002) 'The essence of history in the early years', in Miller L., Drury R. and Campbell R. (Eds) *Exploring Early Years Education and Care*. London: David Fulton.

Welch G. F. and Adams P. (2004) 'How is music learning celebrated and developed? A professional user review of UK and related international research undertaken for the British Educational Research Association (BERA)'.

Westwood P. (1997, 3rd Edition) *Commonsense Methods for Children with Special Needs*. London: Routledge.

Wood D. (1998, 2nd Edition) *How Children Think and Learn*. Oxford: Blackwell.

Woodfield L. (2004) *Physical Development in the Early Years*. London: Continuum.

Index